Thomas Archer

About my Father's Business

Thomas Archer

About my Father's Business

ISBN/EAN: 9783337779566

Printed in Europe, USA, Canada, Australia, Japan

Cover: Foto ©Suzi / pixelio.de

More available books at **www.hansebooks.com**

"About my Father's Business"

WORK AMIDST THE SICK, THE SAD, AND THE SORROWING

BY

THOMAS ARCHER

AUTHOR OF

"Strange Work," "A Fool's Paradise," "The Terrible Sights of London,"
"The Pauper, the Thief, and the Convict," etc., etc.

CONTENTS.

	PAGE
THE RARITY OF CHRISTIAN CHARITY	1
WITH THE CHILDREN OF THE STRANGER	9
WITH THE CHILDREN'S CHILDREN	18
WITH THE STRANGER IN A STRANGE LAND	34
WITH THOSE WHO ARE LEFT DESOLATE	43
WITH THEM THAT GO DOWN TO THE SEA IN SHIPS	53
WITH THEM WHO WERE READY TO PERISH	62
CASTING BREAD UPON THE WATERS	74
WITH THE FEEBLE AND FAINT-HEARTED	84
WITH THE LITTLE ONES	100
IN THE KINGDOM	112
WITH LOST LAMBS	125
WITH THE SICK	135
BLESSING THE LITTLE CHILDREN	144
WITH THEM THAT FAINT BY THE WAY	156
IN THE VALLEY OF THE SHADOW OF DEATH	165
WITH THE HALT AND THE LAME	173

CONTENTS.

	PAGE
WITH THEM WHO HAVE NOT WHERE TO LAY THEIR HEADS	190
TAKING IN STRANGERS	200
FEEDING THE MULTITUDE	209
GIVING REST TO THE WEARY	220
WITH THE POOR AND NEEDY	227
GIVING THE FEEBLE STRENGTH	248
HEALING THE SICK	261
WITH THE PRISONER	274

"ABOUT MY FATHER'S BUSINESS."

THE RARITY OF CHRISTIAN CHARITY.

WOULD it not be useful to ask ourselves the question whether we are forgetting the true meaning of "charity" in the constant endeavour to take advantage of organized benevolent institutions, about the actual working of which we concern ourselves very little? As the years go on, and what we call civilisation advances, are we or are we not losing sight of "our neighbour" in a long vista of vicarious benefactions, bestowed through the medium of a subscription list, or casual contributions at an "anniversary festival?"

At the speeches that are made on such occasions, when the banquet is over, and the reading of the amounts subscribed is accompanied by the cracking of nuts and a crescendo or decrescendo of applause, in proportion to the liberality of the donors, we are so frequently reminded of "the good Samaritan," that we begin to feel that we may claim some kind of relationship to him; and may shake our heads with solemn sorrow at the inexcusable conduct of the priest and the Levite. It would be worth while, however, to ask ourselves whether we quite come up to the mark of him who, finding the man wounded and helpless by the wayside, dismounted that he might convey the sufferer to the nearest inn; poured out oil for his wounds and wine for his cheer; left him with money in hand for the supply of his immediate needs; and did not scruple—with a robust and secure honesty—even to get into debt on his behalf: since the crown of good-will would be the coming again to learn of the patient's welfare. The debt was a pledge of the intention.

That was the Lord Christ's way of looking at charitable responsibility, and at benevolent effort; and even granting that He illustrated the answer to the question, "Who is my neighbour?" by an extreme case of sudden distress, the longer we look at the peculiar needs of the man who was on his way from Jerusalem to Jericho, the more perhaps we shall be convinced that there are greater, far greater evils, and more terrible accidents, than to fall among thieves, who temporarily rob, strip, and disable their victim.

The present fashion of dealing with such an unfortunate traveller would very much depend on which particular class of philanthropists the modern Samaritan who found him by the road-side happened to belong to.

Of course, it would be a scandal to our Christianity to follow either priest or Levite, although our cowardly sympathies might lie between the two; so, in order to make all safe, we hit on a compromise, and, according to our circumstances, try to find a medium line of conduct between Samaritan and Levite, or Samaritan and priest. We are ashamed to pass on without doing something, and so we call at the inn on our way, and leave the twopence there, in case anybody else should think fit to bring on the man who is lying, stunned and bleeding, in the roadway. Or else, having contrived to rouse the poor fellow to a little effort, we borrow an ass and take him back with us, to find some organised institution for the relief of those who fall among thieves, where the wine and oil are contracted for out of the funds. And there we leave him, without remembering anything whatever about the twopenny contribution which would represent our own share in the benefaction.

It is an awful thought, and one which it may be hoped will soon become intolerable, that, with the mechanical perfection of means for relieving the necessities of those who are afflicted, there seems to grow upon us a deadly indifference to the very deepest need of all—that personal, human sympathy, without which all our boast of benevolence is but as the sounding of brass and the tinkling of a cymbal. Can it be possible that we are approaching a condition when, refusing to have the poor and the afflicted, the widow and the orphan always with us, we shut them away out of our sight, leaving the whole duty of visiting them, of clothing them, of giving them meat and drink, to be done by an official committee; a charitable board, distributing doles, exactly calculated, on a carefully devised scale, and divided to the ounce or the inch, in supposed proportion to the individual need of each recipient? Will there ever come a time when we shall persuade ourselves that we fulfil the law of Christ by paying so much in the pound for a charity rate, and leaving all the actual "relief" to be effected by an official department, or a series of official committees?

The present aspect of charitable administration would be truly appalling if this were likely to be the result, for there are far too many evidences of that deadly indifference which will get rid of all real personal responsibility by paying a subscription, and will pay handsomely, too, at the same time smiling grimly, and half satirically, at the recollection that there are a number of people who always have on hand "cases," of whom they are anxious to rid themselves by placing them in any institution that will receive them without payment.

Let it not be imagined that these latter words of mine are intended to apply to those workers among the poor, who, with small means of their own, cannot do much more than speak words of advice and comfort, and give their earnest help to better the condition of sordid homes and of neglected children. There are scores of true, tender-hearted women who, spending much time amongst the sick and the afflicted, feel their hearts sink within them as they see how much more might be done, if they had but the wherewithal to appease the actual physical needs of those to whom they try to come spiritually near.

If but the miracle so easy to others were first performed, and the five thousand fed, then indeed might follow that still greater miracle, the earnest listening of the once turbulent multitude to the words of the Bread of Life.

But there are those who pursue what they regard as "charitable work" as an excitement—an amusement—just as children are sometimes set to play with Scripture conversation cards, and puzzles out of the Old Testament, with a kind of feeling that the employment comes nearly to a religious exercise. There is as much danger of these persons missing the true work of charity as there would be in the employment of paid officials—indeed, the latter would have one advantage ; they would be less likely to be imposed upon by those who to obtain some special advantage would cringe and flatter.

The first great difficulty in visiting and temporarily relieving the lower class of destitute poor, is to disabuse their minds of an inveterate notion that the benevolent visitor and distributor is paid by some occult society, of which the recipients of bounty know nothing, and for which they care very little. Unfortunately, the sharp determined amateur visitor, who "does a district" as other people with leisure do a flower show or a morning concert——but, alas! these very words of mine show how common is that lack of true charity of which I designed to speak. Who am I that I should sum up the disposition and the heart of my brother or my sister? Only I would say that this suspicion on the part of the ignorant poor, which is so often complained of—the notion that their interviewers are paid for the work of charity—can only yield to the conviction that the work itself is undertaken with warm living human sympathy. Before the true relief shall come to any man, it must come by faith. "With the heart man believeth unto righteousness," and *in* righteousness also.

The two tendencies that are driving us away from charity to a kind of selfish economy, are the habit of "relieving our overcharged susceptibilities by secreting a guinea," and thinking we have thereby fulfilled the claims of religion and humanity, and the practice of going about seeking where we may find candidates for other people's guineas, and so becoming a kind of charitable detectives, with an eye to reputation and advancement in the force.

We are forgetting that heartfelt sympathy, that clasp of the hand and beam of the eye which will make even a cup of cold water a benefaction, if we have no more to give, or if the need goes no further than a refreshing draught, that shall be turned from water into wine by the power of loving fellowship. Or we may be saying, "Be ye clothed, and be ye fed," trusting to some other hand to do the necessary work, without having ourselves first wrought for the means of taking our part in it, either by a deep personal interest in the relieving institution or in the destitute recipient.

"Yet one thing thou lackest,"—even though out of thy great possessions a large proportion is given to the poor; "follow thou me." "Go about doing good," do not think to have fulfilled the law without love—that which you call charity; the mere *giving*—is but to offer a stone when bread is required of you, unless it be done with love in your heart—personal, human, and therefore Divine love. "If ye have not been faithful in that which is another man's, who shall give you that which is your own?" Use the benefits of institutions—even though you use them only for others—as you would use your own property. Recommend only cases that are known to you to be worthy and necessitous, and, should the institution depend on voluntary support, let a contribution accompany your "case," if you can any way afford it, as an act of justice as well as of mercy.

Don't join in the traffic in votes, and never go begging for "proxies," in order to have an exchangeable stock on hand, that you may secure a candidate for any particular institution. This kind of gambling is a cancer that is eating the heart out of genuine, pure, charitable effort, and is making way for the cold impersonal system of distribution, which is now being advocated by those who would make the relief of human wretchedness and distress a mechanical organisation without the soul of love. At the same time, let us not forget that no charitable effort which would be efficacious in affording relief to the widely-spread distress by which we are surrounded, could be even so much as attempted without associations established for the express purpose of relieving particular forms of suffering. This, indeed, is the glory of our country, that humanity is so strong among us as to lead us not only to combine, but to emulate. The absolute concentration and centralization of charitable effort would be a calamity. The breaking up of the best of our institutions, which have grown from small beginnings in almsgiving into wide and influential centres of benevolent effort, would be destruction.

If anything that may be written hereafter concerning some representative (large and small, but still truly representative) efforts to do the work that Christianity demands as its first evidence of reality, should lead to a deeper and wider personal interest in their behalf, it will be matter for rejoicing. The larger the number of people who ask what is being done, the greater will be the desire to continue the good work, or to declare it. The attention that might in this way be directed to the mode of affording relief would exercise so keen an influence in the reformation of abuses, and the adoption of improvements, that all our charities would soon become truly "public." With the more earnest conviction of the duty of personal inquiry, and real sympathetic interest in the individual well-being of our poorer brother or sister, would come the satisfaction that we belonged to an association, or to a chain of associations, which will afford to him or to her the very relief which otherwise we should despair of securing.

I purpose in another chapter to ask you to read the story of an institution that was in its day wonderfully illustrative, and even now serves to take us back for two centuries of history. Only yesterday I was speaking to some of its inmates. One of them had nearly completed her own century of life, most of them had seen far more than the threescore years and ten which we call old age; but they come of a wonderful race, the men of fire and steel; the women of silent suffering—the old Huguenots of France.

WITH THE CHILDREN OF THE STRANGER.

 HUNDRED and eighty-seven years ago a French army invaded England and effected a landing at various places on the coast. Smaller divisions of that army had previously obtained a footing in some of the chief towns of Great Britain; and for about fifty years afterwards other contingents arrived at intervals to find the compatriots settled among the people, who had easily yielded to their address and courage, and by that time were apparently contented to regard them as being permanently established in the districts of which they had taken possession. The strange part of the story is, that for a large part of this time England was successfully engaged in war with the country of the invaders, and not only with that country, but with a discarded prince of its own, who, having received assistance from France, strove to regain the throne which he had abdicated by raising civil war in Ireland. Then was to be seen a marvellous thing. A detachment of the French army of occupation in England went with King William to the Boyne, and when the mercenaries who were at the back of James in his miserable enterprise came forth to fight, they beheld the swords of their countrymen flash in their faces, and

heard a well-known terrible cry, as a band of veteran warriors cut through their ranks, fighting as they had been taught to fight in the Cevennes and amidst the valleys and passes of Languedoc. For the army that invaded England in 1686, and for four or five years afterwards, was the army of the French Huguenots, against whom the dragoons of Louis XIV. and the emissaries of Pope and priests had been let loose after the revocation of the Edict of Nantes.

Four hundred thousand French Protestants had left their country during the twenty years previous to the revocation of that pact, which had been renewed after the siege of Rochelle, and though the attempt to escape from the country was made punishable by the confiscation of property and perpetual imprisonment in the galleys, six hundred thousand persons contrived to get out of France, and found asylums in Flanders, Switzerland, Holland, Germany, and England, after the persecutions were resumed.

Comparatively few of the men who came in the second emigration had fought for the religion that they professed. They had learned to endure all things, and with undaunted courage many of them had suffered the loss of their worldly goods, the burning of their houses, hunger, poverty, and the imprisonment of their wives and daughters in distant fortresses, because they would not forswear their faith. Hundreds of their companions were at the galleys, hundreds more had been tortured, mutilated, burned, broken on the wheel. Women as well as men endured almost in silence the fierce brutalities of a debased soldiery, directed by priests and fanatics, who had, as it were, made themselves drunk with blood, and seemed to revel in cruelty. With a resolution that nothing seemed able to abate, pastors like Claude Brousson went from district to district, living they knew not how, half famished, in perpetual danger, and with little expectation of ultimately escaping the stake or the rack. Nay, they refused to leave the country, while in the woods and wildernesses of the Gard great congregations of their brethren awaited their coming, that they might hold services in caves and " in the desert," as they called that wild country of the Cevennes and of Lozére. These men were non-resistants. They met with unflinching courage, but without arms. Those of them who remained in France stayed to see the persecutions redoubled in the attempt to exterminate the reformed faith. They were the truest vindicators of the religion that they professed. Up to the time of the siege of Rochelle, and afterwards, Protestantism was represented by a defensive sword, but these men discarded the weapons of carnal warfare. Only some years later, when the persecutors (rioting in the very insanity of wrath because their declaration that Protestantism was abolished was falsified by constant revivals of the old Huguenot worship) directed utter extermination of the Vaudois, did the grandeur of the non-resisting principle give way before the desperation of men who came to the conclusion that, if they were to die, they might as well die fighting.

It must be remembered that some of them knew well how to fight. Some of their leaders—men of peace as they were, and men of an iron determination, which was shown in the obstinacy with which they refused to take up the sword—had come of stern warriors and were *Frenchmen*—Norman Frenchmen—Protestant Norman Frenchmen. A rare combination that;—cold hard steel and fire.

But it was not till some time afterwards that these men became the leaders of the peasantry, the chestnut-fed mountaineers who came down from their miserable huts and joined what had then become an organised army of insurrection. Before this time arrived a strange aberration seemed to move the people. The old simple non-resisting pastors had been done to death by torture and execution, and the people met, it is true, but often met amid the ruin of their homes, or in desert places, and as sheep having no shepherd. Then a wild hysterical frenzy appeared among them. Men, women, and even children claimed to be inspired, and at length fanaticism leaped into retaliation. On a Sunday in July, 1702, a wild mystic preacher, named Séguier went down with a band of about fifty armed men to release the prisoners. They were confined in dungeons beneath the house of one Chayla, a priest, who directed the prosecutions, and invented the tortures which he caused to be inflicted for the conversion of heretics. The Protestants broke open his door, forced the prison, and ultimately set fire to the house, in attempting to escape from which Chayla was recognised and killed. This was the beginning of a series of retaliations by the tormented people, the success of which changed the whole attitude of the Protestants of the district. They had formerly endured in silence; now they were desperate enough for insurrection. And the insurrection followed. Séguier was captured, maimed, and burnt alive; but others took his place. The war of the "Camisards" had commenced. Then it was that the leaders of the Protestant army in the Cevennes arose ;—Roland and Cavalier, and the men who for a long time waged successful warfare against the royal forces, till defeat came accompanied by a new *régime*.

The rumbling of the revolutionary earthquake was already shaking the throne and the persecuting church. Voltaire, educated by the Jesuits, and hating religion, was helping to deliver the martyrs of the Protestant faith even before he began to "philosophise."

The struggle of the Camisards can only be said to have ceased when the persecutions were nearly at an end, and France itself was tottering. But what of that great Huguenot contingent which had invaded Britain, and was growing in number year by year as the *émigrés*, leaving houses and land, shops, warehouses, and factories, fled across the frontier, or got down to the shore, and came over the sea in fishing-boats and other small craft, in which they took passage under various disguises, or were stowed away in the holds, or packed along with bales of merchandise, to escape the vigilance of the emissaries who were set to watch for escaping Protestants? It is a little significant that of these non-combatant Protestants eleven regiments of soldiers were formed in the English army; but the truth is that of the vast number of *émigrés* who left France, some 30,000 were trained soldiers and sailors, and doubtless a proportion of these came to England, though probably fewer than those of their number who served in the Low Countries. At any rate, in 1687, two years after the revocation of the Edict of Nantes, there arrived in England 15,500 refugees, some of whom brought with them very considerable property, and most of them were men of education, or skilled in the knowledge of the arts, or of those manufactures and handicrafts which are the true wealth of a nation. At Norwich and Canterbury they quickly formed communities which became prosperous, and helped the prosperity of the districts, where they set up looms, and dyeworks, and other additions to the local industries. In London they formed two or three remarkable colonies, so that when Chamberlain wrote his "Survey of London," there were about twenty French Protestant churches, the greater number of which stood in Shoreditch, Hoxton, and Spitalfields—in fact, above 13,000 emigrants had settled in or near the metropolis. The one French Protestant church founded by Edward VI. was, of course, inadequate to receive them, and their immediate necessities were so great that a collection was made for their relief, and a sum of 60,000*l.* was by this means obtained in order to alleviate their distress.

Among these *émigrés* were many noblemen and gentlemen of distinction, who, with their wives, were reduced to extreme poverty by the confiscation of their property. These had learned no trade, but with characteristic courage many of them set themselves to acquire the knowledge of some craft by which they might earn their bread, while some of their number learned of their wives to make pillow-lace, and so continued to support themselves in decent comfort.

To those who knew the "old French folk," as they came to be called in after years, when the later emigration had again increased the number of the weavers' colony in Spitalfields, nothing was more remarkable than the cheerfulness, one might almost say the gaiety, that distinguished them. Reading the account given by French writers of the old Huguenots in France, one might be disposed to regard them as stern and sour sectaries, but that would be a very erroneous opinion. Perhaps the sudden freedom to which they came, the rest of soul, and the opportunity to endeavour to serve God with a quiet mind raised them to a tranquil happiness which revived the national characteristic of light-heartedness; but however it may have been, the real genuine old French weaver of Spitalfields and Bethnal Green was a very courteous, merry, simple, child-like gentleman. The houses in which these people lived, some of which are still to be seen with their high-pitched roofs and long leaden casements, were very different to the barely-furnished, squalid places in which their descendants of to-day are to be found; and, indeed, the Spitalfields weaver even of seventy years ago was usually a well-to-do person; while in the old time he could take "Saint Monday" every week, wear silver crown-pieces for buttons on his holiday coat, and put on silk stockings on state occasions. This was in the days when French was still spoken in many of the little parlours of houses that stood within gardens gay with sweet-scented blooms of sweet-william, ten-weeks-stock, and clove-pink. When there was still an embowered greenness in "Bednall," and Hare Street Fields were within a stone's throw of "Sinjun"—St. John, or rather St. Jean Street,—or of the little chapel of "*La Patente*," in Brown's Lane, Spitalfields. Even in later times than that, however, I can remember being set up to a table, and shown how to draw on a slate, by an old gentleman with a face streaked like a ruddy dried pippin. I was just old enough to make out that the tea-table talk was in a strange tongue; but I can remember that there were evidences of the refinements that the old refugees had brought with them across the sea. Not only in their neat but spruce attire, in their polite grace to women, in their easy, good-humoured play and prattle to little children, in their cultivation of flowers, their liking for birds, and their taste for music, but in a score of trifling objects about their tidy rooms, where the click of the shuttle was heard from morning to night, these old French folk vindicated their birth and breeding. By tea-services of rare old china, rolls of real "point" lace, a paste buckle, an antique ring, a fat, curiously-engraved watch, a few gem-like buttons, delicately-coloured porcelain and chimney ornaments; by books and manuscript music, or by flute and fiddle deftly handled in the playing of some old French tune, these people expressed their distinction without being aware of it. It has not even yet died out. Unfortunately, many of their descendants—representatives of a miserably paid, and now nearly superseded industry—have deteriorated by the influences of continued poverty; and even so long ago as the evil war-time of Napoleon I., many of the old families anglicised their names in deference to British hatred of the French, but there are still a large number of people in the eastern districts of London whose names, faces, and figures alike proclaim their origin.

But we must go back once more to the time when the great collection was made. It is at least gratifying to know that the £60,000 soon increased to £200,000, and was afterwards called the "Royal Bounty," though Royalty had nothing to do with it during that reign. In 1686-7 about 6000 persons were relieved from this fund, and in 1688 27,000 applicants received assistance, while others had employment found for them, or were relieved by more wealthy *émigrés* who had retained or recovered some part of their possessions. But there were still aged and sick people, little children, widows, orphans, broken men, homeless women, and lonely creatures who had become almost imbecile or insane through the cruelties and privations that they had suffered. For these a refuge was necessary, and at length —but not till 1708—an institution was founded in St. Luke's, under the name of the French Hospital, but better known to the " old folks" as the " Providence."

Of what it was and is I design to tell in another chapter.

WITH THE CHILDREN'S CHILDREN.

THAT great invading French army of nobles, gentry, artists, traders, handicraftsmen, of which some account has already been given, was added to from time to time, even as lately as the Revolution, and the restoration of the dynasty after the downfall of Napoleon, when a strange reaction against the Protestants was commenced, partly as a pretence for concealing political animosity. The department of the Gard was once more the scene of horrible atrocities, against which Lord Brougham invoked the aid of the English Parliament, and obtained the help of Austrian bayonets to protect the people, who were being murdered, tortured, or outraged, in defiance of feeble local authorities. But by this time there was a new generation of the first great Anglo-French colony in London. Spitalfields had grown to the dimensions of a township. Bethnal had begun to lose its greenness. There was, as there still is, a remarkable settlement about Soho. "Petty France" was as well known as the exhibition of needlework in Leicester Square, or Mrs. Salmon's wax figures in Fleet Street.

Those poor refugees who fled to escape from the horrors of Sainte Guillotine, or the ruthless cruelties at Nismes, came to brethren many of whom had never seen the glowing valleys and golden fields of Languedoc, whence their forefathers escaped only with life and hands to work. They had preserved their national characteristics; they attended churches and chapels where the pastors still spoke their native tongue, and where they had established schools for their children; but they had settled down to a quiet, though a busy life, in the heart of the great workshop of the world, and only a few of them—principally the gentry, some of whom had regained a portion of their property—felt frequent or urgent impulses to return. More than a hundred and twenty years had elapsed since the "Royal Bounty" had been expended in the relief of the 27,000 *émigrés* who yet were without any permanent refuge for the destitute, the sick, the aged, and the insane among their number. This was in 1688, and it was not till nearly twenty-eight years afterwards that any regular institution was organized. The earlier refugees had become aged or had died, after having obtained such temporary help as could be afforded by subscriptions or the large benefactions of their more wealthy fellow-countrymen. Still, the later emigrations increased the number of applicants for permanent relief. At last, in 1718, a great concourse of French refugees assembled in a chapel which formed a special portion of a building only just completed, but which had already received the dignity of forming the subject of a Royal charter granted by His Majesty King George I. to his "right trusty and right well-beloved cousin, Henry de Massue, Marquis de Ruvigny, Earl of Galloway, and a number of trusty and well-beloved gentlemen, all naturalized refugees, who made the first governor and directors of the "Hospital for Poor French Protestants and their descendants residing in Great Britain;" otherwise known as the French Hospital, but soon to be spoken of with simple pathetic brevity as "La Providence."

The idea of founding such a charity was due to a distinguished refugee in Holland—no less a personage than M. de Gastigny, Master of the Hounds to Prince William of Orange; a ruddy, jovial-looking gentleman withal, whose portrait, should you go to see it, will set you wondering whether he could ever have been classed among the "sour sectaries" to whom it was the fashion to attribute a disregard of social pleasures. A bequest of a thousand pounds sterling from the bluff keeper of the kennels was to be divided into equal sums—£500 for the building, and the interest of the remaining £500 to be spent on its maintenance.

Not a very adequate provision, truly, for any such purpose; but sufficiently suggestive to set the more prosperous members of the great Anglo-French colony to increase the amount. The astute Master of the Hounds must surely have foreseen this result when he left this legacy to the management of the trustees of the already existing relief fund, still miscalled "the Royal Bounty." They exhibited that prudence in money matters which is a French characteristic, and let the thousand pounds accumulate for eight years, after which a general subscription was invited from successful merchants and traders, while with a just appreciation of the benefits which had been conferred by these good citizens on the land of their adoption, some wealthy Englishmen added their contributions to the general fund.

Thus it came about, that a piece of land was purchased in the Golden Acre—a queer old half-countrified precinct of St. Giles, Cripplegate—that a building was erected for the reception of eighty poor persons, that a charter was granted, and that the new charitable association was consecrated in the new chapel by Philippe Menard, the minister of the French Church of St. James's and secretary of the enterprise.

This was, indeed, something worth working for. The aged or afflicted poor among the refugees were no longer mere mendicants living on precarious alms. Out of their abundance the more prosperous gave cheerfully. In 1736 another adjoining site was purchased, and another side of the great open quadrangle of garden ground was built upon, so that by 1760 the "Providence" numbered 230 inmates. This, however, was its culminating point of usefulness. Religious persecution had diminished, and at length may be said to have ceased altogether. Even as early as 1720 only 5000 persons required relief from the "Bounty," so that eventually the trustees were enabled to devote part of it to the assistance of those who fled from the Revolution—many of whom were the descendants of those who had been the persecutors of the Protestants. The great industrial colony, prudent, temperate, and industrious, had almost grown beyond its earlier needs—and all that it required was that some adequate provision should be made for infirm or aged men and women, who being widowed or unmarried, and without means of support, required a refuge in which they might peacefully end their days. The same causes which had diminished the number of applicants had also reduced the amount of current subscriptions, so that some portion of the building was removed, as being no longer necessary, and in order to secure a sufficient endowment an Act of Parliament was obtained, empowering the directors to let their land on building leases. By that time the neighbourhood was known not as "the Golden Acre," but as St. Luke's, and on the ground once purchased by the Marquis de Ruvigny and his trusty and well-beloved companions, grew Radnor Street, Galway Street, Gastigny Place, and part of Bath Street, while the number of inmates was reduced to sixty—that is to say, about twenty men and forty women, all of whom were to be above sixty years of age, of French extraction, and professing the Protestant religion. It was a queer old range of building, that retreat; pleasant enough, perhaps, when as a rather blank series of red brick houses, it looked across its own formal walled garden to the pleasant fields and open country, but strangely silent, and with a crumbling, dreary look about it, when the lunatic asylum of St. Luke's dominated all the surrounding tenements of a crowded, sordid neighbourhood. Only the initiated could easily find the little low black door that opened in the bare wall, and led to the large irregular space, which was laid out in weedy beds and stony borders, distinguished by an air of decay rather than of production—especially where in certain dank corners a tangle of sapless stalks and tendrils indicated some faintly hopeful attempt to rear an arbour, in which persons of robust imagination might fancy they were sheltered from impending blacks that issued from the manufactory chimneys close by. The visitor to this out-of-the-way corner of the great city, seeing the old people walking up and down the paved causeway in front of the row of crooked-paned lower windows, or airing themselves at the doorsteps, might be excused for the fancy that they had the imaginative faculty of children; and were expected to "make believe" a good deal before they could quite reconcile themselves to the notion that this dingy area of quadrilateral plots and paths, in which the wet stood in small puddles, was ever a "pleasaunce" gay with garden blooms, and smelling of knotted marjoram and fragrant thyme. Yet there were still evidences of the invincible cheerfulness of the old French nature, among the old creatures with faces streaked like winter apples, and hands which, even though they trembled, were swift of gesture and of emphasis.

There were old fellows there who had still about them indications of true comeliness and grace that distinguished them from all vulgar surroundings;—ancient gentlemen, who would go out on wet days to sweep away any rainpools that might lie before the doors of the old ladies, and so besmirch an otherwise immaculate shoe. It should be remembered, too, that there was no livery there. Those who had some one to help them to the garb of gentility wore what pleased them; those who were dependent on the charity for clothing, were neither bound in one pattern, nor condemned to the uniform of poverty. Neat or lively cotton prints, or warm stuff gowns, with proper hose and caps and kerchiefs, for the women; plain Oxford mixture, black, steel grey, or brown, for the men, and each one measured for his suit. Those who entered there were not the recipients of a dole grudgingly conceded. It was no poorhouse, but the "Providence." Only eleven years ago there were some evidences of the old meaning of the place in the remnants of the antique furniture which adorned the queer rooms. They were not wards or dormitories, but veritable bedrooms; and each one had its own peculiarities, even in the bedsteads with spindle posts and dimity hangings, the boxes and cupboards, and special chairs which distinguished it from the rest. Some of these things had evidently been heirlooms either of the institution or of the individual; and, indeed, the preservation of individuality was a cheerful feature of the place, despite its dim and somewhat dreary surroundings.

The Board Room was, in its way, one of the most extraordinary apartments in London: with its tables supported by a tangled puzzle of legs, its high-backed, polished chairs with leather seats, worn till they reminded one of the cover of an antique ledger bound in unfinished calf; its wonderful old black-framed prints representing the meetings of the Huguenots in the Clerk's field in the times when men and women carried their lives in their hands, and dragoons rode congregations down and slashed them with sabres as they fell. Its dimly-seen portraits of the noble, broad-browed, dark-eyed Ruvigny (the first governor), who refused to go back to France even at the invitation of the King; of the gentle Pastor Menard, with high, capacious forehead, and calm, strong mien; of hale, shrewd, ruddy Gastigny; and of some men of later date, with Frenchman written in every line of their finely-marked faces.

The little room set apart as a chapel—a barely-furnished place enough, with desk and raised platform and plain seats—was venerable because of all the meaning that lay in its studied absence of all ornament, and because of the significance it must once have had to the sad-eyed men who crowded into it, some of them thinking, perhaps, how it had come about that they could stand there in peace and without a hand upon the hilt of a sword.

There were, even at that later time, old men and women in the dim old building who could repeat family legends of the emigration—for they lived to a great age, these French folk, many of them being still alert of eye and ear, and foot, even though they had heard the click of the shuttle and the rattle of the loom eighty years before.

Some of them have survived the old place itself; for while they are in a new home, the ancient building has changed, if even it be not altogether dismantled. The leases paid good interest, and eight years ago a new French hospital arose—away from the dingy old precinct of the Golden Acre.

To see this later "Providence" aright, you must come through the very heart of that neighbourhood which was once the great Silk Colony, thread the bye-ways of Poverty Market, note the tall silent houses where the looms no longer rattle, nor the sharp whirr of the shuttle stirs cage-birds to sing; pass across the debatable land lying on the edge of Shoreditch, where human beings live in sties built in the backyards of other houses, in streets that are still with the blank silence of misery and want. You should walk amidst pigeon and dog fanciers; call in at certain dingy, slipshod taverns, where at night a slouching company will meet to hear bullfinches pipe for wagers, and where starving men and women stand and drink away the pence that are all too few to buy food for the starving brood at home, and so are flung upon the sloppy counter in exchange for the drugged drink that feels like food and fire in one. Through Bethnal Green, with its "townships" and its "Follies," extending in sordid rows of tenements built to one dreary pattern. Over districts which, only a few years ago, were fields and open spaces, leading to farm lands and hedgerows, and so away to the great expanse of marsh land where the dappled kine wade knee-deep in the lush pastures, and the stunted pollards stand like patient fishermen upon the river's brink.

Yes, the present "French Hospital"—the New Providence—was built ten years ago in the border-land beyond the Weaver's Garden, that great garden and pleasure-ground known as Victoria Park. It is the only garden left to the descendants of those old craftsmen who once dwelt in houses every one of which had its gay plot of flowers, its rustic arbour, or its quaint device of grotto-work, built up of oddly-shaped stones and pearl-edged oyster-shells. Do you think there is now no remnant of the old French folk left? Come for a stroll among the grand beds and plantations of this East-end playground, and you shall see. On holidays and alas! on those days when (to use the expressive term handed down from prosperous times) the weaver is "at play"— that is to say, waiting for woof and weft, and so wiling away the sad and often hunger-bringing hours—you will see him, with his keen well-cut face, his dark appreciative eye, his long delicate hands, his well-brushed, threadbare coat and hat; and the mark of race is plainly to be noted in his intensity of look and his subdued patient bearing. He comés of a stock which had it not been of the hardiest and the most temperate and enduring in the world, would have disappeared a century ago. On Sunday mornings, when the bells are sounding round about him, he is to be met with lingering (with who shall say what inner sense of worship) by the strange shrubs and flowering plants, or standing with a pathetic look of momentary satisfaction on his lean, mobile face, to mark the rare glow and gush of colour made by the blooms in a "ribbon" device of flowers on a sunny border by a dark background of cedar. But come and see what his forefathers might have called, in their Scripture phraseology, "the remnant of the children of Israel;" the old inmates of that French Hospital founded so long ago when De Ruvigny was the "beloved cousin" of George I., and Philippe Menard preached at St. James's; when the Duchess de la Force brought donation after donation to the work, and Philippe Hervart, Baron d'Huningue gave £4,000, all in one splendid contribution, to the building fund. Could they have seen (who knows that they have not?) this great French château rising beyond the park palings in a neighbourhood fast filling with houses, but still open to the air that blows from the Weavers' Garden and from the great expanse of land leading towards the forest, they would have recognised the familiar style of those grand mansions which in France succeeded the castles of the feudal nobility when Henry Quatre was king. The high-pointed roof with its irregularly picturesque lines, the quaint towers and spires, the slate blue and purple, and rosy tints of colour in slope and wall and gable; the various combinations of form and hue changing with every point of view, make this modern copy of the old French chateau a wonderful feature in any landscape, and the unaccustomed visitor seeing it as it stands there in its own ornamental ground, surrounded by a quaint wall decorated in coloured bands, wonders what can be the meaning of a building so full of suggestion; while if he be of an imaginative turn, he may fall into a day-dream when he peers through the gate that stands by the porter's lodge.

But let us pass through this gate, and so up to the

entrance-hall, and we shall seem to leave behind us not only the Weavers' Garden, but most things English. The hall itself, paved with encaustic tile, leads to a flight of broad, shallow steps, beneath an arched ceiling of variegated brick and two screen arches. These steps conduct us at once to a central corridor, extending for the entire length of the building, and rising to the greatest height of the open roof of timber with its lofty skylights. In front of us is a double stone staircase, one branch being for the old ladies, the other for the men; and immediately at the foot of the former division is the entrance to the refectory, a large handsome dining-hall, where, at two long tables, this wonderful company assemble, only the very infirm having their meals carried to the upper ward, where they are waited on by paid attendants. Separate staircases are provided for the servants of the establishment, whose rooms are in the tower above the main wards—or rather, let us say, principal apartments, for they are not so much wards as a series of twenty-two large bedrooms, linen-rooms, and two bath-rooms. The steward of the hospital, a venerable gentleman with the courteous air and speech of some seneschal of olden time, has also his own apartments, reached by a third stair, his sitting-room and office occupying a space close to the entrance. On the right of the main staircase and at the end of the corridor is the ladies' sitting-room, a fine high-windowed light and lofty place, admirably warmed, as indeed all the building is, and so furnished that at each large square table four old ladies can sit and have not only ample space for books or needlework, but on her right hand each can open a special separate table-drawer with lock and key, wherein to keep such waifs and strays—shreds, patches, skeins, and unconsidered trifles—as children and old women like to accumulate. There is another day-room beside this, and a similar, though not quite so large an apartment is provided for the men, both rooms being furnished with sundry books and a few sober periodicals of the day.

It must not be forgotten though that many of the old gentlemen have grown accustomed to the use of tobacco, and here in the basement is a smoking-room, quite out of the way of the ordinary sitting and dining-rooms, and not far from the laundry and drying-rooms, which form an important part of the establishment.

But, hush! there is a hymn sounding yonder in the refectory; a hymn sung by voices, many of which are yet fresh and clear, though the singers number more than eighty years of life, and of life that has often been hard and full of heaviness.

It is the grace before meat, and the hot joints, with the fresh vegetables from their own garden, have just come up from the big kitchen by means of a lift to the serving-room.

There are no servants to wait at table, and the family dinner-party is a private one, inasmuch as it is the custom here for the most active of the inmates to agree among themselves who shall be butler, or *beaufetière*, for each day during the week. So the dinner-time goes pleasantly and quickly, the meat, the vegetables, and the capital household beer, of which each man has a pint twice a day, and each woman half a pint, being the only articles that require serving.

The good old-fashioned family custom of everybody having his or her own teapot is observed here. A great gas-boiler stands on one side the refectory, and a row of convenient lockers on the other; and each inmate has tea and coffee from the stores, while bread and butter are also served out for consumption according to each individual fancy, and not in rations at each meal time. Thus those old ladies and gentlemen who have spending money, or friends to bring them some of the little luxuries that they so keenly appreciate, can add a relish to their breakfast or to the evening beer.

We will not go in while they are at dinner, for there are those here yet who "might have been gentlefolk" but for the mutability of mortal affairs. Stay! here come the old ladies, with old-fashioned curtseys, which are more than half a bow, and not a mere vulgar "bob." There is no mistaking some of their faces. You may see their like in French pictures, or in old French towns still. Some of them with eyes from which the fire had not yet died out; with deftly-moving fingers; with a quick, springy step; with an inherited remnant of the French *moue* and shrug, as they answer a gentle jest about their age and comeliness.

"Eighty-four; and I don't know how it is, but I don't seem to see so well in the dark as I used. When I went out to see my brother-in-law, I was quite glad he came part of the way home with me."

"Turned eighty, but I can't get upstairs as I used to do."

"You speak French, madame?"

"Pas beaucoup, monsieur;" this from one of the only two actual French women now in the establishment, the rest being lineal descendants only. The oldest, who is now going quietly and with a very pretty dignity out of the refectory, is ninety-four, and can not only hear a low-toned inquiry, but answers it in a soft, pleasant voice. She bears the weight of years bravely, but the burden has perhaps been heavy; and she speaks in a mournful tone, as one looking forward to a mansion among the many—to a house not made with hands, may sometimes speak when even the grasshopper becomes a burden.

As to a young person of sixty-five or thereabout, nobody regards her as having any real business to mention such a trifling experience of life; while of the men—most of whom semed to have filed off for their pipe or newspaper—one remains finishing his dinner, for he has been on duty for the day, and is now winding up with a snack of bread-and-butter and the remainder of his mug of porter—a stoutly-built, hale, stalwart-looking gentleman, who, sitting there without his coat, which hangs on the back of a chair, might pass for a retired master mariner, or a representative of some position requiring no little energy and endurance. I fancy, for the moment that he must be an official appointed to serve or carve and employed on the establishment.

"Eighty-four," and one of the old weaving colony of Bethnal Green.

There can be no mistake about it. Every inmate provides certificates and registers enough to make the claim undoubted; and as to the right by descent, half the people here carry it in their faces, and to the initiated, are as surely French, as they are undoubtedly weavers.

The morning here begins with family prayers, which the steward reads from a desk in the refectory, and so the day closes also. The Sunday services are in the chapel, and such a chapel! To those who remember the dim, barely-furnished room in the old building at St. Luke's, this gem of architectural taste and simple beauty at the end of the main corridor comes with no little surprise. Its beautiful carved stone corbels, mosaic floor, and charming ornamentation; its broad gallery entered immediately from the upper floor, so that the feeble and infirm may go to worship directly from their sleeping-rooms; its glow of subdued colour and sobered light from windows of stained glass; its simple decorations, and its spotless purity, are no less remarkable than the plainness which characterises the general effect. It is to be noticed, too, that there is no "altar," but "a table;" that neither at the back of the communion nor on the carving of the lectern, nor even in the windows, is there to be seen a cross. Where the Maltese cross would occur amidst the arabesques of the stained glass, we see the fleur-de-lis. French Protestantism, has perhaps, not yet lost its intense significance, at all events here, in this chapel where the service of the Church of England is observed, and an ordained clergyman ministers to the family of the children's children of the ancient persecuted people of Languedoc, the symbol under which the Protestants were burned and tortured and exiled has no place. This is probably in accordance with the traditions left by De Ruvigny, by Gastigny, by Menard, and by their successors, whose portraits still hang in the fine board-room of the new "Providence."

Of course, no contributions or subscriptions are now asked for to support this old French charity. With it are associated one or two gifts of money, such as that of Stephen Mounier for apprenticing two boys; and the bequest of Madame Esther Coqueau for giving ten shillings monthly to ten poor widows or maidens; but the directors do not seek for external aid. To the charity when it was first chartered was added a portion of the accumulations of the benefactions of the French Church at

Norwich, and it may here be mentioned that at Norwich, where a contingent of the army of refugees had settled, the Society of Universal Goodwill was also established by Dr. John Murray, a good physician, who strove to extend to a large organisation a plan for relieving distressed foreigners. This was but ninety years ago, and it was less successful than its promoter desired, so that part of the funds accumulated were judiciously handed to another admirable society in London, of which I shall have something to say, "The Society of the Friends of Foreigners in Distress."

WITH THE STRANGER IN A STRANGE LAND.

O we ever try to realise the full meaning of the declaration that they who are afar off shall be made near by the blood of Christ? Surely it does not stop at the nearness to God by redemption, for the only true redemption is Christ-likeness, and nearness to God assumes nearness to each other in the exercise of that loving-kindness which is the very mark and evidence of our calling.

It would be well if we sometimes ceased to separate by our vague imaginations "the next world," or "the other world," from the present world, which is, perhaps in a very real sense, if we could only read the words spiritually, "the world to come" also;—as it is obvious that the world means the people around us—ourselves, those who are near and those who seem to be afar off; and no world to come that could dispense with our identity would be of any particular significance to us as human beings.

Let us then, for the present purpose, try to see how effectually Christ-likeness should bring near to us those who are afar off, by taking us near to them; how He who came not to destroy but to fulfil, looks to us to entertain strangers; and to "be careful" in the performance of that duty, as to Him who will say either, "I was a stranger, and ye took me in," or the reverse.

At the beginning of the present century, with the exception of the French Protestant organisation, there existed in London no established association for the relief of destitute foreigners who, having sought a refuge here, or being, as it were, thrown upon our shores, were left in distress, hunger, or sickness,—unheeded, only obtaining such temporary casual relief as a few charitable persons might afford, if by any chance their necessities were made known to them. At that time the foreign Protestant clergy, to whom alone many of these destitute men and women could apply for relief, were themselves mostly the poor pastors of congregations consisting either of refugees or of artisans and persons earning their livelihood by precarious labour connected with the lighter ornamental manufactures. The means at their disposal for charitable purposes outside their own churches were consequently very small, and they were unable to render any really effectual assistance, even if they could have undertaken, what would at that time have been the difficult task of verifying the needs for which relief was claimed.

Some attempt had already been made by Dr. John Murray, a good physician of Norwich, to extend to London the benefits of his "Society of Universal Goodwill;" but the scheme had been only partially successful. To him, however, the credit is due of having striven to give definite shape to an association which was afterwards to take up the good work of caring for strangers. The foreign Protestant clergy settled in London met to consider how they might best organise a regular plan for relieving the wants of those who had so often to apply to them in vain; and having settled the preliminaries, which were heartily approved by several foreign merchants, and others, who were willing to assist in any scheme that would include inquiry into the circumstances of those who sought assistance, called a public meeting in order to found a regular institution. This was on the 3rd of July, 1806, and the result of the appeal was the formation of the society of "The Friends of Foreigners in Distress." By the following April, a committee had been formed and the Charity was in working order, nor were funds long wanting with which to commence the work in earnest. The cases requiring relief were so numerous, however, and the demands on the society's resources were so constant, that though some large donations were afterwards obtained from senates, corporations, wealthy merchants, ambassadors, noblemen, and Royal benefactors, a considerable subscription list became necessary in order to enable the society to grant even partial relief to cases, the urgent claims of which were established by careful inquiry.

There is a wonderful suggestiveness in the list of "Royal Benefactors (deceased)," headed by his late Majesty King William IV., and her late Majesty the Queen Dowager Adelaide. More than one of the Royal donors themselves died in exile; and several of those who shared their misfortunes, and were their faithful followers, have shared the small benefits which the Society had to bestow. "His late Majesty King Charles X. of France" contributed £300; "His late Majesty Louis Philippe," 100 guineas; the unfortunate Maximilian, Emperor of Mexico, £25; and his late Imperial Majesty Napoleon III., £50: while their Magnificencies the Senates of the Free German Towns, as well as the humbler companies of London's citizens, appear to have given liberally. Notwithstanding all this, however, the Society has not been able to retain funded property to any considerable amount, and it is to the annual subscription list—to which our Queen contributes £100, the Emperor of Germany £100, and the Emperor of Austria £100—that the charity must look for support.

Unhappily there are evidences that these annual subscriptions are fewer than they should be. There seems still to be some reluctance on the part of the general public steadily to support an effort which has a very distinct and pressing claim upon Englishmen, who pride themselves, justly enough, upon the free asylum which this country affords to foreigners, and who appear ready to give largely in the way of occasional aid. The disparity between the number of handsome donations and of very moderate annual subscriptions is a painful feature of the Society's report, and even public appeals have hitherto been followed rather by increased applications from persons recommending cases for relief, *without accompanying the recommendation with a subscription*, than by any decided augmentation of the funds. The Friends of Foreigners in Distress are principally to be found amongst prosperous foreigners in London, and doubtless this is no less than just; but until larger aid is given by the English public, we have no particular reason to include this association in any boastful estimate of British charity.

That the committee does its work carefully, and that cases of distress are relieved only after due inquiry, and with no such careless hand as would encourage idle dependence or promote pauperism, is evident enough to anybody who will take the trouble to inquire into the method of assistance. Let us go and see.

Perhaps not one Londoner in a thousand could tell you offhand where to find Finsbury Chambers. It is probably less known even than Prudent Passage, or what was once Alderman's Walk; and may be said to be less attractive than either, for it is a dingy, frowsy, little out-of-the-way corner in that undecided and rather dreary thoroughfare—London Wall. It is, in fact, a space without any outlet, and looks as though it ought to have been a builder's yard, but that the builder took to erecting houses on it as a speculation which never answered, even though they were let out as "chambers;" that is to say, as blank rooms and sets of offices, the supposed occupiers whereof committed themselves to obscurity by causing their names to be painted on the doorposts, and leaving them there to fade till time and dirt shall wholly obliterate them.

And yet it is in one of these lower rooms, occupying the ground floor of No. 10, that a good work is going on; for here, in an office almost representatively bare and dingy even in that place, the Society of Friends of Foreigners in Distress holds its weekly meetings of directors, and the secretary, Mr. William Charles Laurie, or his assistant, Mr. C. P. Smith, gives daily attendance (Saturdays excepted), between eleven and one o'clock. Assuredly, the funds of the charity are not expended in luxurious appointments for its headquarters. Even a German commission agent just commencing business could scarcely have a more simply-furnished apartment. The objects which first strike the visitor's attention are a row of japanned tin candlesticks, meant for the use of the board at any of their Wednesday meetings which may be prolonged till after dusk. The furniture, if it was ever new, must have been purchased with a regard for economy in the very early history of the society. The work is evidently so organised as to require no long daily attendance. The place is furnished only according to the temporary necessities of business quickly dispatched. Neither in official salaries, nor in expensive official belongings, are the funds of the institution wasted.

The system is, in fact, simple enough, and is conducted on the principles laid down by the first meetings of the committee above seventy years ago, with one important exception. Formerly, applicants for relief must have been for some time resident in England; but changes in transit, and the more rapid intercommunication of nations, have made it necessary that some ready aid should be granted to those who find themselves cast upon the terrible London wilderness without a friend to help them, ignorant to whom to apply for help, and little able even to make known their sufferings.

Every Wednesday, then, the directors meet for receiving applications for relief, and reports of cases that have been investigated by the Visiting Committee.

The plan adopted is to issue to the governors of the charity a number of small tickets, each of which, when signed and bearing the name of the applicant for relief, entitles the latter to apply to the weekly committee for an investigation of his case. Every subscriber of a guinea is regarded as a governor for a year, and there are, of course, life governors also. Both these are entitled to recommend cases either for what may be termed casual relief, or for election as pensioners to receive weekly assistance (of from 2s. to 5s., and in cases of extreme old age or great infirmity, 7s. 6d. a week), sick allowances, or passage money to enable applicants to return to their own country.

It may easily be believed how a small weekly contribution will often save a destitute man or woman, or a poor family, from that utter destitution which would result from the inability to pay rent even for a single room; while in cases of sickness, the regular allowance even of a very trifling sum will enable many a poor sufferer to tide over a period of pain and weakness, during which earnings, already small, are either reduced or cease altogether.

In cases of urgent necessity four superintendents are appointed from the board of directors, with the power to grant immediate relief; and of course many applicants receive temporary assistance from the governor who recommends them, until their case is investigated by the committee, and they are on the list of the worthy and indefatigable " visitor."

After the expulsion of the Germans from Paris during the late war, that little dingy quadrangle in London Wall was filled with a strange crowd of lost and helpless foreigners, whose condition would admit of only a temporary inquiry, and indeed needed little investigation, since want and misery were written legibly enough in their faces. For a large number of these, passage money had to be paid, and the relief was continued till the press of refugees from France abated. There was a special subscription for the relief of these poor creatures, raised chiefly among German merchants living in London, and even now the Society has to extend a helping hand to some who still remain.

Any one wandering by accident into Finsbury Buildings

on a Wednesday forenoon, would wonder what so many
subdued and rather anxious-looking men were waiting
about for in such an out-of-the-way locality—some of
them leaning against the wall inside, others sitting in the
bare room, just within the barer passage. Every one of
these has had his circumstances carefully inquired into,
and is in attendance to receive what may be called temporary relief. During the official year of my latest visit 150
homeward passages had been paid, and in the two years
from 1871 to 1873 the number of persons who received relief
was 21,333, who with their wives and families represented
a considerable community of poverty. During the year
1,983 grants were made of sums varying from less than
10*s*. to 1,324 persons, 10*s*. to 431, 15*s*. to 47, £1 to 135,
and so on to £5, which was allowed in a few instances,
while sick allowances were granted in 292 cases. One important and suggestive feature of this excellent Society is
that it numbers among its members not only subscribers to
other charitable institutions, but members of the medical
and legal professions, who frequently render their aid
to applicants free of expense, in order either to relieve
them from suffering, or to protect them from the errors
or impositions to which their ignorance and helplessness
might expose them.

There is no restriction either as regards creed or
nationality, and though each case is matter for inquiry,
the only persons disqualified for receiving relief are those
who are detected as impostors—persons who are deemed
to have sufficient support from any other source, those
who cannot give a good reason for having come to this
country, and proof of their having striven to obtain work
and to labour for a maintenance, those who are proved

to have been guilty of fraud or immoral practices, and beggars, or drunken, dissolute persons.

As regards the numbers of persons who have received relief since the institution was founded, there is the tremendous total of 21,645 applicants on behalf of 129,299 individuals. What an army it represents! Of these Germany (which till recently included Austria, Hungary, and Bohemia) represents 71,913; Sweden and Norway, 9,422; Holland, 8,878; France, 7,339; Russia, 7,006; Italy, 5,415; Belgium, 4,578; Denmark, 4,215; the West Indies, 1,716; Switzerland, 1,685; and so on in a diminishing proportion till we come to " Central Africa !" —a very recent case, no doubt.

Can any one question the good that has been effected by an institution so careful not only to relieve with rigid economy, but also to do its work on so truly voluntary a principle? If the temporary and comparatively casual aid afforded to poor and destitute strangers works so beneficially, however, the pensions, to which only very extreme cases are elected, are even still more in the nature of help given to those who are ready to perish, Here are some specimen cases:

A watchmaker of Frankfort, seventy-four years old, and nearly seventy years in this country, disabled by paralysis, with a wife, who is a waistcoat maker, unable to compete with the sewing-machine; one son, twenty years old, who, having some small situation, lives with them, pays the rent, and "does what he can;" a boy of fourteen who works as an errand boy.

An Italian looking-glass maker, seventy-three years old, and fifty-three years in this country. Has lately lived by making light frames, but health and strength fail, and he is suffering from asthma. His wife, an

Englishwoman, and aged sixty-six, works as a charwoman. He has two sons, each married and with large families, so that they can do nothing for him.

A French widow, sixty-seven years old, and thirty-two years in this country, and paralysed for the last thirteen years. Her only daughter who is in delicate health, earns her "living" by needlework, but can only gain enough for her own maintenance.

These are only three of the first cases in the official report of pensioners, and they are not selected because of their peculiarly distressing character. When it is remembered that this society has not, in a general way, sufficient means to grant more than *two shillings a week* in the way of relief, and when we take the trouble to observe that in the majority of cases where a pension is granted the recipients have been so long resident here that they may be said to have lost their nationality in ours, will it be too much to ask of England —alike the asylum for the persecuted and the teacher of liberty and of charity—that the "Friends of Foreigners in Distress" shall be regarded as the friends of all of us alike in the name of Him of whom it was said, "Can any good thing come out of Nazareth?"

But I have not quite done with the pensioners. I must ask the reader to go with me to Lower Norwood, where amidst a strange solitude, that is almost desolation, we will visit three ladies of the *ancien régime*, one of whom, at least, began life nearly ninety years ago as a fitting playmate for the daughter of a king.

WITH THOSE WHO ARE LEFT DESOLATE.

THERE is something about the aspect of Nature as seen from the railway station at Lower Norwood on a damp and misty day which, if not depressing, can scarcely be regarded as conducive to unusual hilarity. I speak guardedly because of my respect for the district, and lest I should in any way be suspected of depreciating any particular locality as an eligible place of residence. In the latter regard I may mention that the immediate neighbourhood of Lower Norwood Station is not at present converted into a small township by the erection of long rows of tenements on freehold or long leasehold plots. My remarks apply only to the general outlook from the road, amidst an atmosphere threatening drizzle, and beneath a sky betokening rain. As far as houses are concerned, there seemed to me, on the occasion of my last visit, far more probability of pulling down than of building. In fact, I went for the purpose of inspecting a whole series of very remarkable tenements which I had heard were soon either to disappear from the oozy-looking green quadrangle of which they formed three sides, or were to be converted to another purpose than that of the dwelling-places of a few elderly ladies who occupied one dreary side, whence they could look at the desolation of the closed houses on the other.*

* Since this was written the Almshouses have been closed, and their two or three remaining inmates "lodged out."

It will not be without regret that I shall hear of this intention being carried out, for the houses are devoted to the sheltering of alms-folk; and the alms-folk are the elder pensioners of that admirable association, the Society of the Friends of Foreigners in Distress, which, for above ninety years, has been doing its useful work among those who, but for its prompt and judicious aid, would feel that they were "alone in a strange land."

As a part of its original provision for the relief of some of the applicants who, after long residence in this country, had fallen into a distressed condition at an age when they were unable any longer to maintain themselves by their own exertions, the society instituted the almshouses at Lower Norwood. There is now an impression among the directors of the charity that their intentions may be carried out in future by some better method than placing a number of aged and frequently infirm persons in a comparatively remote group of dwellings, where they are peculiarly lonely, and lack frequent personal attention and general sympathy. There can be no doubt that almshouses have frequently been associated a little too closely with that monastic or conventual practice with which they mostly originated, and that the retirement, almost amounting to seclusion, into which the inmates of such places are removed, may be very far from affording to the aged the kind of asylum which they most desire. Alas, in many instances, to be placed in an almshouse is to be put out of the way,—to be conveniently disposed of; with the inference that every possible provision has been made for comfortable maintenance. Thus, susceptibilities are quieted. The aged pensioners are supposed to be periodically visited; their wants attended to by somebody or other who "sees that they are all right," and the whole matter is conveniently forgotten, except when a casual traveller passes a quaint, ancient, mouldy-looking, but still picturesque block of buildings, and inquires to what charity they belong; not without a kind of uneasy fancy that there is a custom in this country of burying certain old people before their time—shutting them out of the light and warmth of every-day companionship; or, to change the metaphor, making organised charity a kind of Hooghly, on the tide of which the aged, who are supposed to be nearing the end of their mortal life, are floated into oblivion until the memory of them is revived by death.

It is no part of my intention to represent that the almshouses at Lower Norwood bore such a significance, but the conditions to which I have referred appear to be so inevitable where places like these are concerned, that I cannot question the good sense of the directors of the Charity in determining to supersede them, and to carry on the work by annual or monthly pensions only. On behalf of the few remaining inmates of these queer, half-deserted, and failing tenements, it was desirable that the proposition should be acted on at once, and a more comfortable provision be made, at least, for those who wait on, with constantly deferred hope, doubly heart-sickening when so little time is to be counted on, in which something will be done before the houses themselves, crumbling to decay, become but a type of their own forlorn old age.

It is with some such thoughts as these that I stand at the entrance to the green, with last year's weedy aftermath still dank and tangled with wind and rain. The queer little one-storied dark-red houses of the quadrangle bear a melancholy resemblance to a set of dilapidated and discarded toys, the box for which has been lost. They are built, too, on a kind of foreign-toy pattern, with queer outside staircases, leading to street-doors under a portico, which is the only entrance to the upper storey, the lower doors in the quadrangle communicating only with the ground-floor. The crunch of my footsteps along the moist path, gives no echo; the place seems to be too dull and lifeless even for that kind of response. The left wing and far the greater portion of the centre block are still with the silence of desertion. Peering through the dim leaden casements, I see only small, bare, empty rooms. There is a sense of mildew and of damp plaster peeling from the walls,—of leaky water-pipes, and a humid chill, which no glowing hearth nor bright July weather could utterly subdue. Such is the feeling with which the whole place strikes me on this leaden wintry day, when the vapour from the engine on the railway trails slowly upward to meet the ragged edge of the dun cloud that streams slowly downward; when a big, black dog crouches on the threshold of the village chandler's shop, to get out of the drizzle; and the butcher, who has sold out, closes his half-hatch, with the certainty that he may take his afternoon nap by the fire, undisturbed by customers.

Even when I pause before one of the little narrow portals to which I have been directed, there are few more signs of life, except that at the same moment I hear other footsteps behind me, and a baker stop to deliver a loaf. This is promising, as far as it goes, and enables me to present myself unostentatiously, under cover of the baker's basket, to a lady who opens the door. Unless I am greatly mistaken, that lady has a French face, and as it is a French lady for whom I am to inquire, I begin to think I have come to the end of my quest. It is evident, however, from the surprised questioning look which greets my appearance, that visits from strangers are not of very frequent occurrence there. I can trace in the rather shrinking recognition accorded to my request to see the lady to whom I bring an introduction, the sensitiveness that belongs to that kind of poverty which has learned to endure in seclusion reverses that would be less bearable if they were exposed to a too obtrusive expression of sympathy. It is a positive relief to be left alone for a minute, standing in that narrow lobby, looking into a room which has the appearance of a disused scullery, while my errand is made known in another room on the right, to which I am presently bidden. It is a poor little place enough; poor, and little, and dim, even for an almshouse, and scarcely suggestive of comfort though a bright fire is burning in a grate, which somewhat resembles a reduced kitchen-range, and though the table which stands beneath the casement bears some preparations for the evening meal, and the cheap luxury of a cut orange on a plate. The walls are dim, the ceiling cracked and discoloured by the evident overflow of water in the room overhead; the furniture consists of a kind of couch which may do duty for a bed by night, and of two or three windsor chairs, one of which has already been placed for me. It is a poor place enough; and yet the lady to whom I am at once introduced is ready to do its honours with a grace and dignity that well become her appearance and her name. Madame Gracieuse B——, for more than forty years resident in England, and speaking English with a purity of accent that is only rivalled by the more perfect music of the French in which she addresses me, has passed the threescore years and ten which are counted as old age. Yet seeing her sweet, calm face; her smooth, broad, intelligent brow; the mild, penetrating scrutiny of her gentle eyes; the soft hair put back under the quaint French cap, shaped like a hood; those years remain uncounted; until, with a pleasant smile, only just too placid for vivacity, she tells how she came to this country in 1830, after the ruin of the fortunes of her house by the revolution which dethroned Charles X., and made her a governess in England, where so many of the old nobility sought a refuge and a home.

But before this is said, she has presented me to a third lady—to whom, indeed, my original introduction extended—already long past the limit of that short period which we call long life; for she is more than eighty years old, and by reason of the infirmity which has lately come upon her, does not rise to receive me, but remains seated in the couch by the fire. It is a very limited space in which to be ceremonious; but were this lady sitting in one of a suite of grand rooms in some aristocratic mansion, with all the surroundings to which her birth, her high connections, and the recollection of her own personal accomplishments entitle her, she might not lack the homage which too often only simulates respect.

It is possible that she may long ago have learned to assess it at its true value, for she has seen it at a court where it could not save a king from banishment; and if we may judge from a face with strong determined lineaments, a brow of concentrated power, and eyes the light of which even the recent paralysis of age has not extinguished, she has been one who could undergo exile, poverty, and even the sadder calamity of being forgotten, with a wonderful endurance.

Yes, Madame la Comtesse Maria de Comoléra, friend and fellow-student of that Madame Adelaide whose name has become historical, when your father was Monsieur l'Intendant of the Duc d'Orléans, and when you lived within the atmosphere of the French court, spending quiet days at the easel in your painting-room, or preparing the delicate *pâte* of Sèvres porcelain, on which to paint the roses and lilies that you loved, the grim visions of exile and poverty may never have troubled you. When the house of Bourbon crumbled, and you escaped from the ruin it had made, you had still your art left to solace, if not to gladden you; and for a time at least you lived by it, and took a new rank by the work that you could do. There were flowers in England, and your hands could still place their glowing hues on canvas. Witness those pictures of yours that now hang on the walls of the gallery of the Crystal Palace, or adorn some private collections. Witness, too, the recognition of some of our own painters when Sir Charles Eastlake was president of the Royal Academy, and when you found a friendly patron in Queen Adelaide of gentle memory. Alas, the nand has lost its cunning; and if its work is not altogether forgotten, those who look upon it are unaware that you are living here in this poor room—pensioner of a charity which, were it but supported as it might be, could better lighten your declining years. Yet I will not call you desolate, madame. Two faithful friends are with you yet. The sunset of your calm life, whereof the noon was broken by so terrible a storm, is dim enough; but it goes not down in complete darkness. Gentle and admiring regard survives even in this dull place; and with it the love that can bring tears to eyes not over ready to weep on account of selfish sorrows, and can move ready hands to tend you now that your own grow heavy and feeble.*

As I become more accustomed to the subdued light of the room, I note that amidst the confusion of some old pieces of furniture or lumber there are pictures, unframed and dim, leaning against the walls. One of them—a large painting of some rare plant, formerly a curiosity in the Botanical Gardens at Regent's Park, while the rest are groups of flowers and fruit. Just opposite me, on the high mantel-piece, the canvas broken here and there near the edges, obscured by the dust and smoke that have dulled their surface, are two oil-paintings which I venture to take down for a nearer inspection. Surely they must have been finished when madame was yet in the prime of her art. Exquisite in drawing, delicate in colour, and with a subtle touch that gives to each petal the fresh crumple that bespeaks it newly-blown, and to fruit the dewy down that would make even a *gourmet* linger ere he pressed the juice. It is almost pain to think that they are left here uncared for; and yet, who knows what influence their presence above that dingy shelf may have upon the wandering thoughts and waning dreams of her who painted them when every new effort of her skill was a keen delight?

Nay, even as I hold them to the light, and in a pause of our chat (wherein Madame la Comtesse speaks slowly and with some difficulty) say some half-involuntary words of appreciation, she has risen, and stands upright by the fire with an earnest look in her face and a sudden gesture of awakened interest. The artistic instinct is there still, after more than eighty years of life, and the appreciation

---

* Since these lines were written, Madame Comoléra has gone to her rest.

of the work animates her yet. Not with a mere vulgar love of praise (for Madame is still la Comtesse Comoléra even though she spends her days in an almshouse), but with a recognition that I have distinguished the best of the work that is left to her to show. I shall not readily forget the sudden look of almost eager interest, the effort to speak generous words of thanks, as I bow over her hand to say farewell, and feel that I have been as privileged a visitor as though madame had received me in a gilded *salon*, at the door of which a powdered lacquey stood to " welcome the coming—speed the parting guest."

And so with some pleasant leave-takings, and not without permission to see them again, I leave these ladies —the fitting representatives of an old nobility and an old *régime*—to the solitude to which they have retired from a world too ready to forget.

If by any means for the solitude could be substituted a pleasant retirement, and for the sense of desolation and poverty a modest provision that would yet include some grace and lightness to light their declining days, it would be but little after all.

WITH THEM THAT GO DOWN TO THE SEA IN SHIPS.

T is possible that those portions of the sacred history which have reference to the association of our Lord Jesus Christ with ships, and the wonderful portions of the great narrative where the Divine Voice seems, as it were, to come from the sea, may have a special attraction for us who live in an island and claim a kind of maritime dominion.

Surely the words "Lord, save me, or I perish," and the instant response of the outstretched hand of the Saviour of men, must have been read with an awful joy by many a God-fearing sailor on the homeward voyage. "It is I, be not afraid," must have come with an intensity of meaning to many a heart which has known the peril of the storm, wherein the voice of man to man has been almost inaudible.

There is something very solemn in the prayers we send up for those at sea. Most of us feel a heart-throb when we lie awake listening to the mighty murmurs of the wind, and waiting for the shrill shriek with which each long terrible blast gathers up its forces—a throb which comes of the sudden thought of lonely ships far out upon the ocean, where men are wrestling with the elements, and looking with clenched lips and straining eyes for the lingering dawn.

Yet, with all this, it is a national reproach to us that until a comparatively recent date we have done little or nothing for our sailors—little for those who have been ready to maintain the old supremacy of our fleet—almost nothing for that greater navy of the mercantile marine to which we are indebted for half the necessaries and for nearly all the luxuries which we enjoy.

A national reproach, because not only have charitable provisions for destitute, sick, infirm, or disabled sailors been neglected, but subscriptions demanded by the State from seamen of the merchant service were never properly applied to relieve the distress of those for whom they were professedly received. Considerably over a million of money has been contributed by merchant seamen, by deductions of sixpences from their monthly pay for the maintenance of Greenwich Hospital, and in addition to this there have been accumulated in the hands of the Government the examination fees of masters and mates passing the Board of Trade examination, and the penny fees paid by common seamen on shipment and unshipment, while the unclaimed wages and effects of seamen dying abroad are calculated at about £8000 a year.

Now there can be no doubt that Greenwich Hospital was originally intended to include merchant seamen in its provisions, for the preamble to the original scheme of William III. recites, " Whereas the King's most excellent Majesty being anxiously desirous to promote the Trade, Navigation, and Naval strength of this Kingdom, and to invite greater numbers of his subjects to betake themselves to the sea, hath determined to erect a hospital," &c. For this purpose sixpence per man per month was to be paid out of the wages of all mariners to the support of the Hospital, and every seaman was to be registered. Why? That the charity might be "for the relief, benefit, or advantage of such the said registered Marines, or Seamen, Watermen, Fishermen, Lightermen, Bargemen, Keelmen, or Seafaring Men, who by age, wounds, or other accidents shall be disabled for future service at sea, and shall not be in a condition to maintain themselves comfortably; and the children of such disabled seamen; and the widows and children of such of them as shall happen to be slain, killed, or drowned in sea service, so far forth as the Hospital shall be capable to receive them, and the revenue thereof will extend."

So far as words went, therefore—and subsequent Acts of Parliament confirmed them—Greenwich Hospital was open to all registered seamen. The fact has always been, however, that it was barely able to meet the claims made by the disabled and infirm sailors of the Navy alone, and therefore the mercantile marine was practically excluded, while the payments were still demanded.

Now let us see what past Governments did for the relief of those old, infirm, or disabled men who having "seen wonders on the great deep," came home and sought help.

A charitable trust, called the "Merchant Seamen's Fund," had been established by merchants and shipowners of the City of London, who gave large sums to it, in order to try to make up for the injustice by which these sailors were virtually excluded from Greenwich Hospital, to which the men of the mercantile marine still had to pay sixpence a month. By a remarkably knowing piece of legislation, an Act was passed (the 20th of George II.) which incorporated the Merchant Seamen's Fund, appointed president and governors, and gave authority to purchase land for building a hospital, to help pay for which another sixpence a month was claimed from the pay of merchant seamen and masters of merchant vessels.

Not till the year 1834, by an Act passed in the reign of William IV., were the merchant sailors relieved from compulsory payment to Greenwich. They had contributed to the hospital for 138 years without having derived any direct benefit from it; and though they were not unwilling to subscribe for their brethren in the Royal Navy, the injustice which demanded their contributions, though their own fund was inadequate to pay for the promised building for which it was intended, became too glaring to be continued. It was therefore determined that a grant of £20,000 should be made to Greenwich Hospital out of the Consolidated Fund, and that the merchant sailors should go on paying their shilling a month for their own benefit (masters paying two shillings), and that a provision for widows and children should be included in the charity, the benefits of which were to be extended to Scotland and Ireland.

The hospital never was built. The Board of Trade taking the management of the contributions, appointed trustees, who were altogether incompetent, and did their duty in a perfunctory or careless manner. In 1850, only £20,000 was distributed among old, infirm, and disabled seamen, while £41,000 was bestowed on widows and children; the allowances varying at different ports from £1 to £7, each place having its own local government. Of course a collapse came. The fund was bankrupt; and in the following year an Act was passed for winding it up—for, says the Board of Trade Report, "the Government has had no control over the matter. The London

Corporation and the trustees of outports could not by any mangement have prevented the insolvency of the fund, as long as they were guided by the principles which the several Acts of Parliament laid down . . . . . the whole system was vicious."

By the winding-up Act of 1851 compulsory contributions ceased; but those who chose to continue to subscribe voluntarily might do so. It is hardly to be wondered at that the merchant seamen lost confidence in the paternal protection of the Board of Trade. A few thousand pounds were left from the compulsory contributions, and when this came to be inquired for, nobody knew anything about it. It had somehow slipped out of the estimates, and nobody could tell what had become of it.

That is what past governments have done for poor mercantile Jack.

What has the great British public done for him? Not so very much after all. The truth is, that the sailor, who has always been spoken of as "so dreadfully improvident," has been practically regarded as being most self-helpful. All the time that we have been shaking our solemn heads, and lifting up our hands at the improvidence, the folly, and the extravagance of these frequently underpaid and sometimes overworked men, we have made even the help that we were willing to extend to them in their deeper necessities partially dependent on their own constant and regular subscription to the same end.

Poor improvident Jack!—poor thoughtless, incorrigible fellow!—it was necessary for the Government of his country to look after him, in order to protect him against his own want of forethought, and the result has been to run the ship into shoal water, and go hopelessly to wreck without so much as salvage money.

Jack ashore! Don't we all still look at the sailor in the light of the evil war-times, when the king's men were said to draw pocketsful of prize-money and to spend it in low debauchery or wild wanton folly? Even now we repeat the stories of frying watches along with beefsteaks and onions, or eating bank-note sandwiches. Nay, to this day in the fo'c's'le of merchant vessels some of the melancholy old songs in which sailors are wont to satirise themselves are occasionally sung, telling how

> "When his money is all spent,
> And there's nothing to be borrowed and nothing to be lent,
> In comes the landlord with a frown,
> Saying, 'Jack! get up, and let *John* sit down,
> For you are *outward* bound.'"

There's a world of meaning in that grim suggestive summary; but, thank God! it has less meaning now than it once had. Until quite lately, sailors of merchant ships could be kept for days waiting to be paid, and, sickened with lingering for long weary hours about the office of the broker or agent who withheld their money, fell into the hands of the harpies who were, and still are constantly on the look-out to plunder them. Men with all the pure natural longing for home and reunion with those near and dear to them, were compelled to loiter about the foul neighbourhood of the dock where their ship discharged its cargo, lodging in some low haunt with evil company, and liable to every temptation that is rife in such places, till too often so large a portion of their hardly-earned wages had been forestalled, that in a dreary and desperate madness of dissipation they were tempted to fling away the small balance remaining to them, and to awake to reason only when, naked and nearly destitute, they were compelled to go to sea again, with a slender stock of clothes, and a week's board and lodging paid for with advance notes.

From long confinement and monotony on shipboard, the sailor even now comes to a sense of temporary freedom, giddy with the unaccustomed sense of solid ground and the wild toss and uproar of the ocean of life in a great city. What are still the influences which in many seaports await him directly his foot touches the shore, and sometimes even before he has come over the vessel's side? With a boy's recklessness, a man's passions, and the unwonted excitement of possessing money and boundless opportunities for spending it, a shoal of landsharks are lying ready to batten on him. The tout, the crimp, and all the wretches, male and female, who look upon him as their prey, will never leave him from the time when they watch him roll wonderingly on to the landing-stage, till that desperate minute when he flings his last handful of small change across the tavern counter, and calls for its worth in drink, since "money is no use at sea."

This was far more frequently the termination of mercantile Jack's spell ashore, before the new regulations as to prompt payment of seamen's wages came into force. At that time you had only to take a morning walk across Tower Hill, where the bluff lay figure at the outfitter's door stands for Jack in full feather, and thence to America Square, or the neighbourhood of the Minories and Rosemary Lane, to see dozens of poor fellows lounging listlessly about the doors of pay-agents, waiting day after day at the street-corners, with an occasional visit to the public-house, and the perpetual consumption of "hard" tobacco. It was easy afterwards to follow Jack to Ratcliffe, Rotherhithe, Shadwell, and the neighbourhood, where his "friends" lay in wait for him to spend the evening; in the tap-rooms of waterside taverns, where he sat hopelessly drinking and smoking during a hot summer's afternoon; to frowsy, low-browed shops of cheap clothiers, to hot, stifling dancing-rooms, to skittle-alleys behind gin-shop bars, where a sudden brawl would call out knives, and the use of a "slung-shot" as a weapon would make a case of manslaughter for the coroner; to very minor theatres, where he could see absurd caricatures of himself in the stage sailors, dancing hornpipes unknown at sea; to the dreadful dens of Bluegate Fields and Tiger Bay—to any or all of these places you might have followed Jack; and may even yet follow his fellows who have not yet been redeemed from the evil ways of those bad times, when there were no homes for sailors amidst the bewildering vice and misery of maritime London, and other seaport towns of this great mercantile island.

It so happened that I made my first intimate acquaintance with the one real, publicly representative "Sailors' Home" in Well Street, near the London Docks, after having seen Jack under several of the terrible conditions just referred to, so that, with this painful knowledge of him and his ways, it was with a kind of delighted surprise that I suddenly walked into the great entrance-hall of the institution, where he and his fellows were sitting on the benches by the wall with the serious, contemplative, almost solemn air which is (in my experience) the common expression of sailors ashore, and during ordinary leisure hours. There they were, a good ship's crew of them altogether, sitting, as I have already said, in true sailor fashion—stooping forward, wrists on knees, lolling on sea-chests and clothes-bags, taking short fore-

and-aft walks of six steps and a turn in company with some old messmate, smoking, growling, chatting, and generally enjoying their liberty; not without an eye, now and then, to the smart officer who had come in to see whether he could pick up a brisk hand or two for the mail service.

This was some five or six years ago, and it is a happy result of the plan on which the Home was first established (which was intended ultimately to make the institution self-supporting, if the cost of building were defrayed) that the whole scheme has been so enlarged since that time, that anybody who would see what our mercantile seamen are like, may now go and see them, in a largely increasing community, in this great institution. So many come and go and reappear at intervals represented by the length of their voyages, that 10,120 officers and men had partaken of its inestimable benefits during the year from the first of May, 1872, to the end of April, 1873.

But the institution itself was founded in earnest faith, and built with the labour that is consecrated by prayer. Both to the Home and to its companion institution, the Refuge for Destitute Seamen—we will pay a visit on our next meeting.

WITH THEM WHO WERE READY TO PERISH.

N the 28th of February, 1828, a very terrible calamity happened in the place known as Wellclose Square, Whitechapel. A new theatre called the Brunswick, had been erected there on the site of a former building, known as the Old Royalty. It had been completed in seven months, and three days afterwards, during a rehearsal, the whole structure gave way and fell with a crash, burying ten persons amidst the ruins, and fearfully injuring several others. Such a catastrophe was very awful, and the people of the neighbourhood looked with an almost solemn curiosity at the wreck of an edifice in which they themselves might have met with death suddenly.

Very soon, however, they began to regard the heap of ruins with surprise, for early one morning there appeared two officers of the Royal Navy, surrounded by a gang of labourers with picks and shovels, and before these men (some of whom were Irish Roman Catholic) began to work they listened attentively while one of the officers offered up an earnest prayer to God for a blessing on the results of the labour they were about to undertake. Morning after morning their labour was thus sanctified, and evening after evening it was celebrated by the voice of thanksgiving, till at length the ground was cleared, and on the 10th of June, 1830, the first stone of a new building was laid. The building was to be a Home for Sailors, and as a necessary adjunct to the Home, it was intended to establish a Destitute Sailors' Asylum.

The two naval officers were Captain (now Admiral) George C. Gambier, and Captain Robert James Elliot, now gone to his rest, who with Lieutenant Robert Justice afterwards Captain, and now with his old comrade, in the heavenly haven, had been seeking how to ameliorate the condition of seamen, numbers of whom were to be seen homeless, miserable, and frequently half naked and destitute, in that foul and wretched neighbourhood about the Docks and beyond Tower Hill.

The task was a difficult one, and might have daunted less brave and hopeful men, for it was intended to demolish the piratical haunts where the enemies of the sailor lay in wait for his destruction; where crimps and thieves and the keepers of infamous dens held their besotted victims in bondage, while they battened on the wages that had been earned during months of privation and arduous toil.

It was necessary, therefore, first to provide a decent and comfortable lodging-house for the reception of sailors coming into port,—a place where they might safely deposit their clothes and their wages, and where they could "look out for another ship" without the evil intervention of crimps or pretended agents. It was a part of the intended plan also to establish a savings bank, for securing any portion of their wages which they chose to lay by, or for safely transmitting such sums as they might wish to send to their relations. In short, the design was to provide a home for the homeless, and hold out helping hands to those who were ready to perish.

Those ruins of the theatre stood on the very spot for such an establishment, and the two captains, Gambier and Elliott, began by buying the ground and the wreck that stood upon it, not by asking for public subscriptions, but mostly with their own money, to which was added a few contributions from any of their friends who desired to join in the good work.

It is impossible to use more earnest or touching words than those in which the late Rear-Admiral Sir W. E. Parry spoke of the labours of his friend and fellow-supporter of the Sailors' Home, in an address to British seamen at Southampton, in 1853. "And now," he said, "let me just add that, from the first moment in which Captain Elliot stood among the ruins of the Brunswick Theatre, till it pleased God to deprive him of bodily and mental energy, did that self-denying Christian man devote all his powers, his talents, his influence, and his money, to this his darling object of protecting and providing for the comfort of sailors. Connected with a noble family, and entitled by birth, education, and station, to all the advantages which the most exalted society could give him, he willingly relinquished all, took up his abode in a humble lodging, surrounded by gin-shops, near the 'Home:' denied himself most of the comforts, it may almost be said some of the necessaries of life, in order the more effectually to carry out his benevolent design; and for eighteen years of self-denial and devotion, made it the business of his life to superintend this institution."

For the noble officer lived to see the building for which he had wrought and prayed, complete and successful. In 1835 300 sailors could be received and welcomed there.

The piratical lairs began to empty of some of those who had been shown a way of escape, and the good work went on. In the adjoining Seamen's Church the congregation was largely augmented by the boarders from the Sailors' Home, while the Honorary Chaplain and the Missionary attached officially to the institution, became not only parson and preacher, but friendly adviser and instructor, ready to speak, to hear, and to forbear. The addition of a book depository, where various useful publications may be purchased, and Bibles are sold at the lowest possible prices, and in various languages, was a valuable auxiliary to moral and religious instruction, and at once increased the home-like influences of the place.

The institution having gone on thus prosperously, under the direction of a goodly number of officers and gentlemen, added to its possessions by acquiring other plots of freehold ground, extending backward to Dock Street; and in 1863 Lord Palmerston laid the stone of an entirely new block of building, which was inaugurated by the Prince of Wales in 1865, since which time 502 boarders can be received, each being provided with his separate cabin.

Since the opening of the institution in 1835 it has received 246,855 seamen of various countries and from all parts of the world. Of these 72,234 have been old or returned boarders, and most of them have conducted their money transactions through the "Home," and have made good use of the savings-bank.

There are 270 inmates under that protecting roof as I step into the large entrance hall in Well Street to-day; and the two hundred and seventy-first has just gone to look after his kit and sea-chests, which have been carefully conveyed from the Docks by one of the carmen belonging to the institution, who has " The Sailors' Home, Well Street," worked in red worsted on his shirt, and painted on the side of the van from which he has just alighted.

It is evident that our friend No. 271 has been here before, for he knows exactly where to present himself in order to deposit some of his more portable property with the cashier or the superintendent. He scarcely looks like a man who will want an advance of money, for he is a smart, alert, bright-eyed fellow, with a quiet air of self-respect about him which seems to indicate an account in the savings-bank; but should he be "hard-up," he can ask for and receive a loan not exceeding twenty shillings directly his chest is deposited in his cabin. Just now the chest itself, together with its superincumbent bundle, stands against the wall along with some other incoming or outgoing boxes, more than one of which are associated with brand new cages for parrots, and some odd-shaped cases evidently containing sextants or other nautical instruments. There is a whole ship's crew, and a smart one too, in the hall to-day; while a small contingent occupies the clothing department, where one or two shrewd North-countrymen are being fitted each with a "new rig," knowing well enough that they will be better served there than at any of the cheap outfitters (or the dear ones either) in the neighbourhood. Fine blue broadcloth, pilots, tweeds, rough weather, and petershams are here to choose from " to measure," as well as a wonderful collection of hats, caps, underclothing, hosiery, neckties, boots, and shoes so unlike the clumsy specimens that swing along with the tin pots and oilskins in some of the little low-browed shops about the district, that I at once discover the reason for the smartness and general neatly-fitted look of most of the men and lads now pacing up and down, talking and smoking. It is quiet talk for the most part, even when half a dozen of the inmates adjourn to the refreshment-room, where they can obtain a glass of good sound beer (though there is a much more general appreciation of coffee) and sit down comfortably at a table like that at which two serious mates are already discussing some knotty point, which will probably last till tea-time.

Tea-time? There is the half-past five o'clock signal gong going now, and light swift steps are to be heard running up the stairs into the large dining-hall, where the two hundred and seventy-one, or as many of them as are at home, sit down like fellows who know their business and mean to do it. It is a pleasant business enough, and one soon despatched; for there are so many big teapots, that each table is amply provided by the alert attendants, who dispense bread-and-butter, watercresses, salads, and savoury bloaters and slices of ham and tongue, the latter having been already served by a carver who is equal to the occasion. It is astonishing how quickly the meal is over when its substantial quality is taken into account; but there is no lack of waiters, the number of attendants in the building being sixty-five, some of whom, of course, belong to the dormitories and to other departments.

The meals here are, of course, served with the utmost regularity, and without limit to quantity. Breakfast, with cold meat, fish, bacon, and general "relishes," at eight in the morning; dinner at one: consisting of soup, roast and boiled meats, ample supplies of vegetables, occasional fish, stupendous fruit-pies and puddings, and a good allowance of beer. After tea comes a substantial snack for supper, at nine o'clock, and the doors of the institution are kept open to half-past eleven at night; those who wish to remain out later being required to obtain a pass from the superintendent.

Of course it is requested that the boarders come in to meals as punctually as possible; but those who cannot conveniently be present at the regular time, can have any meal supplied to them on application. Indeed, two or three belated ones are arriving now, as we go to the end of the long and lofty refectory to look at the crest of the late Admiral Sir William Bowles, K.C.B., which, supported by flags, is painted upon the wall, as a memorial of a gallant officer and a good friend to this institution and to all sailors.

Leaving the dining-hall, we notice a smaller room, set apart for masters and mates who may desire to have their meals served here; and on the same extensive storey is a large and comfortable reading-room well supplied with periodicals, and containing a capital library consisting of entertaining and instructive books.

The board-room is close by, and is of the size and shape to make an excellent mission-room, where week-night services and meetings of a religious character are held, and well attended by men who, having seen the wonders of the Lord upon the great deep, join in His reasonable service when they are at home and at rest. This vast floor also contains two dormitories: but most of the sleeping cabins are in the second and third floors.

There are few sights in London more remarkable than these berths, which are, in fact, separate cabins, each closed by its own door, and containing bed, wash-stand, chair, looking-glass, towels, and ample space for the sea-chest and personal belongings of the occupant. The cabins extend round a large area rising to a great height, and surrounded above by a light gallery reached by an outer staircase, round which are another series of berths exactly resembling the lower ones; so that there are, in fact, double, and in one or two dormitories treble tiers of cabins, and the upper ones may be entered without disturbing the inmates of those below. One of the three-decker areas is of vast size, and, standing in the upper gallery and looking upward to the lofty roof, and then downward to the clear, wide, open space between the lower rooms, the visitor is struck by the admirable provision both for light and ventilation; the former being secured at night by means of properly distributed gas jets, which are of course under the care of the night attendants, who are on watch in each dormitory, and may be summoned at once in case of illness or accident.

Not only is there provision against fire by a length of fire-hose attached to hydrants on each storey, but the water supply to lavatories and for other purposes is secured by a cistern holding 4,000 gallons at the top of the building; so that there is complete circulation throughout the various parts of the building.

It is time that we paid a visit to the basement of this great institution, however; for, in more senses than one, it may be said to be at the foundation of the arrangements. Yes, even with respect to the amusements provided for the inmates—for while chess, draughts and backgammon are to be found in the library and reading-room, and billiards and bagatelle hold their own on the great landings of the first storey, we have down here a skittle-alley of a character so remarkable, that some of us who have read Washington Irving think of the reverberations of the giants' pastime in the mountains, while we wonder where sailors can first have acquired a taste for this particular amusement. It is a good and healthy one, however, and is wisely provided, since it adds one more efficient inducement to the men to take their pleasure among their true friends instead of seeking it amidst the evil influences of a filthy tavern, or in the garish heat of some vile Ratcliff Highway bowling-alley, where men are maddened with drugged drink, and greeted with foul imprecations by the harpies who seek to rob and cheat them.

There is much to see in this basement, and to begin with here is No. two hundred and seventy-one sending his chest up by the great luggage-lift to the second floor, where he will find it presently in his cabin. We cannot stay to speak to him, however, for we are on the very verge of the kitchen, to which we are, as it were, led by the nose; for wafted thence comes an appetising perfume of new bread just taken from one of the great ovens devoted to the daily baking. There are lingering odours also of to-day's dinner, though the meat ovens and the great boilers and hot plates are clean and ready for the morrow. The pantry door, too, is open, and there are toothsome varieties of "plain-eating" therein, while the storerooms savour of mingled comforts, to which the gales of Araby the blest offer no parallel, and the butcher's shop has a calm and concentrated sense of meatiness which is suggestive to a robust appetite not already satiated with a chunk from one of a whole squadron of soft, new currant-cakes. After a peep at the large and busy laundry with its peculiar moist atmosphere, the coal and beer cellars, the pumping machinery and boiler-room may be passed by, and little curiosity is excited by this long and convenient apartment where hot and cold baths are prepared to order at a merely nominal charge. There is a door close by, however, where we stop instinctively, for there is a cheerful light inside, and a sound of easy and yet interrupted conversation which can belong to only one department of society. There can be no mistake about it— a veritable barber's shop, and a gentleman with a preternaturally clean chin complacently surveying himself in a looking-glass of limited dimensions, while another waits to be operated upon by the skilled practitioner who carries in his face the suggestion of a whole ropery of "tough yarns," and was—or am I mistaken—tonsor to the *Victory* or to some ship of war equally famous when the British seaman shaved close and often, and pigtails had hardly gone out of fashion. There is no time for testing the great artist's skill this evening, though I could almost sacrifice a well-grown beard to hear some rare old fo'c's'le story. But no story could be more wonderful than the plain truth that for all the generous provision in this excellent institution the rescued sailor brought within its wholesome influence pays but fifteen shillings a week. Yes, men and apprentices, fifteen shillings; and officers, eighteen and sixpence.

The evening lowers over the outer world of Mint Street and Leman Street, and the great blank void of the Tower ditch is full of shadow. Standing again in the large entrance hall, which reminds one more of shipboard, now that the lights are dotted about it, leaving it still a little dim, I hear the trickling of a drinking-fountain, and associated with its fresh plash hear as pleasant a story as any yarn that ever the barber himself could have spun for my delight.

The fountain, which is of polished Aberdeen granite,

was opened last November in proper style, a platform being erected, and the chair being taken by the Secretary to the "Metropolitan Drinking Fountains Association," supported by several ladies and gentlemen. Mr. Lee made an appropriate speech, and called attention to the gift, and pointed to the inscription; and it was quite an emphatic little observance for the inmates who had gathered in the hall on the occasion. And well it might be, for the fountain bears this modest inscription:—" The gift of William McNeil, Seaman, in appreciation of the great benefits he has derived on the various occasions during which he has made the Institution his *Home*, for upwards of 25 years.

I think very little more need be said for the Sailors' Home than is indicated by this plain, earnest testimony to its worth. Yet it is necessary to say one more word. This Sailors' Home is in a way self-supporting, and at present seeks only the kindly interest of the public in case it should ever need another response to an appeal for extending its sphere of usefulness. Not a farthing of profit is permitted to any individual engaged in it, and even fees to servants are prohibited, though the crimps and touts outside endeavour to bribe them sometimes, to induce sailors to go to the common lodging-houses, where land-rats seek their prey. All the profits, if there are any at all, are placed to a reserve fund for repairs, improvements, or extensions. At any rate, no public appeals are being made just now.

But there is another institution next door—another branch of the stem which has grown so sturdily from the seed planted by the good captain—the Destitute Sailors' Asylum. That is a place full of interest, though there is nothing to see there. Nothing but a clean yard, with means for washing and cleansing, and a purifying oven for removing possible infection from clothes, and a great bare room, just comfortably warmed in winter, and hung with rows of hammocks, like the 'tween-decks of a ship.

That is all; but in those hammocks, sometimes, poor starved and destitute sailors go to sleep, after they have been fed with soup and warmed and comforted; and in the morning, when they turn out, they are fed again with cocoa and bread, and if they are naked they are clothed. There are not very many applicants, for, strange as it may appear, since sailors' homes have come in fashion there are but few destitute seamen; but there *need be no unrelieved destitute sailors at all in London,* for anybody can send such a one to the Asylum in Well Street, London Docks, and he will be admitted. Here then, is an institution that may claim support.

CASTING BREAD UPON THE WATERS.

NE of the old Saxon commentators on the Holy Scriptures, in referring to the passage, " Cast thy bread upon the waters, and it shall be found after many days," ventures to suggest as a meaning—" Give succour to poor and afflicted seamen." Whatever may be the conclusions of critical Biblical expositors, there can be no doubt that the pious annotator was right in a true—that is, in a spiritual interpretation of the text.

Should it be necessary to appeal twice to the English nation—which has, as it were a savour of sea-salt in its very blood—to hold out a helping hand for those who, having struggled to keep our dominion by carrying the flag of British commerce all round the world, are themselves flung ashore, weak, old, and helpless, dependent on the goodwill of their countrymen to take them into some quiet harbour, where they may, as it were be laid up in ordinary and undergo some sort of repairs, even though they should never again be able to go a voyage? It is with feelings of something like regret that an average Englishman sees the old hull of a sea-going boat lie neglected and uncared for on the beach. Not without a pang can we witness the breaking-up of some stout old ship no longer seaworthy. Yet, unhappily, we have hitherto given scant attention to the needs of those old and infirm seamen, who having for many years contributed out of their wages to the funds of the Naval Hospital at Greenwich, and having been again mulcted of some subscriptions which were to have been specially devoted to found an asylum for themselves, are left with little to look forward to but the workhouse ward when, crippled, sick, or feeble with age, they could no longer tread the deck or crack a biscuit.

It is true that there are now hospitals or sick-asylums in connection with some of the sailors' homes at our seaports, and to the general hospitals any sailor can be admitted if he should be able to procure a letter from a governor. The 'tween-decks of the *Dreadnought* no longer form the sole hospital for invalided merchant seamen in the Port of London; but even reckoning all that has been done for sailors, and fresh from a visit to that great building where three hundred hale and hearty seamen of the great mercantile navy find a home, we are left to wonder that so little has been accomplished for those old tars who, having lived for threescore years or more, going to and fro upon the great deep, can find no certain anchorage, except within the walls of some union where they may at last succeed in claiming a settlement. Surely there is no figure which occupies a more prominent place in English history than that of the sailor— not the man-o'-war's man only—but the merchant seaman, the descendant of those followers of the great old navigators who were called " merchant adventurers," and who practically founded for Great Britain new empires beyond the sea. In the poetry, the songs, the literature, the political records, the social chronicles, the domestic narratives of England, the sailor holds a place, and even at our holiday seasons, when our children cluster on the shingly shore or the far-stretching brown sands of the coast, we find still that we belong to a nation of which the sailor long stood as the chosen representative. Nay, in the midst of the life of a great city we cannot fail to be reminded of the daring and the enterprise which has helped to make London what it is.

The poet, who, standing on the bridge at midnight, and listening to the chime of the hour, found his imagination occupied with serious images and his memory with solemn recollections, would have been no less moved to profound contemplation had he been a temporary occupant of one of the great structures that span the silent highway of the Thames. There is something in the flow of a broad and rapid stream which has a peculiar association with thoughts of the struggle and toil of human life, and as we look on the ever-moving tide, we ask ourselves what have we done for the brave old toil-worn men who have seen the wonders of the great deep for so many years, and have brought so much to us that we can scarcely speak of food or drink without some reminder of their toilsome lives and long voyages? Well, a little has been done,—very little when we reflect how much yet remains to be accomplished; and yet much, regarded as a fair opportunity for doing a great deal more. I have already recounted some part of the sad story of what a provident Government did when it thought to undertake the affairs of poor improvident Jack. How it collected his money, and neglected to give him the benefit of the enforced subscription; how it administered and laid claim to his poor little effects and arrears of pay, if he died abroad and nobody came forward to establish a right to them; how it demanded additional contributions from his monthly wages, in order to show him how to establish a relief fund; and how somehow the scheme went "by the board" (of Trade), and the balance of the money was lost in the gulf of the estimates.

As long ago as 1860 it became clear to a number of leading merchants, shipowners, and officers of the mercantile marine that nothing was to be looked for from the State when the subject of making an effort to provide for aged and infirm sailors was again urgently brought forward; but it was determined to make a definite movement, and "The Shipwrecked Mariners' Society," which had then 40,000 officers and seamen among its subscribers, was appealed to as a body having the power to form the required association.

It was not till 1867, however, that the actual work of providing an asylum for old sailors was commenced. The society had then put down the sum of £5,000 as a good beginning, a committee had been appointed, of which the late honoured Paymaster Francis Lean was the indefatigable honorary secretary, and Captain Thomas Tribe the secretary, whilst the list of patrons, presidents, vice-presidents, and supporters included many eminent noblemen and gentlemen who took a true interest in the undertaking.

Several public meetings were held, and "a Pension and Widows' Fund" was first established. Then the committee began to look about them for a suitable house in which to begin their real business, and had their attention directed to a large building at that time for sale, situated on the breezy height above Erith, and formerly well known as the residence of Sir Culling Eardley, who had named it Belvidere. The property, including twenty-three acres of surrounding land, cost £12,148, and £5,000 having already been subscribed, the balance of £7,148 was borrowed at five per cent. interest. Not till the 5th of May, 1866, however, was the institution inaugurated and handed over to a committee of management.

It is admirably suggestive of its present occupation, this fine roomy old mansion, standing on the sheltered side, but near the top, of the lofty eminence, whence such a magnificent view may be obtained, not only of the surrounding country, but of the mighty river where it widens and rushes towards the sea. Here on the broad sloping green, where the tall flagstaff with its rigging supports the Union Jack, the old fellows stroll in the sun or look out with a knowing weather-eye towards the shipping going down stream, or sit to smoke and gossip on the bench beneath their spreading tree opposite the great cedar, while the cow of the institution chews the cud with a serious look, as though it had someway caught the thoughtful expression that characterises "turning a quid." A hundred infirm sailors, each of whom is more than sixty years old, are serenely at their moorings in that spacious square-built house, where the long wards are divided into cabins, each with its neat furniture, and many of them ornamented with the curious knick-knacks, and strange waifs and strays of former voyages which sailors like to have about them. There is of course a sick-ward, where those who are permanently disabled, or are suffering from illness, receive medical attention and a special diet; but the majority of the inmates are comparatively hearty still, though they are disabled, and can no longer "hand reef and steer."

There are a hundred inmates in this admirable asylum,

and ninety pensioners who are with their friends at the various outports of the kingdom, each receiving a pension of £1 a month, called the "Mariners' National Pension Fund," the working management of which, with the "Widows' Annuity Fund," is made over to the "Shipwrecked Mariners' Society."

A hundred and ninety worn-out and disabled seamen now provided for or assisted, and a total of above 300 relieved since the opening of the institution. A good and noble work truly. But can it be called by so great a name as *National*, when we know how large a number of old sailors are yet homeless, and that at the last election there were 153 candidates who could not be assisted because of the want of funds to relieve their distress? Looking at the number of men (2,000 to 5,000) lost at sea or by shipwreck every year, and at the inquiry which has been made, through the efforts of Mr. Plimsoll and others, with respect to the conditions under which the service of the mercantile marine of this country is carried on, is it not a reproach to us that during the nineteen years since this institution was founded, so little has been done? Year by year it has been hoped that the Board of Trade would relinquish its claim to take possession of the effects of sailors dying abroad, and would transfer the £1,200 a year represented by this property to the funds of the society, but hitherto the committee have waited in vain. The donations from all sources are comparatively few; and though the annual subscriptions are numerous, they are rapidly absorbed.

Many masters, mates, seamen, engineers and firemen pay to this institution a subscription of five shillings a year, for which they have a vote at each annual election; or any such subscriber may leave his votes to accumulate for his own benefit when he shall have reached the age of sixty years, and becomes a candidate for admission.

One-fifth of the candidates admitted are nominated by the committee on the ground of their necessities or special claims to the benefit of the charity, while general subscribers or donors have privileges of election according to the amount contributed. Perhaps one of the most touching records of the subscription list is, that not only did the cadets of the mercantile training-ship *Worcester* contribute something like £100 in one official year, but that the little fellows on board the union training-ship *Goliath* lying off Grays, have joined their officers and their commander, Captain Bourchier, to send offerings to the aid of the ancient mariners, of whom they are the very latest representatives. On many a good ship these small collections are made for the same object, and at the Sailors' Home in Well Street there is a box for stray contributions; but much more has yet to be done. Perhaps it is far to go to see this great house on the hill, but most of us have caught a glimpse of its tall towers and its flagstaff in our excursions down the silent highway of London's river, and it might be well to think how little effort is required to give to each cabin its inmate, and to fill the dining-room with tables, each with its "mess" of six or eight old salts, who are ready to greet you heartily if you pay them a visit, and to salute you with a grave seamanlike respect. Would you like to know how this rare old crew lives in the big house under the lee of the wind-blown hill? To begin with, the men who are not invalids turn out at eight in winter and half-past seven in summer, and after making beds and having a good wash, go down to prayers and breakfast at nine' or half-past eight, breakfast consisting of coffee or cocoa and bread-and-butter.

At ten o'clock the ward-men, who are appointed in rotation, go to clean wards and make all tidy, each inmate being, however, responsible for the neatness of his own cabin, in which nobody is allowed to drive nails in bulkheads or walls, and no cutting or carving of woodwork is permitted. The men not for the time employed in tidying up or airing bedding, &c., can, if they choose, go into the industrial ward, where they can work at several occupations for their own profit, as they are only charged for cost of materials. Dinner is served in the several messes by the appointed messmen at one o'clock, and consists on Sundays of roast beef, vegetables, and plum-pudding, and on week-days of roast or boiled meat, soup, vegetables, with one day a week salt fish, onions, potatoes, and plain suet-pudding, and in summer an occasional salad. A pint of beer is allowed for each man. The afternoon may be devoted either to work, or to recreation in the reading and smoking rooms, or in the grounds. Tea and bread-and-butter are served at half-past five in summer and at six in winter, and there is often a supper of bread-and-cheese and watercresses or radishes. The evening is devoted to recreation, and at half-past nine in winter, and ten in summer, after prayers, lights are put out, and every one retires for the night.

None of the inmates are expected to work in the industrial wards, and of course there are various servants and attendants, all of whom are chosen by preference from the families of sailors, or have themselves been at sea. The whole place is kept so orderly, and everything is so ship-shape, that there is neither waste nor confusion, and yet every man there is at liberty to go in and out when he pleases, on condition of being in at meal-times, and at the time for evening prayers, any one desiring to remain away being required to ask permission of the manager. It must be mentioned, too, that there is an allowance of ninepence a week spending money for each inmate.

The men are comfortably clothed, in a decent sailorly fashion, and many of the old fellows have still the bright, alert, active look that belongs to the "smart hands," among whom some of them were reckoned nearly half a century ago. The most ancient of these mariners at the time of my first visit was ninety-two years old, and it so happened that I saw him on his birthday. He came up the broad flight of stairs to speak to me, with a foot that had not lost all its lightness, while the eye that was left to him (he had lost one by accident twenty years before) was as bright and open as a sailor's should be. This is a long time ago, and William Coverdale (that was his name) has probably gone to his rest. Significantly enough, at the time of my latest visit, the oldest representative of the last muster-roll was James Nelson, a master mariner of Downpatrick, eighty-five years of age; while bo's'n Blanchard is eighty-one; able seaman John Hall, eighty; William Terry (A. B.), eighty-two, and masters, mates, quartermasters, cooks, and stewards, ranged over seventy. With many of them this is the incurable disability that keeps them ashore; the sort of complaint which is common to sailors and landsmen alike if they live long enough—that of old age. It will come one day, let us hope, to the young Prince, whom we may regard as the Royal representative of the English liking for the sea. For the asylum for old and infirm sailors at Greenhithe has not been called Belvidere for some years now. Prince Alfred went to look at it one day, and asked leave to become its patron, since which it has been called "The Royal Alfred Aged Merchant Seamen's Institution"—rather a long name, but then it ought to mean so much.

WITH THE FEEBLE AND FAINT-HEARTED.

S there any condition wherein we feel greater need of human help and true loving sympathy than in the slow, feeble creeping from sickness to complete convalescence, when the pulse of life beats low, and the failing foot yet lacks power to step across that dim barrier between health and sickness—not far from the valley of the shadow of death?

In the bright, glowing summer-tide, when the sun warms bloodless creatures into renewed life, our English sea-coast abounds with visitors, among whom near and dear friends, parents, children, slowly and painfully winning their way back to health and strength are the objects of peculiar care. In all our large towns people who have money to spend are, at least, beginning to make up their minds where they shall take their autumn holiday; —in many quiet health-resorts wealthy invalids, and some who are not wealthy, have already passed the early spring and summer;—at a score of pleasant watering-places, where the cool sparkling waves break upon the "ribbed sea-sand," troops of children are already browning in the sun, scores of hearts feel a throb of grateful joy as the glow of health begins to touch cheeks lately pale, and dull eyes brighten under the clear blue sky.

Thousands upon thousands are then on their way to that great restorer, the sea, if it be only for a few hours by excursion train. England might seem to have gathered all its children at its borders, and very soon we hear how empty London is, while a new excuse for a holiday will be that there is "nothing doing" and "nobody is in town." And yet throughout the busy streets a throng continues to hurry onward in restless activity. Only well-accustomed observers could see any considerable difference in the great thoroughfares of London. Shops and factories look busy enough, and if nothing is doing, there is a mighty pretence of work, while the nobodies are a formidable portion of the population when regarded in the aggregate.

Early in August the census of our large towns still further diminishes. Prosperous tradesmen, noting the decrease of customers, begin to prepare to take part in the general exodus. "Gentlefolks" have concluded bargains for furnished houses on the coast and put their dining and drawing-rooms into brown holland. In West-End streets and squares the front blinds are drawn, and all inquiries are answered from the areas, where charwomen supplement the duties of servants on board wages. "London is empty," the newspapers say, and in every large town in the kingdom the great outgoing leaves whole districts comparatively untenanted. Yet what a vast population remains; what a great army of toiling men and women who go about their daily work, and keep up the unceasing buzz of the industrial hive. What troops of children, who, except for Sunday-school treats, would scarcely spend a day amidst green fields, or learn how to make a daisy-chain, or hear the soft summer wind rustling the leaves of overhanging trees.

It would perhaps astonish us if we could have set down for us in plain figures how many men and women in England have never seen the sea; how many people have never spent a week away from home, or had a real long holiday in all their lives. It may be happy for them if they are not compelled by sudden sickness or accident, to fall out of the ranks, and to leave the plough sticking in the furrow. It is not all for pleasure and careless enjoyment that the thousands of our wealthy brethren and sisters go to the terraced houses, or handsomely appointed mansions, which await them all round the English shore. Into how many eyes tears must need spring, when the prayers for all who are in sorrow, need, or adversity are read in seaside churches on a summer's Sunday. By what sick-beds, and couches set at windows whence wistful eyes may look out upon the changeful glory of wood and sea and sky, anxious hearts are throbbing. What silent tears and low murmuring cries on behalf of dear ones on whose pale cheeks the July roses never more may bloom, mark the watches of the silent night, when the waves sob wakefully upon the beach. What thrills of hope and joy contend with obtrusive fears as, the golden spears of dawn break through the impenetrable slate-blue sky, and a touch of strength and healing is seen to have left its mark upon a brow on which the morning kiss is pressed with a keen throb that is itself almost a pang.

The first faltering footsteps back to life after a long illness or a severe shock, how they need careful guidance. Let the stronger arm, the helping hand, the encouraging eye be ready, or they may fail before the goal of safety be reached.

"All that is now wanted is strength, careful nursing, plenty of nourishment, pure air—the seaside if possible, and perhaps the south coast would be best." Welcome tidings, even though they herald slow recovery, inch by inch and day by day, while watchful patience measures out the time by meat and drink, and the money that will buy the means of comfort or of pleasure, becomes but golden sand running through the hour-glass, which marks each happy change.

Yes; but what of the poor and feeble, the faint-hearted who, having neither oil nor wine, nor the twopence wherewith to pay for lodging at the inn, must need lie there by the way-side, if no hand is stretched out to help them?

While at those famous health-resorts, the names of which are to be read at every railway station, and in the advertisement sheets of every newspaper, hundreds and thousands are coming back from weakness to strength, there are hundreds and thousands still who are discharged from our great metropolitan hospitals, to creep to rooms in dim, close courts and alleys, where all the tending care that can be given them must be snatched from the hours of labour necessary to buy medicine and food. How many a poor sorrowing soul has said with a sigh, "Oh! if I could only send you to the sea-side. The doctors all say fresh air's the great thing; but what's the use? they say the same of pure milk and meat and wine."

It may be the father who has met with an accident, and cannot get over the shock of a surgical operation—or rheumatic fever may have left mother, son, or daughter in that terrible condition of utter prostration, when it seems as though we were in momentary danger of floating away into a fainting unconsciousness, which not being oblivion, engages us in a struggle beyond our waking powers.

Alas! in the great summer excursion to the coast these poor fainting brethren and sisters are too seldom remembered. Here and there a building is pointed out as an infirmary, a sea-side hospital, or even as a retreat for convalescents, but the latter institutions are so few, and the best of them are so inadequately supported, that they have never yet been able to prove by startling figures the great benefits which they confer upon those who are received within their walls.

One of the oldest of these truly beneficent Institutions, "The Sea-side Convalescent Hospital at Seaford," has just completed a new, plain, but commodious building, not far from the still plainer House which has for many years been the Home of its grateful patients. So let us pay a visit to the old place just before its inmates are transferred to more ample quarters, to provide for which new subscriptions are needed, and fresh efforts are being made. The visit will show us how, in an unpretentious way, and without costly appliances, such a charitable effort may be worthily maintained.

Curiously enough, Seaford itself is an illustration of declension from strength to weakness, and of the early stages of recovery; for though it is one of the famous Cinque Ports, it has for nearly 200 years been an unnoted retreat.

But it is still a place of old, odd customs, such as the election of the chief of the municipality at an assembly of freemen at a certain gate-post in the town, to which they are marshalled by an officer bearing a mace surmounted with the arms of Queen Elizabeth. It is famous, too, for Roman and other antiquities, and its queer little church dedicated to St. Leonard, has some rare specimens of quaint carving and a peal of bells which are peculiarly musical, while the sounding of the complines on a still summer's night is good to hear. In fact, for a mere cluster of houses forming an unpretentious and secluded town, almost without shops to attract attention, with scarcely the suspicion of a high street, and destitute of a grand hotel, Seaford is remarkably interesting for its legendary lore, as a good many people know, who have discovered its greatest attraction, and take lodgings at the dull little place, where even the martello tower is deserted. The chief recommendation of the place, however, is its healthfulness, and the grand air which blows off the sea to the broad stretch of shingly beach, and the range of cliff and down-land which stretches as far as Beachy Head, and rises just outside the town into one or two bluffs, about which the sea-gulls whirl and scream, as the evening sun dips into the sparkling blue of the water. It is just at the foot of the boldest of these ascents that we see an old-fashioned mansion, once known as Corsica Hall, but now more distinctly associated with the name of the Convalescent Hospital, of which it has long been the temporary home, the London offices of the charity being at No. 8, Charing Cross, London.

The institution, which was founded in 1860, has for its president the Archbishop of Canterbury, and for its patronesses the Duchess of Cambridge and the Duchess of Teck, and it has done its quiet work efficiently and well, under difficulties which must have required staunch interest on the part of its committee.

It is difficult at first to understand that the big many-roomed house just by the spur of the cliff, and peeping out to see over the shingle ridge, is in any sense a hospital; but here is a convalescent who will give us a very fair idea of the work that is being done; a tall fellow who is but just recovering from acute rheumatism, and is now able to go about slowly but with a cheery, hopeful look in his face. Presently, as one comes near the front door, a lad, who having come from a hospital where he has been attended for fractured ancle, has been sent here to recover strength, is hobbling across a poultry-yard, where a grand company of black Spanish, Polish, Cochin China, and other fowls are assembled to be fed, and beneath a pent-house roof in this same yard, on a bench, which would be well replaced by a more comfortable garden-seat if the funds would allow, there is a sheltered and comfortable corner for the afternoon indulgence of a whiff of tobacco. Twenty-five men and twenty-four women are all the inmates, besides attendants, for whom space can be found; and an inspection of the airy and scrupulously clean dormitories, or rather bedrooms, on each side of the building, will show that all the accommodation has been made available. It must be remembered, however, that as the period of each inmate's stay is but a month of twenty-eight days, fresh cases are constantly admitted during all the summer months; so that though as late as at the end of March only fourteen men and six women were distributed in the wards, the average number admitted during the last official year has been 511 (an increase of twenty-four over the year before), while the total number of cases received since the opening of the institution amounts to nearly 5,000.

There are evidences that in this old house, with its long passages, and little supplementary stairs leading to the bedrooms, economy has been studied, and yet all that can be done to adapt the place to its purpose has been effected. The sense of fresh air and cleanliness is the first noticeable characteristic. There are no slovenly corners; in sitting-rooms, corridors, or dormitories, whether the latter be little rooms with only two or three beds, or either of the large apartments, with their wide bay-windows looking forth upon the sea. Plainly and even sparely furnished, they have an appearance of homelike comfort, and it is pleasant to note that in the larger bright cheerful room devoted to women patients there are evidences of feminine taste and womanly belongings, even to the egg-cups holding little posies of wild flowers and common garden blooms that deck the broad mantelshelf in front of the toilet glasses. The same home-like influences are to be observed in other departments, and though this old country house—of which the institution holds only a short term as tenants—is not altogether suited for the purpose to which it has been applied, the arrangements are not without a certain pleasant departure from the too formal and mechanical routine which is observed in some establishments to have a peculiarly depressing influence on the sick.

The kitchen is like that of some good-sized farm-house, with brick floor, an ample "dresser," and a big range, flanked with its pair of ovens, and just now redolent of the steam of juicy South-down mutton and fresh vegetables about to be served for the patients' dinners.

It is a property of the Seaford air to make even persons with delicate appetites ready for three plain meals a day, with a meat supper to follow, and the convalescents are no exception to the rule. Tea and bread-and-butter for breakfast, bread-and-cheese and ale for the men, and cake and ale for the women as a snack in the way of lunch, good roast meat and vegetables for dinner, with occasional pies or puddings, with another half-pint of ale; tea as usual; and a supper consisting of a slice of meat, bread, and another draught of beer—this is the most ordinary diet; but in many cases milk is substituted for ale, and there is also a morning draught of milk, or rum-and-milk, a lunch or supper of farinaceous food, and wine or special diet, according to the orders of the house surgeon, who visits the patients daily, or as often as may be required. Following the odour of the roast mutton, we see the male patients preparing to sit down to dinner in a good-sized room, where, to judge from the pleased and grateful faces of men and lads, they are quite ready to do justice to the repast. Barely furnished, and with table appointments of the plainest kind, the dining-room is not indicative of luxury; but the sauce of hunger is not wanting, and as we bow our leave-taking, there are signs that the money spent at this Seaford Hospital is well represented by the wholesome but expensive medicine of pure food and drink in ample quantities, prescribed under conditions which build up the strength, and restore life to the enfeebled frames of those to whom a month of such living must be an era in their history.

The women's dining-room is, I am glad to see, more ornamental than that of the men. The walls are bright with gay paper, containing large and brilliantly coloured scenery, while the wide windows look seaward, and fill the large room with cheerful light.

This is all the more essential as there is no other sitting-room for the female patients, and the more convenient furniture, especially a low wooden couch covered with a mattress, is adapted to the needs of those who require indoor recreation as well as frequent rest. The men have a separate sitting-room in the basement, not a very cheerful apartment, but one which in the warm summer-time is cool, and adapted for the after-dinner doze, or for reading a book when the weather is not quite favourable for sitting out of doors.

There is, by the bye, a very decided need of entertaining and pleasant books for the patients' library at Seaford, the few which are on the two or three shelves being mostly old, and of a particularly dreary pattern. It is obvious that, in an institution where, in order to meet the constant needs of those who seek its aid, every shilling must be carefully expended, only a small sum can be devoted to literature; but it may only have to be made known that the convalescents really need a few cheerful volumes to help them along the road from sickness to health, and out of the abundance of some teeming library the goodwill offering may be made.

It is time that we—that is to say, the kindly and judicious secretary, Mr. Horace Green, the examining physician, Dr. Lomas, and the present writer—should yield to the influences of the grand appetising climate of this airy nook of the English coast, and after a short turn into the poultry-yard, a glance at the deliberate cow, and a passing greeting to the great black cat with collar and bell and a mew that is almost a deep bass roar, and to the most exacting, ugly, and voracious pet dog it was ever my lot to encounter—we accept the invitation to test the quality of the Southdown mutton and other Seaford fare, with a following of that delicately boiled rice and jam to which the healthy palate returns with childlike appreciation.

On hospitable thoughts intent, the bright and active lady who is superintendent matron of the hospital, has for the time adopted us into her hungry family, and with the knowledge of the effects of the breeze blowing over that high bluff, and curling the waves along the shingle ridge, has set out a repast in her own pleasant parlour, where she does the honours of the institution with a simple cheerful grace that speaks favourably for the administration which she represents. But I should now be writing in the past tense, for the larger building is completed. The inmates will have a better appointed home.

In order to maintain the objects of the charity, and to ensure the comfort of those for whom its provisions are intended, some well-considered regulations have to be adopted and enforced; and the most discouraging circumstances with which the committee and their officers have to contend, are those which arise from the negligence of subscribers nominating patients, or from the demands made on the charity by those who constantly expect more benefits from the institution than their contributions would represent even if they were paid three times over.

It is, perhaps, not to be wondered at that people, anxious to secure for their protégés the advantages of such means of recovery as are represented by a temporary hospital where there has only been one death in five years, should readily contribute their guinea for the sake of gaining the privilege, even though they may add to that small subscription the five shillings a week which is the sum required with each patient. What has to be complained of, however, is that constant attempts are made to introduce cases which are so far from being convalescent, that they are still suffering from disease, and require constant medical or surgical treatment. In order to do this, nominations are frequently obtained from country subscribers, and it has required the constant vigilance of the examining physician and the committee to avoid the distressing necessity of obtaining for such patients admission to other hospitals, or sending them back to their own homes, not only without having received benefit from the institution, but perhaps injured by the journey to and fro when they were in a weak and suffering condition.

It should be remembered that the Seaford Hospital is not for the sick, but for persons recovering from sickness, —those for whom the best medicines are regular and ample meals, grand bracing air, sea-baths, long hours of quiet and restorative sleep, and that general direction of their daily progress towards complete recovery, which will often make them strong and set them up completely, even in the twenty-eight days of their sea-side sojourn.

To send patients who require the medical care and attendance which can only be provided in a hospital for the special disorders from which they suffer, or who are afflicted with incurable diseases, is unjust, both to the poor creatures themselves and to the charity which cannot receive them.

For consumptive patients, except in the early or threatening stage of phthisis, Seaford is unsuitable, but a month at the hospital for patients of consumptive tendency has been known to produce remarkably beneficial results. It is in cases of recovery after rheumatism and rheumatic fever, or when strength is required after painful or exhausting surgical operations, in nervous depression, debility, pleurisy, and recovery from accidents, that the fine air is found to be wonderfully invigorating; for Seaford is high and dry, the subsoil being sand resting on chalk, so that there is little surface evaporation, while the shelter afforded by Beachy Head screens this little bay of the coast from the east wind.

It is not to be wondered at that the Archbishop of Canterbury, the Bishop of London, and the late Bishop of Winchester should have joined many of the London clergy, and more than eighty of the most eminent physicians and surgeons connected with metropolitian hospitals, to recommend this charity as one especially deserving of public support. Those who are ever so superficially acquainted with the homes and difficulties of the poorer classes in London know that the period of debility after sickness, when the general hospital has discharged the patient, or when the parish doctor has taken his leave, is a terrible time. Too weak to work, without means to buy even common nourishment at the crisis when plentiful food is requisite, and stimulated to try to labour when the heart has only just strength to beat, men and women are ready to faint and to perish unless helping hands be held out to them. Try to imagine some poor cabman or omnibus-driver, lying weak and helpless after coming from a hospital; think of the domestic servant, whose small savings have all been spent in the endeavour to get well enough to take another place; of the poor little wistful, eager-eyed errand-boy, scantily fed, and with shaking limbs, that will not carry him fast enough about the streets. Try to realise what a boon it must be to a letter-carrier, slowly recovering from the illness by which he has been smitten down, or to the London waiter, worn and debilitated by long hours of wearying attendance to his duties, to have a month of rest and, re-invigoration at a place like this. In the table of inmates during the last few years are to be found a host of domestic servants, mechanics and apprentices, warehousemen and labourers, 36 housewives (there is much significance in that word, if we think of the poor wife or mother to be restored to her husband and children), 46 needlewomen, 19 clerks, 15 teachers (mark that) 41 school-children, 9 nurses, 1 policeman, 3 seamen and watermen, 1 letter-carrier, 4 errand-boys, 7 Scripture-readers, and others of various occupations.

It is no wonder, I say, that the general hospitals should regard this Convalescent Home at Seaford as a boon; but, unfortunately for the charity, the appreciation which it receives from some of those wealthy and magnificently-endowed institutions operates as a very serious drain on its own limited resources, which are only supplied by voluntary subscriptions, contributions, and legacies. Every subscriber of a guinea annually, and every donor of ten guineas in one sum, has the privilege of recommending one patient yearly, with an additional recommendation for every additional subscription of one guinea, or donation of ten guineas. The payment of five shillings a week by each patient admitted is also required by the guarantee of a householder written on the nomination paper, and the travelling expenses of the patient must also be paid, the Brighton Railway Company most benevolently conveying patients to the hospital by their quick morning train, in second-class carriages at third-class fare.

Now it is quite obvious that the five shillings a week, though it removes the institution from the position of an absolute charity, goes but a very short distance in providing for the needs of the inmates, and when the guinea contribution is added to it, there is still a very wide margin to fill before much good can be effected. Let us see, then, what is the effect of every subscription of a guinea representing a claim, as in the case of the patients sent from the general hospitals.

The cost of those admirable medicines, food and drink, wine, milk, and sea-baths, together with the expenses of administration, and the rental will represent at least £4 8s. per head for each patient, and as Guy's, Bartholomew's, St. Thomas's, and the London Hospitals, each subscribing their ten guineas annually, demand their ten nominations in exchange, the account stands thus :—

For each case, five shillings per week for four weeks, and one guinea subscription=£2 1s., which, deducted from the actual cost (£4 8s.), leaves £2 7s. to be paid out of the funds of the Seaford Institution, which, on ten patients a year, represents £23 10s. as the annual contribution of this poor little charity to each of the four great charitable foundations of the metropolis.

But there is now an opportunity for acknowledging this obligation, and for recognizing the useful career of this really admirable institution. The lease of the present house has already expired, and the committee have been obliged to give up possession. It is therefore necessary to support the new hospital for those who need the aid that such a charity alone can give, and the building has already been erected, only a few yards further in the shelter of the bluff, where it has provided another home. With a commendable anxiety to keep strictly within their probable means, the committee have decided not to imitate a too frequent mode of proceeding, by which a large and splendid edifice would saddle their undertaking with a heavy debt, and perhaps cripple resources needed for carrying on their actual work; but they have obtained from Mr. Grüning, the architect, a plain building which will provide for their needs for some time to come, and may be hereafter increased in accommodation by additions that will improve, rather than detract from, its completeness. A great establishment, with a hundred beds, laundries, drying-houses, and hot and cold sea-baths on the premises, would cost £13,000; and as the actually available funds in hand for building purposes were not more than £5,000, with another probable £1,000 added by special donations expected during the year, the committee, however reluctantly, folded up the original plan, and estimated the cost of a plain unpretentious building, calculated at first to receive thirty-three male and thirty-three female patients, but capable of additions which will raise its usefulness and completeness to the higher demand, whenever there are funds sufficient to pay for them. The expenditure for the new hospital was about £7000, and, should the anticipated donations be increased fourfold, there will be no difficulty in crowning the work, by such provisions as will include the full number of a hundred faint and failing men and women within the retreat where they find rest and healing.

WITH THE LITTLE ONES.

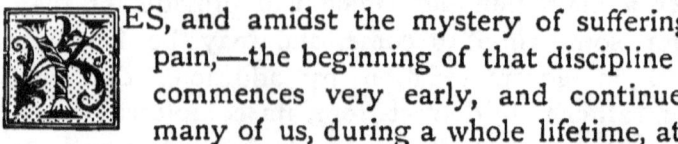ES, and amidst the mystery of suffering and pain,—the beginning of that discipline which commences very early, and continues, for many of us, during a whole lifetime, at such intervals as may be necessary for the consummation which we can only faintly discern when we begin to see that which is invisible to the eyes of flesh and of human understanding, and is revealed only to the higher reason —the essential perception which is called faith.

I want you to come with me to that eastern district of the great city which has for so long a time been associated with accounts of distress, of precarious earnings, homes without food or fire, scanty clothing, dilapidated houses, dire poverty and the diseases that come of cold and starvation. The place that I shall take you to is quite close to the Stepney Station of the North London Railway. The district is known as Ratcliff; the streets down which we shall pass are strangely destitute of any but small shops, where a front "parlour" window contains small stocks of chandlery or of general cheap odds and ends. The doorways of the houses are mostly open, and are occupied by women and children, of so poor and neglected an appearance, that we need no longer wonder at the constant demands made upon the institution which we are about to visit. Just here the neighbourhood seems to have come to a dreary termination at the brink of the river, and to be only kept from slipping into the dark current by two or three big sheds and wharves, belonging to mast, rope, and block-makers, or others connected with that shipping interest the yards of which are, many of them, deserted, no longer resounding to the noise of hammers. The black spars and yards of vessels alongside seem almost to project into the roadway as we turn the corner and stand in front of a building, scarcely to be distinguished from its neighbours, except for the plain inscription on its front, "East London Hospital for Children and Dispensary for Women," and for a rather more recent appearance of having had the woodwork painted. But for this there would be little more to attract attention than might be seen in any of the sail-makers' dwellings, stores, and lofts in the district; and, in fact, the place itself is—or rather was—a sail-maker's warehouse, with trap-doors in the rough and foot-worn floors, steep and narrow stairs, bulks and baulks of timber here and there in the heavy ceilings and awkward corners, not easily turned to account in any other business. Some of these inconveniences have been remedied, and the trap-doors as well as the awkwardest of the corners and the bulks have been either removed or adapted to present purposes, for the business is to provide a home and careful nursing for sick children, and the long rooms of the upper storeys are turned into wards, wherein stand rows of Lilliputian iron bedsteads, or tiny cribs, where forty boys and girls, some of them not only babes but sucklings, form the present contingent of the hundred and sixty little ones who have been treated during the year. Not a very desirable-looking residence you will say, but there are a good many inmates after all; and the scrupulous cleanliness of the place, as seen from the very passage, is an earnest of that plan of making the best of things which has always been characteristic of this hospital at Ratcliff Cross. Some eight or nine grown-up folks, and from thirty to forty children, make a bright, cheerful home (apart from the suffering and death which are inseparable from such a place) in that old sail-maker's warehouse, if brightness and cheerfulness are the accompaniments of good and loving work, as I thoroughly believe they are.

It was during the terrible visitation of cholera, nearly twelve years ago, that this work of mercy was initiated, and the manner of its foundation has about it something so pathetic that it is fitting the story should be known, especially as the earnest, hopeful effort with which the enterprise began seems to have characterised it to the present day. Among the medical men who went about in the neighbourhood of Poplar and Ratcliff during the epidemic, was Mr. Heckford, a young surgeon, who, having recently come from India, was attached to the London Hospital, and who took a constant and active part in the professional duties he had undertaken. In that arduous work, he, as well as others, received valuable and indeed untiring aid from the ready skill and thoughtful care of a few ladies, who, having qualified themselves as nurses, devoted themselves to the labour of love amongst the poor. To one of this charitable sisterhood, who had been his frequent helper in the time of difficulty and danger, the young surgeon became attracted by the force of a sympathy that continued after the plague was stayed in the district to which they had given so much care, and when they had time to think of themselves and of each other. They went away together a quietly married couple; both having one special aim and object in relation to the beneficent career upon which they had entered in company. Knowing from hardly-earned experience the dire need of the district, they at once began to consider what they could do to alleviate the sufferings of the women and children, so many of whom were sick and languishing, in hunger and pain, amidst conditions which forbade their recovery. If only they could make a beginning, and do something towards arresting the ravages of those diseases that wait on famine and lurk in foul and fœtid alleys;—if they could establish a dispensary where women—mothers too poor to pay a doctor—could have medicine and careful encouragement; if they could find a place where, beginning with a small family of say half a dozen, they might take a tiny group of infants to their home, and so set up a centre of beneficent action, a protest against the neglect, the indifference, and the preventable misery for which that whole neighbourhood had so long had an evil distinction.

The question was, how to make a beginning: but the young doctor and his wife had been so accustomed to the work of taking help to the very doors of those who needed it, that all they wanted was to find a place in the midst of that down-east district where they could themselves live and work. Out of their own means they bought the only available premises for their purpose—a rough, dilapidated, but substantial, and above all, a ventilable sail-loft with its adjacent house and store-rooms, and there they quietly established themselves as residents, with ten little beds, holding ten poor little patients supported by themselves, in the hope that voluntary aid from some of the benevolent persons who knew what was the sore need of the neighbourhood would enable them in time to add twenty or thirty more, when the big upper storeys should be cleansed and mended and made into wards. That hope was not long in being realised, and on the 28th of January, 1868, after a determined effort to maintain the institution and to devote themselves to its service, a regular committee was formed and commenced its undertakings, the founders still remaining and working with unselfish zeal. From twenty to thirty little ones were received from out that teeming district, where a large hospital with ten times the number of beds would not be adequate to the needs of the infant population, the mothers of which have to work to earn the scanty wages which in many cases alone keep them from absolute starvation. The struggle to maintain the wards in the old sail-lofts was all the harder, from the knowledge that in at least half the number of cases where admission was necessarily refused, from want of space and want of funds, the little applicants were sent away to die, or to become helpless invalids or confirmed cripples, not less from the effects of destitution—the want of food and clothing—than from the nature of the diseases from which they were suffering.

The young doctor and his wife dwelt there, and with cultivated tastes and accomplishments submitted to all the inconveniences of a small room or two, from which they were almost ousted by the increasing need for space. With a bright and cheerful alacrity they adapted those very tastes and accomplishments to supplement professional skill and tender assiduous care :

the lady—herself in such delicate health that her husband feared for her life, and friends anxiously advised her to seek rest and change—used books and music to cheer the noble work, and always had a picture on her easel, with which to hide the awkward bulges and projections, or to decorate the bare walls and brighten them with light and colour.

It was at Christmas-tide seven years ago that I first visited the hospital, and there were then very pleasant evidences of the season to be discovered in all kinds of festive ornament in the long wards, and especially in the smaller rooms, where this loving woman had attracted other loving women around her, as nurses to the suffering little ones; and was there and then engaged in the superintendence of a glorious Christmas-tree. But the time came when the hoped-for support having arrived, Mr. and Mrs. Heckford felt that they could leave the family of forty children to the care of those who had taken up the work with heartfelt sympathy. They had laboured worthily and well, but, alas!—the reward came late—late at least for him, who had been anxious to take his wife away to some warmer climate, in an endeavour to restore the strength that had been spent in the long effort to rear a permanent refuge for sick children in that dense neighbourhood. It was he who stood nearest to shadow-land,—he who was soonest to enter into the light and the rest that lay beyond. Mr. Heckford died, I believe, at Margate, after a short period of leisure and travel, which his wife shared with him. His picture, presented by her to the charity which they both founded, is to be seen in the boys' ward. Another portrait of him—a portrait in words written by the late Mr. Charles Dickens, who visited and pathetically described the children and their hospital in December, 1868, conveys the real likeness of the man.

"An affecting play was acted in Paris years ago, called the Children's Doctor. As I parted from my Children's Doctor now in question, I saw in his easy black necktie, in his loose-buttoned black frock-coat, in his pensive face, in the flow of his dark hair, in his eyelashes, in the very turn of his moustache, the exact realisation of the Paris artist's ideal as it was presented on the stage. But no romancer that I know of has had the boldness to prefigure the life and home of this young husband and wife, in the Children's Hospital in the East of London."

What the hospital was then, it has remained—but with such improvements as increased funds and a more complete organisation have effected. It is still the ark of refuge for those little ones who, smitten with sudden disease, or slowly fading before the baleful breath of famine or of fever, or ebbing slowly away from life by the fatal influences that sap the constitutions of the young in such neighbourhoods, are taken in that they may be brought back to life, or at worst may be lovingly tended, that the last messenger may be made to bear a smile.

But the hope for the future of this most admirable institution has grown to fill a larger space. It is indeed essential to any really permanent effort in such a district that it should be increased, and the founders looked forward with earnest anticipations of the time when, gathering help from without, they could enter upon a larger building, which will soon be completed, and will be more adequate to the needs of such a teeming population. The area embracing Poplar, Mile End, Whitechapel, St. George's, Limehouse, Ratcliff, Shadwell, and Wapping numbers some 400,000 inhabitants, and strangely enough—as it will seem to those who have not yet learnt the true characteristics of the really deserving poor—many of the distressed people about that quarter will conceal their poverty, and strive as long as they are able—so that when at last they go to ask for aid the case may be almost hopeless, and the delay in obtaining admission may be fatal. There are already so many more applicants than can be received that it may be imagined what must be the vast amount of alleviable suffering awaiting the opportunity of wider means and a larger building. It would be easy to shock the reader by detailing many of the more distressing diseases from which the poor little patients suffer, but on visiting the wards you are less shocked than saddened, while the evident rest and care which are helping to restore and to sooth the sufferers ease you of the greater pain by the hope that they inspire.

It is Sunday noon as we stand here in the dull street where, but for the sudden opening of a frowsy tavern and the appearance of two or three thirsty but civil customers, who are not only ready but eager to show you the way to the "Childun's 'orsepital," there would be little to distinguish it from a thoroughfare of tenantless houses. Ratcliff is at its dinner at present, but we shall as we go back see the male residents leaning against the doorposts smoking, and the women and children sitting at the doors as at a private box at the theatre, discussing the sordid events of the streets and the small chronicles of their poor daily lives.

But we must leave the cleanly-scrubbed waiting-room and its adjoining large cupboard which does duty as dispenser's room. It is dinnertime here too, or rather it has been, and there are evidences of some very jolly feasting, considering that, after all, the banqueters are mostly in bed and on sick diet, which in many cases means milk, meat, eggs, and as much nourishment as they can safely take. Indeed, food is medicine to those who are turning the corner towards convalescence—food and air—of which latter commodity there is a very excellent supply considering the kind of neighbourhood we are in. Here and there we see a little wan, pinched, wasted face lying on the pillow; a listless, transparent hand upon the counterpane—which are sad tokens that the tiny sufferers are nearing the eternal fold beyond the shadowy threshold where all is dark to us, who note how every breath bespeaks a feebler hold on the world of which they have learnt so little in their tiny lives. There are others who are sitting up with picture-books, or waiting to have their abscesses dressed, and arms bandaged, or eyes laved with cooling lotion. Hip-disease and diseases of the joints are evidence of the causes that bring so many of the little patients here, and there are severe cases of consumption and of affections of the lungs and of the glands; but as the little fellow wakes up from a short nap, or catches the eye of the "lady nurse"—a lively and thoroughly practical Irishwoman, who evidently knows how to manage, and has come here, after special training, for the love of doing good—they show a beaming recognition which is very pleasant to witness. With all the nurses it is the same.

They are young women who, receiving small pay, have come to devote themselves to the work for Christ's sake and the Gospel's—that is to say, for the love of humanity and of the good tidings of great joy that announce the love of Him who gave Himself for us.

In the girls' ward there is the same freshness and cleanliness of the place and all its belongings, the same wonderful patience and courageous endurance on the part of the baby inmates, which has been my wonder ever since we went in. Here is a mite of a girl sitting up in bed, holding a moist pad to her eye, her poor little head being all bandaged. She never utters a sound, but the little round face is set with a determined endurance. "What is she sitting up for?" She is "waiting to see muvver." Another little creature, who is suffering from abscesses in the neck, submits to have the painful place poulticed only on the condition that she shall decide, by keeping her hand upon the warm linseed-meal, when it is cool enough to put on. These are scarcely pleasant details, and there are sights here which are very, very sad, and make us shrink —but I honestly declare that they are redeemed from being repulsive because of the evidence of love that is to be witnessed,—the awakening of the tender sympathies and sweet responses of the childlike heart. But for its being Sunday—which involves another reason to be mentioned presently—the beds would be strewed with toys and picture-books, while a rocking-horse, which is a part of the hospital property, and a fit kind of steed to draw the "hospital-carriage," which is represented by a perambulator—would probably be saddled and taken out of the stable on the landing. On the topmost storey we come to the real infants, the little babies, one of whom is even now in the midst of his dinner, which he takes from a feeding-bottle, by the aid of an india-rubber tube conveniently traversing his pillow.

Everywhere there are evidences of the care with which the work is carried on, and as we descend to the waiting-room again we have fresh proofs of the benefits that are being effected in the great district, by the provision made for the little creatures, many of whom would otherwise be left to linger in pain and want. For the waiting-room is filled—filled with mothers and elder sisters and little brothers, tearfully eager and anxious for the weekly visit to the fifty children upstairs. Here is the secret of the brave little patient faces in the beds and cots above.

It is infinitely touching to think how the prospect of "seeing muvver" sustains that chubby little sufferer,—how the expected visit nerves the stronger ones to endurance, and sends a fresh throb of life through those who are still too weak to do more than faintly smile, and hold out a thin pale hand.

If Mr. Ashby Warner, the Secretary at this Hospital for Sick Children at Ratcliff Cross, could but send some responsive thrill into the hearts of those who, having no children of their own, yet love Christ's little ones all over the world,—or could bring home to the fond fathers and mothers of strong and chubby babes the conviction that to help in this good work is a fitting recognition of their own mercies; nay, if even to sorrowing souls who have been bereaved of their dear ones, and who yet believe that their angels and the angels of these children also, do constantly behold the face of the Father which is in heaven, there would come a keen recognition of the blessedness of doing something for the little ones, as unto Him who declares them to be of His kingdom—there would soon be no lack of funds to finish building that great new hospital at Shadwell, which *is* to take within its walls and great airy wards so many more little patients, to help and comfort by advice and medicine so many more suffering mothers and sisters than could be received in the old sail-loft and its lower warehouse at Ratcliff Cross. For the hope of the founders and their successors has at last being realised—a larger building than they had at first dared to expect is to be erected on ground which has been purchased, still within the district where the need is greatest—and when the time comes that the last touch of carpenter and mason shall have been given to the new home, and the picture of Mr. Heckford shall be hung upon another wall, there may well be a holiday "down east"—as a day of thanksgiving and of gratitude, to those who may yet help in the work by giving of their abundance.

IN THE KINGDOM.

"OF such are the kingdom of heaven;" and "whosoever doeth it unto the least of these little ones, doeth it unto Me." Surely there is no need to comment again on these sayings of Him who, in His infinite childlikeness, knew what must be the characteristics of His subjects, and declared plainly that whosoever should enter into the kingdom must become as a little child. One thing is certain, that those who are within that kingdom, or expect to qualify themselves for it, must learn something of the Divine sympathy with which Christ took the babes in his arms and blessed them. Thank God that there is so much of it in this great suffering city, and that on every hand we see efforts made for the rescue, the relief, and the nurture of sick and destitute children. Would that these efforts could relieve us from the terrible sights that should make us shudder as we pass through its tumultuous streets, and witness the suffering, the depravity, and the want, that comes of neglecting the cry of the little ones, and of those who would bring them to be healed and sanctified.

Only just now I asked you to go with me to Ratcliff to see the forty tiny beds ranged in the rooms of that old sail-maker's warehouse which has been converted into a Hospital for Sick Children. There is something about this neighbourhood of Eastern London that keeps us lingering there yet; something that may well remind us of that star which shone above the manger at Bethlehem where the Babe lay. The glory of the heavenly light has led wise men and women to see how, in reverence for the childlikeness, they may work for the coming of the kingdom, and those who enter upon this labour of love, begin—without observation—to find what that kingdom really is, and to realise more of its meaning in their own hearts.

To the cradle in a manger the wise men of old went to offer gifts. To a cradle I would ask you to go with me to-day; to a whole homeful of cribs; which is known by a word that means crib and manger and cradle all in one—"The Crèche."

There is something, as it seems to me, appropriate in this French word to the broad thoroughfare (so like one of the outer boulevards of Paris) out of which we turn when we have walked a score or two of yards from the Stepney Station, or where some other visitors alight from the big yellow tramway car running from Aldgate to Stepney Causeway. The Causeway itself is a clean, quiet street, and is so well known that the first passer-by can point it out to you, while, if the inhabitants of the district can't quite master the *crunch* of the French word, they know well enough what you mean when you ask for the "babies' home," or for "Mrs. Hilton's nursery." The home itself is but a baby institution, for it is only five years old, but it might be a very Methuselah if it were to be judged by the tender, loving care it has developed, and the good it has effected, not only on behalf of the forty sucklings who are lying in their neat little wire cots upstairs, like so many human fledglings in patent safety cages, and for the forty who are sprawling and toddling about in the lower nursery, or for the contingent who are singing a mighty chorus of open vowels on the ground-floor; but also in the hopeful aid and tender sympathy it has conveyed to the toiling mothers who leave their little ones here each morning when they go out to earn their daily bread, and fetch them again at night, knowing that they are fresh and clean, and have been duly nursed and fed, and put to sleep, and had their share of petting and of play.

The sound of the forty singing like one is not perceptible as we approach the house, which, with its large high windows open to the soft, warm air, lies very still and quiet. The wire-blinds to the windows near the street bear the name of the institution, and over the doorway is inscribed the fact that the Princess Christian has become the patroness of this charity, which appeals to all young mothers, and to every woman who acknowledges the true womanly love for children. Each day, from twelve to four o'clock, visitors are welcomed, except on Saturdays, when the closing hour is two o'clock, as, even in some of the factories down east, the half-holiday is observed, and poor women working at bottle-warehouses and other places have the happiness of taking home their little ones, and keeping them to themselves till the following Monday morning. Do you feel inclined to question whether these poor, toil-worn women appreciate this privilege? Are you ready to indulge in a cynical fear that they would rather forego the claim that they are expected to assert? Believe me you are wrong. One of the most hopeful and encouraging results of the tender care bestowed upon these babes of poverty is that of sustaining maternal love, and beautifying even the few hours of rest and family reunion in the squalid rooms where the child is taken with a sense of hope and pride to lighten the burden of the day. Early each morning the little creatures are brought, often in scanty clothing, sometimes shoeless, mostly with a ready appetite for breakfast. Then the business of matron and nurses begins. But, come, let us go in with the children, and see the very first of it, as women, poorly clad, coarse of feature, and with the lines of care, and too frequently with the marks of dissipation and of blows upon their faces, come in one by one and leave their little living bundles, not without a certain wistful, softened expression and an occasional lingering loving look.

The house—stay, there are actually three houses, knocked into one so as to secure a suite of rooms on each floor—is as clean as the proverbial new pin; and as we ascend the short flights of stairs, there is a sense of lightness and airiness which is quite remarkable in such a place, and is by some strange freak of fancy associated with the notion of a big, pleasant aviary—a notion which is strengthened by our coming suddenly into the nursery on the first-floor, and noting as the most prominent object of ornament a large cage containing some sleek and silken doves, placed on a stand very little above the head of the tiniest toddler there.

There is enough work for the matron, her assistant, and the four or five young nurses who receive these welcome little guests each morning. The rows of large metal basins on the low stands are ready, and the morning's ablutions are about to commence, so we will return presently, as people not very likely to be useful in the midst of so intricate an operation as the skilful washing and dressing of half a hundred babies.

There is plenty to see in the neighbourhood out of doors, but we need not wander far to find something interesting, for on the ground-floor of these three houses which form the Crèche—the babies' home—provision has also been made for babies' fathers, in the shape of "a British Workman," or working-man's reading, coffee, and bagatelle room, with a library of readable books, and liberty to smoke a comfortable pipe.

Of the servants' home, which is another branch of this cluster of charitable institutions, we have no time to speak now, for our visit is intended for the Crèche, and we are already summoned to the upper rooms by the sound of infant voices. Doubt not that you will be welcomed on the very threshold, for here comes an accredited representative of the institution, just able to creep on all fours to the guarded door, thence to be caught up by the gentle-faced young nurse, who at once consigns the excursionist to a kind of square den or pound, formed of stout bars, and with the space of floor which it encloses covered by a firm mattrass. There, in complete safety, and with two or three good serviceable and amiably-battered toys, the young athletes who are beginning to practise the difficult feat of walking with something to hold by, are out of harm's way, and may crawl or totter with impunity. They have had their breakfast of bread and milk, and are evidently beginning the day, some of them with a refreshing snooze in the little cribs which stand in a row against a wall, bright, as all the walls are, with coloured pictures, while in spaces, or on low tables here and there, bright-hued flowers and fresh green plants are arranged, so that the room, necessarily bare and unencumbered with much furniture, is so pleasantly light and gay, that we are again reminded of a great bird-cage. Out here in a little ante-room is a connected row of low, wooden arm-chairs, made for the people of Lilliput, and each furnished with a little tray or table, and, drumming expectantly and with a visible interest in the proceeding, sit a line of little creatures, amidst whom a nurse distributes her attentions, by feeding them carefully with a spoon, just as so many young blackbirds might be fed. Already some of the little nurslings are sitting up in their cribs, quietly nodding their round little heads over some cherished specimen of doll or wooden horse. One wee mite of a girl, quite unable to speak, except inarticulately, holds up the figure of a wooden lady of fashion, with a wistful entreaty which we fail to understand, till the quick-eyed lady who accompanies us spies a slip of white tape in the tiny hand, and at once divines that it is to be bound about the fashionable waist, as an appropriate scarf, and at once performs this finishing stroke of the toilet, to the immeasurable satisfaction of everybody concerned. This is in the upper room, the real baby nursery, where the age of some of the inmates is numbered by weeks only, and there is in each swinging cot a sweet, sleepy sense of enjoyment of the bottle which forms the necessary appliance of luncheon-time.

At the heads of several of these cots are inscribed the names of charitable donors, happy parents, bereaved mothers, sympathetic women with babies of their own, either on earth or in heaven, who desire to show gratitude, faith, remembrance, by this token of their love for the childlikeness of those they love and cherish in their deepest memories, their most ardent hopes. In more than one of the little beds there are signs of the poverty or the sickliness in which the children were born, and the effects of which this home, with its freshness and light and food, is intended to remedy. No cases of actual disease are here, however, since a small infirmary for children suffering from more serious ailments has been added to the institution, and the Sick Children's Hospital is but three street lengths distant.

The first most remarkable experience which meets the visitor unaccustomed to observe closely, is the freshness and beauty of the children in this place. Squalid misery, dirt, neglect, starvation, so disguise and debase even the children in such neighbourhoods, that squeamish sentimentality turns away at the first glance, and is apt to conclude that there are essential differences between the infancy of Tyburnia or Mayfair and the babyhood of Ratcliff and Shadwell. Yet I venture to assert that if Mr. Millais or some other great painter were to select his subjects for a picture from these rooms of the old house in Stepney Causeway, he would leave the galleries of Burlington House echoing with "little dears," and "what a lovely child!" and popular prejudice would conclude that from birth the little rosebud mouths were duly fitted with silver spoons instead of being scant even of the bluntest of wooden ladles.

At this Crèche at Stepney Causeway the reasons of the true childlike freshness, alacrity, and even the engaging impetuosity and loving confidence which characterise these little ones, is not far to seek. As you came up you noticed row after row of blue check bags, hanging in a current of fresh air on the wall of the staircase. Those bags contain the clothes in which these children are brought to the Home in the morning. They are changed with the morning's ablutions, and clean garments substituted for them until the mothers come in the evening to fetch away their bairnies, and by that time they have been aired and sweetened. It is noticeable that this has the effect in many instances of inducing the women to make praiseworthy efforts to improve the appearance of the children, and, indeed, the whole tendency of the treatment of the little ones is to develop the tenderness and love which lie deep down in the hearts of the mothers. Even the endearing nicknames almost instinctively bestowed upon the tiny darlings have a share in promoting this feeling, and the pretty rosy plump little creatures, or the quaint expressive bright-eyed babies, who are called " Rosie," " Katie," " Pet," " Little Old Lady," and so on, all have a kind of happy individuality of their own in the regards of the dear lady who founded and still directs the institution, and in those of the nurses who tend them. Sometimes the names arise from some little incident occuring when the children are first brought there, as well as from the engaging looks and manners of the little ones themselves. " The King," is a really fine baby-boy, the recognised monarch of the upper nursery, but his sway is strictly constitutional ; while a pretty little wistful, plump lassie, is good-humouredly known as " Water Cresses," and has no reason to be ashamed of the name, for it designates the business by which a hard-working mother and elder sister earn the daily bread for the family.

Did I say that the charge for each child is twopence daily? Nominally it is so ; and let those who desire to know something of the real annals of the poor remember that even this small sum—which of course cannot adequately represent anything like the cost—is not easily subtracted from the scanty earnings of poor women engaged in slopwork, or selling dried fish, plants, crockery, and small wares in the streets, or going out to work in warehouses, rope-walks, match-making, box-making, and other poor employments, where the daily wages will not reach to shillings, and sometimes are represented only in the pence column. Let it be remembered, too, that the husbands of these women (those who are not prematurely widows, or whose husbands have not deserted them) are employed as dock labourers, and are often under the terrible curse of drink, or are in prison, while the women struggle on to support the little ones, who but for this institution, would perhaps be left—hungry, naked, and sickly—to the care of children only two or three years older than themselves; or would be locked in wretched rooms without food or fire till the mother could toil homeward, with the temptation of a score of gin-shops in the way.

Each of the bright intelligent little faces now before us has its history, and a very suggestive and pathetic history too.

Look at this little creature, whose pet name of Fairy bespeaks the loving care which her destitute babyhood calls forth; she is only ten months old, and her mother is but nineteen, the widow of a sailor lost at sea two months before the baby was born.

Katie, of the adult age of five years, is the child of a man who works on barges. Rosie, one of the first inmates, has a drunken dock-labourer for a father, and her mother is dead. Dicky represents the children whose father, going out to sea in search of better fortune for wife and children, is no more heard of, and is supposed to be dead. "The King" is fatherless, and his mother works in a bottle-warehouse. The pathetic stories of these children is told by Mrs. Hilton herself, in the little simple reports of this most admirable charity. They are so touching, that I cannot hope to reproduce them in any language so likely to go straight to the heart as that in which you may read them for yourself if you will either visit the Crèche, or send ever so small a donation, and ask for a copy of the modest brown-covered little chronicle of these baby-lives. Standing here in the two nurseries, where the dolls and Noah's arks, the pictures and the doves, nay, even the baby-jumpers suspended from the ceilings, are but accessories to the clasp of loving arms and the softly-spoken words of tender womanly kindness, I wonder why all one side of Stepney Causeway has not been demanded by a discriminating public for the extension of such an institution. Loitering in the lower room, where one little bright face is lifted up to mine, as the tiny hands pluck at my coat-skirt, and another chubby fist is busy with my walking-stick, I begin to think of the workhouse ward, where mothers are separated from their children night and day ; of a prison, where I have seen a troop of little boys, and a flogging-room provided by a beneficent Government for the recognition by the State of children who had qualified themselves for notice by the commission of what the law called crime.

A pleasant odour of minced beef, gravy, and vegetables, known as "Irish stew," begins to steal upon the air. The wooden benches in one of the rooms are suddenly turned back, and like a conjuring trick, convert themselves into tiny arm-chairs, with convenient trays in front for plates and spoons. The little voices—forty like one—strike up a fresh chant, and a whisper of rice-pudding is heard. So we go out, wondering still, and with a wish that from every nursery where children lisp "grace before meat," some gracious message could be brought to aid and strengthen those who believe with me that the most profitable investment of political economy, the most certain effort of philanthropy, is to begin with the men and women of the future, and so abate the fearful threatenings of coming pauperism, and the still more terrible menace of a permanent "criminal class."

The policy of the authorities, says Mrs. Hilton, in her interesting narrative of the Crèche, in stopping outdoor relief to poor widows with children is causing much sorrow. The 2*s*. 6*d*. or 3*s*. received from the parish secured their rent, and they managed, with shirt-making or trouser-finishing, to earn a bare subsistence; but now the battle for a mere existence is terrible. Doubtless, the children would be better cared for in the House, but mothers cannot be persuaded to give them up. One such case has just passed under my notice; but the woman shall speak for herself. "'Oh, Mrs. Hilton, they have taken off my relief!—I, with four little ones who cannot even put on their shoes and stockings. They offer me the House; but I never can give up my chidren. Look at baby; he is ten months old; his father died of small-pox six months before he was born; he was only ill five days.' I told her I was afraid she would not be able to earn enough to keep them all. 'Well,' she said, 'I must try—I will never go into the House.'"

"But these women have very little feeling for their children, they are so low and brutalised." Are they? Let those who think so visit this Cradle Home, and witness the bearing of the mothers who come to take their little ones home, or to nurse the sucklings at intervals snatched from work. Let them hear what such poor women will do for children *not* their own, even to the extent (as recently took place, in one instance, at least) of sharing with their less necessitous babes the natural sustenance that the mother cannot always give.

Sixty-five children received daily and a hundred or more on the books, with space needed for many more than can be admitted; children who, some of them infants as they are, have learned to lisp profane oaths and babble in foul language, and to give way to furious outbursts of passion, the result of neglect and evil example, and the life of the street and the gutter. It is but a short time, however, before this strange dreadful phase of the distorted child mind disappears, and the pet name is bestowed along with the gentle kindness that obliterates the evil mimicry of sin. The baby taken home from this purer atmosphere of love becomes a messenger of grace to many a poor household, as the short annals of the Crèche will tell; and even the pet names themselves are adopted by the mothers in speaking of and to their own children. One short story from the first report sent out by Mrs. Hilton, and we will go our way with a hope that some words of ours may win a fresh interest for these little ones.

"A precious babe died, and the mother, too poor to bury it, sent for a parish coffin. The child was very dear to us, and we had named her our nursery Queen which had degenerated into ' Queenie.' It was a sore trial to us to see the golden curls mingled with sawdust, which is all that was placed in the coffin; and yet we could not spend public funds on the funeral, and feared to do it privately. In a few hours a mother came and said, ' Come and look at your Queenie now.' We went and saw that loving hands had softened all the harsh outlines. A little bed and pillow had been provided, a frill placed round the edge, and some children had lain fresh-gathered flowers on the darling's breast. The cost had been $9\frac{1}{2}d.$, paid for by those mothers, and although so freely and lovingly given, it was the price of more than a meal each."

If every mother in London with a well-stocked larder would give the price of a meal for the sake of a living child—but, there! my duty is not to beg, but to describe.

WITH LOST LAMBS.

NLY quite lately I had to write about the old French colony in Spitalfields, and of the changes that have come over entire neighbourhoods which were once associated with what is now a failing industry, or rather with one which, so far as London is concerned, has nearly died out altogether.

Not that the public has ceased to hear sundry reports of those quarters of the metropolis of which the name of Bethnal Green is an indication as suggesting dire poverty, neglected dwellings, poorly-paid callings, and constant distress. Some few years ago it became quite a fashion for newspaper special reporters (following in the wake of one or two writers who had begun to tell the world something of the truth of what they knew of these sad regions) to make sudden amateur excursions beyond Shoreditch, for the purpose of picking up material for "lurid" articles about foul tenements, fever, hunger, want, and crime. Bethnal Green became quite a by-word, even at the West End, and certain spasmodic efforts in the direction of charitable relief were made by well-meaning people, so that for a time there was danger of a new kind of demoralisation of the "low neighbourhood," and the price of lodgings, even in the wretched tenements of its notorious streets, were expected to rise in proportion to the demand made by emigrants from other less favoured localities, to which the special correspondent had not at that time penetrated. One good work was effected by the attention of sanitary authorities being called to the fever dens during a time of terrible epidemic, and a certain provision of medical aid, together with purification of drains, whitewashing of rooms, and clearing of sties and dustheaps, was the result. This was but temporary, however; and those who best know the neighbourhood lying between Shoreditch and Bethnal Green, and disclaimed by the local authorities of both because of its misery and dilapidation, are also aware that in various parts of the whole great district from the Hackney Road to Bishopsgate, and so embracing Spitalfields and part of Whitechapel, far away to Mile End and "Twig Folly," there can be discovered more of want, hunger, and disease than could exist in any free city under heaven, if men were not such hypocrites as to defy and disregard the laws which yet they claim to have a hand in framing, and a power to enforce.

Only those who are personally acquainted with such a district can conceive what is the condition of the children of its streets, and yet every ordinary wayfarer of the London thoroughfares may note to what a life some of them are committed. About the outskirts of the markets, round the entrances to railway stations, cowering in the shadows of dark arches, or scrambling and begging by the doors of gin-shops and taverns, the boys—and what is even worse, the girls—are to be seen daily and nightly, uncared for, till they have learnt how to claim the attention of a paternal government by an offence against the law. When once the child, who is a mere unnoted fraction of the population, has so far matriculated in crime as to warrant the interposition of the police, he or she becomes an integer of sufficient importance to be dealt with by a magistrate. Let an infancy of neglect and starvation lead to the reckless pilfering of a scrap of food from a counter, or the abstraction of something eatable or saleable from a market-cart or a porter's sack, and the little unclassified wretch is added as another unit to a body recognised, and in some sense cared for, by the State. As a 'member of the great "criminal class," the juvenile thief becomes of immediate importance. Even though the few juvenile criminal reformatories be full, the gaol doors are open, and the teachings of evil companionship are consummated by the prison brand. The individual war against society gains strength and purpose, for society itself has acknowledged and resented it. The child has entered on a career, and unless some extra legal interposition shall succeed in changing the course of the juvenile offender by assuming a better guardianship, the boy may become an habitual thief, a full-fledged London ruffian; the girl——?

It was with a deep sense of the terrible significance of this question, that a small party of earnest gentlemen met, twenty-seven years ago, in that foul neighbourhood to which I have referred, to consider what should be done to rescue the deserted and destitute girls, some of whom had already been induced to attend a ragged school, which was held in a dilapidated building that had once been a stable.

These thoughtful workers included among them two men of practical experience; one of them, Mr. H. R. Williams, the treasurer of the present institution, the other the Rev. William Tyler, whose bright genial presence has long been a power among the poor of that district, where even the little ragged children of the streets follow him, and lisp out his name as the faithful shepherd, who both gives and labours in one of the truest "cures of souls" to be found in all great London. To them soon came the present honorary secretary, Mr. J. H. Lloyd, a gentleman already familiar with teaching the poor in a neighbouring district no less wretched and neglected. They were the right men for the business in hand, and therefore they began by moving sluggish boards and commissions to put in force the sanitary laws—and, in spite of the opposition of landlords with vested interests in vile tenements let out to whole families of lodgers from garret to basement, and of the malignant opposition of owners of hovels where every abomination was rife, and pigs littered in the yards, while costermongers shared the cellars with their donkeys—insisted on the surrounding streets being paved and drained, and some of the houses being whitewashed and made weatherproof.

Nothing less could have been done, for the terrible cholera epidemic was already raging in that tangle of courts and alleys. Application was at once made for a share from the Mansion House Relief Fund, and the committee had to use every available shilling in order to supply food and medicine, blankets and clothing, to the wretched families; to visit whom, a regular relief corps was organised, carrying on its beneficent and self-denying work, until the plague began to be stayed. Then with scarcely any money, but with unabated hope and fervid faith, this little company of men and women began to consider what they should do to found a Refuge for the children (many of them orphans, and quite friendless) who were everywhere to be seen wandering about, or alone and utterly destitute in the bare rooms that had been their homes. There were already certain institutions to which boys could be sent, for then, as now, the provision for boys was far greater than for girls. This is one of the strange, almost inexplicable conditions of charitable effort, and at that time it was so obvious which was the greater need, that the committee at once determined to commence a building on a waste piece of land which had been purchased close by, and to devote it to the reception of thirty destitute girls, who should be snatched from deadly contamination, and from the association of thieves and depraved companions.

Surely, if slowly, the work went on, the plan of the building being so prepared that it could be extended as the means of meeting the growing need increased. Almost every brick was laid with thoughtful care, and when subscriptions came slowly in, the funds were furnished among the committee themselves rather than the sound of plane and hammer should cease; till at last, when the King Edward Ragged School and Girl's Refuge was completed, a large edifice of three spacious storeys had superseded the old ruinous stable amidst its fœtid yards and sheds, and, what was more, the building was paid for, and a family of children had been gathered within its sheltering walls. At the time of my first visit to the institution no more than twenty, had been taken into this Refuge; but every foot of the building was utilised until the money should be forthcoming to add to the dormitories, and enable the committee to fulfil the purpose that it had in view.

In the large square-paved playground forty happy little members of the infant-school were marching to the slow music of a nursery song; and the numbers on the books were 196, in addition to 304 girls who came daily to be instructed in the great school-room, where they were taught to read, and write, and sew. A hundred and twenty boys were also being taught in the Ragged Church opposite, while seventy children over fifteen years of age attended evening classes, forty-two young men and women were in the Bible class, and a penny bank, a library of books, and a benevolent fund for the relief of poor children in the neighbourhood, were branches of the parent institution.

This, however, was seven years ago, and since that time so greatly has the work flourished, that the Ragged and Infant Schools have premises of their own on the other side of the way; and the great building having been completed by the addition of an entire wing, its original purpose is accomplished, and it is "The Girl's Refuge," of the King Edward Certified Industrial and Ragged Schools, Albert Street, Spitalfields.

It is to the receipt of munificent anonymous donations that the committee owe the completion of the building, and in order to extend the usefulness of their Refuge they have certified it under the provisions of the Industrial Schools Act of 1866. That this was in accordance with their ruling principle of making the most of every advantage at their command may be shown by the fact that when the School Board, almost appalled at the need for making immediate use of any existing organisation, began to send cases to existing "Homes," only eight of these institutions could receive the children, and in these eight no more than forty-four vacancies existed for Protestant girls. The consequence of opening the King Edward Refuge under the Act was that it received nearly all the cases of the year, and that in the twelve months it was certified ninety new inmates after found an asylum within its walls.

If you were to go there with me to-day, you would not wonder that the supporters of this institution were anxious to erect another building in some part of London, where another hundred lambs straying in this great wilderness could be taken to the fold. Passing through the neat dormitories, with their rows of clean white beds; peeping into the big toy cupboard, where the kindly treasurer has recently placed a whole family of eighty dolls, and other attractive inventions to induce children to play, some of whom have never known before what play really meant; looking at the lavatory with its long rows of basins let into slate slabs, and each with its towel and clean bag for brush and comb; noting the quiet "Infirmary," with its two or three beds so seldom needed, and remarking that from topmost floor to the great laundry with its troughs and tubs, a constant supply of hot water provides alike for warmth and cleanliness, I begin to wonder what must be the first sensations of a poor little dazed homeless wanderer on being admitted, washed, fed, and neatly clothed. Why, the two kitchens—that one with the big range, where most of the cooking is done, and the other cosy farmhouse-looking nook, with its air of comfort—must be a revelation to all the senses at once. Then there are the highly-coloured prints on the walls, the singing of the grace before meat; the regular and wholesome food;

the discipline (one little rebel is already in bed, whither she has been sent for misconduct, and an elder girl demurely brings up her slice of bread and mug of milk and water on a plate); the provision for recreation; the occasional visits of parents (many of them unworthy of the name) at stated seasons; the outings to the park, the Bethnal Green Museum, and other places; the Christmas treat; the summer presents of great baskets of fruit; the rewards and prizes; the daily instruction in such domestic work as fits them for becoming useful household servants. What a wonderful change must all these things present to the children of the streets, whose short lives have often been less cared for than those of the beasts that perish! Everywhere there are marks of order, from the neat wire baskets at the foot of each bed in which the girls place their folded clothes before retiring to rest, to the wardrobe closets and the great trays of stale bread and butter just ready for tea. Everywhere there are evidences of care and loving kindness, from the invalid wheel-chair—the gift of the treasurer to the infirmary—to the splendid quality of the "long kidney" potatoes in the bucket, where they are awaiting the arrival of to-morrow's roast mutton, three days being meat dinner days, while one is a bread and cheese, and two are farinaceous pudding days.

As we sit here and sip our tea—for I am invited to tea with the committee—and are waited on by three neat and pretty modest little women—one of them, a girl of eight, so full of child-like grace and simplicity, that there would be some danger of her being spoiled if she were not quite used to a little petting—who can help looking at the inmates now assembling quite quietly at the other end of the room, and thinking that in some of those faces "their angels," long invisible because of neglect and wrong, are once more looking through, calm, happy, and with a hope that maketh not ashamed. Do you see that still rather sullen-looking girl of thirteen. She came here an incorrigible young thief—her father, a tanner's labourer, and out at work from five in the morning—her mother bedridden—her home was the streets—her companions a gang of juvenile thieves such as haunt Bermondsey, and make an offshoot of the population of a place till recently called "Little Hell."

That girl, aged ten, was sent out to beg and to sing songs, and was an adept in the art of pretending to have lost money. There is the daughter of a crossing-sweeper, who cut his throat, and yonder a child of nine, driven from home, and charged with stealing, as her sister also is, in another Refuge; and close by are two girls, also sisters, who were found fatherless and destitute, wandering about famishing and homeless, except for a wretched room, with nothing in it but two heaps of foul straw. I need not multiply cases: and but for the known power of love and true human interest, in which the very Divine love is incarnated, you would wonder where some of these children obtained their quiet docile manner, their fearless but modest demeanour, their bright, quiet, sweet faces.

One case only let me mention, and we will go quietly away, to think of what may be done in such a place by the discipline of this love and true Christian interest. Do you see that emaciated little creature—the pale, pinched shadow of a child sitting at a table, where some of her companions tend her very gently? She is the daughter of a woman who is an incorrigible beggar. She has never known a home, and for four out of her eight years of life has been dragged about the street an infant mendicant; has slept in common lodging-houses; and in her awful experience could have told of thieves' kitchens, of low taverns, and of the customs of those vile haunts where she had learnt the language of obscenity and depravity. But that has become a hideous, almost forgotten dream, and she is about to awaken to a reality in a world to which the present tenderness with which she is cared for is but the lowest threshold. It is only a question of a month or two perhaps. One more bright sunny holiday with her schoolmates in the pleasant garden of the treasurer, at Highgate—whither they all go for a whole happy day in the summer—and she will be in the very land of light before the next haytime comes round. She wants for nothing—wine and fruit and delicate fare are sent for her by kind sympathetic hands; but she is wearing away, not with pain, but with the exhaustion of vital power, through the privations of the streets. From the Refuge she will go home—a lost lamb found, and carried to the eternal fold.

But another building has been found; a large, old-fashioned mansion in St. Andrew's Road, close to the Canal Bridge at Cambridge Heath, and there the more advanced inmates of this original home in Spitalfields are to be drafted into classes whence they will go to take a worthy part in the work of the world, so soon as the necessary subscriptions enable the committee to increase the number of lambs rescued from the wolves of famine and of crime.

WITH THE SICK.

HE memory of the pleasant summer holiday remains with many of us when we have come back again to the duties of the work-a-day world, and it will be good for us all if the gentle thoughts which that time of enjoyment brought with it remain in our hearts, to brighten our daily lives by the influences that suggest a merciful and forbearing temper.

It is perhaps remarkable that few of the charitable institutions at places to which holiday-makers resort are to any commensurate extent benefited by the contributions of those visitors who, while they are engaged in pursuing their own pleasures, seldom give themselves time to think that as they have freely received so they should freely give. Considering that while we are engaged in the absorbing business of money-making, or in the exacting engagements of our daily calling, we can afford little time for the investigation of those claims which are made upon us to help the poor and the needy, it might not altogether detract from the higher enjoyment of a period of leisure if we devoted a few spare hours to inquiring what is being effected for the relief of suffering in any place wherein we take up our temporary abode.

With some such reflection as this I stand to-day on

the spot which to ordinary Londoners is most thoroughly representative of the summer "outing," without which no true Cockney can feel that he is content—a spot, too, which has become, for a large number of English men and women, and notably for a whole host of English children, the synonym for renewed health and strength—the head of Margate jetty.

It is a strange contrast, this moving crowd of people, with their bright dresses and gay ribbons fluttering in the breeze; the smiling faces of girls and women amidst a toss and tangle of sea-blown tresses; the green sparkle of the sea beneath the shining sky; the voices of sailors, the shrill laughter of boys and girls coming from the sands below; the gleam of white sails; the flitting wings of fisher-birds; the gay tumult of the High Street; the traffic of hucksters of shells and toys—a strange contrast to the scene which may be witnessed in and around that large building which we passed only yesterday as the Margate boat stood off from Birchington, and passengers began to collect coats and bags and umbrellas as they saw friends awaiting them on the landing-stage of this very jetty.

It seems a week ago; and just as these few hours seem to have separated us far from yesterday's work, and the routine of daily life, does the short distance along the High Street and past the railway station seem to separate us by an indefinite distance from the sickness and pain that is yet in reality so near. Even as we think of it in this way, the division is less marked, the contrast not so strange, for in that building Faith, Hope, and Charity find expression, and bring a cheerful radiance to those who need the care of skilful hands and the sympathy of loving hearts.

The name of the place is known all over England, for within its walls are assembled patients who are brought from the great towns of different shires, as well as from mighty London itself, that they may be healed of that dread malady, the most potent cure for which is to take them from the close and impure atmosphere of their crowded homes, and exchange the stifled breath of courts and alleys for the boundless æther of the sea.

For the building, to visit which I am here to-day, is the "Royal Sea-Bathing Infirmary, or National Hospital for the Scrofulous Poor, near Margate," and there are at this moment 220 men, women, and children within its sheltering wards. Stay — let me be accurate. I said within its wards; but here, as I pass the gates and the unpretentious house of the resident surgeon to the broad sea front of the building, I note that under the protecting screen of the wall that bounds the wide space of grass-plot and gravel-paths a row of beds are placed, and in each of them a patient lies basking in the warm sunlit air; while a little band of convalescents saunter gently, some of them with the aid of crutch or stick, with the enjoyment of a sense of returning strength. If I mistake not, there are two or three "Bath chairs" crunching the gravel paths a little further on, and down below upon the space marked out and separated from the outer world upon the beach, the two bathing-machines of the establishment are occupied by those for whom convalescence is growing into health.*

The full meaning of such a change can only be realised by those who know how terrible a disease scrofula becomes, not only in the deadly insidious form of consumption, but in the various deformities and dis-

* This was written in the latter part of July, 1874.

tortions of the limbs of which it is the cause; and in those cases where, to the pain and depression of the disorder itself is added some terrible affection of the skin, which the sensitive patient knows can scarcely fail to be repulsive to those who witness it, unless, indeed they have learnt to regard it only as a reason for deeper compassion and for more earnest consolation.

Almost every form of the disorder is to be seen out here in the wide northern area of this inclusive building, which has long ago been bought and paid for, along with the three acres of freehold ground on which it stands.

Of the deep sympathy with which it has been supported by those who early learned to take an interest in its beneficent work, the fountain which has been erected in the centre of the green to the memory of the late Rev. John Hodgson, one of its trustees, is a mute witness. Mr. Hodgson laboured earnestly to secure those casual interests which might be obtained from the vast number of persons who visit Margate every year. In order to make the most of small regular contributions, he appealed for "five shillings a year," and since his death in 1870 this fund has increased, so that in one year nearly 6,000 subscribers had contributed £1,405 7s. 4d. Never was holiday charity more appropriately applied, as anybody who will visit the institution itself may witness in those long wards beyond the open passage, to which the card of Dr. Rowe, one of the three visiting surgeons, has directed me.

Since the first establishment of the institution, seventy-seven years ago, when sixteen cases were treated as a beginning, above 29,000 patients, from London and all parts of the country, have received relief; and to-day the number in the institution (taking no account of a contingent of "out-patients") includes 42 men, 50 women, and 120 children, none of whom are local cases, but all from other parts of England, whence they come frequently from a long distance.

In each of the six wards, of which four are on the ground floor, there is a head-nurse and an assistant, with six helpers for the children's, and four for the adult department, beside the night nurses, who sit up in case of any emergency. There is accommodation for 250 sufferers and for the 40 nurses, attendants, and domestics required for the service of the hospital; so the 220 patients there now, represent the approaching period when a new wing will have to be added, even if only the urgent cases are to be admitted.

The year's list of occupants of the 250 beds shows a total of 721 patients, of whom 614 had been discharged in January, 399 being either cured or very greatly benefited, 171 decidedly benefited, and only 44 obviously uncured; a very large amount of actual gain to humanity, when we reflect on the conditions of the disease to remedy which the institution is devoted.

If out of 721 cases 399 are either cured or have received such marked benefit as to render their ultimate cure highly probable, it is an achievement worthy of the earnest work of which it is the result, a contribution to beneficent efforts well worth the £7,966 which has necessarily been expended in the provision, not only of the appliances which give comfort and rest, but of the generous food and drink which, with the glorious air from the sea, is the medicine necessary to build up the feeble frames and renew the impoverished blood of those to whom meal-times come to be welcome events in the day, instead of merely languid observances.

Down in the kitchen, with its great cooking range and its capacious boilers, there are evidences of that "full diet" which is characteristic of the place; and it is difficult to decide which are the most suggestive, the long row of covered japanned jugs which hang conveniently to the dresser-shelf, and are used for the conveyance of "gravy," or the mighty milk-cans standing in a corner, ready to be taken away when the evening supply comes in from the Kentish dairies. Half a pound of cooked meat for dinner is the daily allowance for each man and for every boy over fourteen years of age, while women and girls receive six ounces, and children four ounces. Breakfast consists of coffee and bread-and-butter, varied in the afternoon by tea, and supper of bread and cheese for adults, and bread and butter for children. Roast and boiled meat is served on alternate days, with accompanying vegetables, and there are three "pudding days" for those who can manage this addition to the fare; while every man and woman may have a pint of porter, and each child a pint of table ale, at the discretion of the doctors. This, of course, represents the ordinary diet, in which specific differences are made for special cases where other or daintier food is required. Perhaps I should have said that this is the scale adopted in the refectory, a large airy room, to the long table in which the patients who are able to "get about" are now advancing with a cheerful premonition of dinner. There is no space to spare, and there are at present no funds to spend in additional building, so that this great airy refectory is used as chapel and assembly room. The Bread of Life, as well as the temporal bread, is distributed here; and those who would object to the necessity may either contribute to build another room, or may come and learn how every meal in such a place, and for such a cause as this, should become a sacrament. Many varieties of the forms taken by scrofulous disease may be seen here; and yet the hopeful looks, the cheerful influence of the bright summer weather, the green glimpses of the sea through doors and windows, and the fresh bracing air, impart to these sufferers an expressive lively briskness, which somehow removes the more painful impressions with which we might expect to witness such an assembly.

It is so perhaps in a still greater measure in these large airy wards, where children sit or lie upon the beds, some of them wholly or partially dressed, where the disease has produced only deformities under surgical treatment, or such forms of skin disease as affect the face. Of the latter there are some very severe and obstinate cases, and from these the unaccustomed visitor can scarcely help turning away, but often only to *re*-turn, and mark how cheerfully and with what a vivid alacrity the little patients move and play, and look with eager interest on all that is going on. For here—in the boys' ward—there is no repression of youthful spirits, so that they be kept within the bounds of moderate decorum, nor do the patients themselves seem to feel that they are objects of melancholy commiseration. To speak plainly, even the worst cases are not reminded that there are people who may be revolted at their affliction. Indeed I, who am tolerably accustomed to many experiences that might be strange to others, am rather taken aback by one little "case," whose face and limbs, though apparently healed, have been so deeply seamed and grooved by the disorder, which must have claimed him from babyhood, that he has evidently learned to regard himself as an important surgical specimen, and, on my approach to his bed, begins with deliberate satisfaction to divest himself of his stockings, in order to exhibit his legs. Hip and spinal disease are among the most frequent and often the most fatal forms of scrofula. One boy, with delicate and regular features, his fragile hand only just able to clasp in the fingers the small present I am permitted to offer him, shows the shadow of death upon his face. In his case the disorder has shown itself to be beyond medical, as it has already been beyond surgical aid, and his short hurried breathing denotes that before the summer days have been shortened by the autumn nights, and the leaves are lying brown and sere, he will be in a better and a surer home, and healed for evermore.

It will be a peaceful end, no doubt, and he will yet have strength enough to be taken home to die, where other than strangers' hands will minister to him at the last, but not more tenderly, it may be, than those that smooth his pillow to-day.

As we leave the boys' wards—clean, and bright, and fresh as they are—we encounter a cosy little party of juvenile convalescents, who are comfortably seated on the door-mat, engaged in a stupendous game of draughts.

There is more of beauty than deformity, more of life than of death, more perhaps of living eager interest than of sadness and sorrow to be seen here, after all; and this is particularly remarkable in the large-windowed spacious ward where the girls can look fairly out upon the gleaming sea. Properly enough, the room occupied by these young ladies has been made more ornamental than that of the boys. The walls are gay with coloured prints, and there are flowers, and a remarkably cheerful three-sided stove, which gives the place an air of comfort, though, of course, it has now no fire in it. Then some of the girls (with those thoughtful delicate faces and large wistful inquiring eyes which are so often to be observed among lame people) are engaged in fancy needlework as they lie dressed upon the beds to which they are at present mostly confined, because of deformities of the feet or legs requiring surgical treatment. There is a library (which needs replenishing), from which patients are allowed to take books; and those children who are able to leave the wards, and are not suffering from illness, are taught daily by a schoolmaster and a schoolmistress, while a visiting chaplain is of course attached to the hospital.

BLESSING THE LITTLE CHILDREN.

I CANNOT yet leave that sea-coast where so great a multitude go to find rest and healing. The Divine Narrative may well appeal to us in relation to such a locality, for it was by the sea-shore that the Gospel came to those who went out to seek Jesus of Nazareth; it was there that the poor people heard Him gladly; there that the sick who were brought to Him were made whole: there that He fed the great company who lacked bread.

All the deeds of humanity were recognised by Him who called himself the "Son of Man." The blessing of little children is one of those needs of true human life which the Lord recognised gladly. He recognises it still; and His solemn mingling of warning and of promise with regard to its observance, has an intensity that may well appeal to us all, now that, after eighteen centuries of comparative neglect and indifference, we are discerning that the only hope of social redemption is to be found in that care for children which shall forbid their being left either morally or physically destitute.

There is a house, standing high above the sea, in that great breezy suburb of Margate, known as Cliftonville—to which I want you to pay a visit when the bright, cheerful, airy wards, the light, spacious dining-room, and comfortable, home-like enlivening influences of the place will entitle it to be regarded as the fitting consummation of two other admirable institutions for the nurture and maintenance of orphan and fatherless children.

The modest little building referred to is named "The Convalescent and Sea-side Home for Orphans," Harold Road, Margate. The parent institutions are "The Orphan Working School," at Haverstock Hill, and that most attractive series of pretty cottages on the brow of the hill at Hornsey Rise, which have been more than once spoken of as "Lilliput Village," but the style and title of which is "The Alexandra Orphanage for Infants"—a name, the distinguishing feature of which is that it is immediately associated with its first patroness, the Princess of Wales.

Of the Home at Margate I need not now speak particularly, except to note that it is for the reception of the little convalescents, who—suffering, as many of them do, from constitutional and hereditary weakness, which is yet not actual sickness, and recovering, as many of them are, from the feeble condition which has been to some extent remedied by the careful nurture, good food, and healthy regimen, of the large institutions near London—are not fit patients either for their own or any other infirmary wards, and yet require to be restored to greater strength before they can join the main body of their young companions in the school or the playground.

Enough that it is picturesque and substantially pretty, as becomes a place which is to become the home of thirty children, taken from among nearly six hundred, the parents of nearly half of whom have died of consumption, and so left to their offspring that tendency to a feeble constitution which can be best remedied by the grand medicine of sea-air, wholesome nutritious food, and a judicious alternation of healthful exercise and rest.

It is to Mr. Joseph Soul—the late indefatigable secretary of the Working School, with which he has been connected for nearly forty years, and the honorary secretary of the Alexandra Orphanage, of which he may be regarded as the virtual founder—that the proposal to establish this Convalescent Home was due, and its affairs are administered at the office of the two charities, at 63, Cheapside.

But it is necessary to tell as briefly as possible the story of the oldest of the two institutions of which this building is to be an accessory—not only the oldest of these two, but probably *the oldest* voluntarily supported orphan asylum in London, since it dates from 116 years ago, when George II. was King, when Louis XV. was scandalising Europe and preparing the Revolution, when Wesleyan Methodism was commencing a vast religious revival, when Doctor Johnson had but just finished writing his dictionary, and when William Hogarth was painting those wonderful pictures which are still the most instructive records of society and fashion as seen in the year 1758.

It was in that year, on the 10th of May, that fourteen periwigged and powdered gentlemen met at the George Inn, in Ironmonger Lane, in order to discuss how they might best found an asylum for forty orphan children—that is to say, for twenty boys and twenty girls.

They soon came to a solemn decision that there was a "sufficient subscription for carrying the scheme into execution," and a record to that effect was soberly entered in the very first clean page of the first minute-book of the Charity, with the additional memoranda that a committee was chosen, and a treasurer appointed to collect and take care of the money necessary to support the undertaking.

The early minute-books of this charity, by the way, are models of serious penmanship. Grave achievements of caligraphy, with engrossed headings, elaborate flourishes, and stiff formal hedge-rows of legal verbiage, suggestive of the fact that the secretaries were either attorneys or scriveners, and regarded the entries in a minute-book or the opening of a new account as very weighty and important events not to be lightly passed over. In this they were probably right: and, at all events, just so much of the old methodical exactitude has come down to the present day in the history of the institution, that the published accounts of the Orphan Working School have been referred to by the *Times* as models of condensation with a clearness of detail, which may be regarded as the best indication of a well-ordered and economical administration.

It might not be too much to say that the old principle of carrying a scheme into execution only when there are sufficient subscriptions still characterises the operations of the institution. At all events, Mr. Soul had secured enough money for the completion of the new building at Margate before the actual work commenced, and his experience told him that funds would be forthcoming to maintain it.

The founders of the original Orphan Working School, however, laid their wigs together to obtain a house ready built, and at last found one adapted to the purpose, in what was then the suburban district known as Hogsden —since gentilised into Hoxton. Like all really good work, the enterprise began to grow—there were so many orphans, and this was still the only general asylum maintained by subscriptions—so that, as funds came in, two other adjoining houses were rented, and in seventeen years the number of inmates had increased from forty to 165.

Reading the formal and yet most interesting records of this parent institution for the care of the orphan and the fatherless, I fall into a kind of wonder at the enormous change in the method of "nurture and admonition," of teaching and training, which has taken place in the past eighty years. Even in this house at Hoxton, whereof the founders appear to have been kindly old gentlemen, the discipline was enormously suggestive of that stern restriction and unsympathetic treatment which was thought necessary for the due correction of the "Old Adam" in the young heart. We know how great an outcry has quite lately been made at the discovery of the remains of that mode of chastisement which seems to have been abandoned almost everywhere, except by a special revival in gaols, and at two or three of the public schools to which the sons of gentlemen are consigned for their education.

The discipline at the Orphanage at Hogsden was cold and repellent enough, perhaps—had very little about it to encourage the affections, or to appeal to the loving confidence of a child—but it was less barbarous than the code which at that time found its maxim in the saying, "Spare the rod, spoil the child." Only very flagrant disobedience, persistent lying and swearing, were punished with public whipping. But even in the case of ordinary falsehood, a child was placed with his face to the wall at meal-time, with a paper pinned to his back with the word "Lyar" written on it, till he was sufficiently penitent to say, in the presence of all the rest of the children, "I have sinned in telling a lie. I will take more care. I hope God will forgive me."

The name, "Working School," was then interpreted so strictly, that there was comparatively little margin for education. Arithmetic appears to have been regarded with peculiar jealousy by the founders of this institution, who, being perhaps bankers, accountants, and capitalists, looked upon such instruction as calculated to give the poor little boys and girls notions beyond their station.

For ten years the teaching of figures was altogether ignored; and it was only when some of the children, having heard that there was a science called "summing'" known to the outer world, begged to be taught, that a solemn meeting of the Governors was called to consider the question, when it was conceded, after great deliberation, and no little opposition from the anti-educational part of the Committee, that arithmetic should be permitted to be taught, as far as addition.

Thus, to their few and rigidly ordered recreations, their hours of manual labour in making nets, list-carpets, slippers, and other cheap commodities, to their instruction in plain reading, and to their times for partaking of plain and even coarse food, served in not too tempting a way, was added the art of writing, and of the first two rules of arithmetic.

This was the condition of the orphans in 1775; but still the charity grew—grew out of house-room; and as the funds grew also, it was determined that it should have a building of its own, on a plot of ground in the City Road, where, improvements having set in, the grand old charity moved with the march of modern improvement. Life became less hard, and instruction more extended. The influences of modern thought and education had superseded the old severity, and new Governors succeeded the bewigged and powdered founders, who had, after all, so well ordered their work, that it increased with the growth of intelligence.

During the seventy-two years from 1775 to 1847, the institution had received 1,124 orphans; and again the dimensions of the house were unequal to the demands of the inmates; while the house itself, and the ground on which it stood, had become so valuable, that it was determined to buy a plot of land at Haverstock Hill, and there to found a truly representative Home for 240 orphan boys and girls—a number which has now increased (as the building itself has been extended) till 400 orphans are taught, fed, and clothed in one of the most truly representative charities in all great London.

The obvious distress and suffering of those who are destitute, and whose claims are constantly before us, may lead us to forget the frequent needs of a large number of people who represent uncomplaining poverty. There is a tendency to identify general appeals to benevolence with efforts for the relief of that extreme necessity which demands immediate and almost undiscriminating aid, and requires the prompt distribution of alms or the provision of a meal, warmth, and shelter. Doubtless, the actually homeless and destitute claim our first attention —especially in the case of deserted and neglected children —and I have tried to show what is being done for those little ones, whose presence in the streets of this great wilderness of brick and stone should of itself be an appeal strong enough to move the heart of humanity in their behalf.

There is, however, another class of poverty, which makes no sign, and bears distress dumbly. There is a need, which, without being that of actual destitution, requires a constant struggle to prevent its representing the want of nearly all the luxuries, and some of those things which most of us regard as the necessaries of life.

We find this among that large section of the middle class represented by persons holding inferior clerkships, small official appointments, and situations where the salaries are only sufficient to yield a bare subsistence, and there is little or no probability of their improvement, because, among the number of candidates who are eager to fill such positions, there exists a degree of distress not easily estimated, even by the appearance of those who are the sufferers. Of course, relief cannot reach such people through the poor-law, or by any direct legislation. They are far above the reach of almsgiving, or even of societies for distributing bread and coals. They have a just pride in maintaining a position of independence; and though they may sometimes look with a feeling too near to envy at the more prosperous mechanic or the skilled artisan, who can earn "good wages," dress in fustian or corduroy, send his children to the Board School, and regulate working hours and weekly pay by the rules of a Trade Union, they mostly keep bravely on, hoping that as the children grow up, they may get the boys "into something," and find some friend to help them to place the girls in situations where they may partly earn their own living.

With rent and taxes often absorbing a fourth part of his entire income, with market cliques combining against him to keep up the prices of food, with dear bread, dear potatoes, boots and shoes always wearing out, and respectability demanding cloth clothes, even though they be made of "shoddy," how is the clerk, the employé, the small tradesman, the struggling professional man, to follow the prudent counsel which wealthier people are always ready to bestow upon him—and "lay by for a rainy day?" Rainy day! why his social climate may be said to represent a continual downpour, so far as the necessity for pecuniary provision. He lives (so to speak) with an umbrella always up, and it is only a poor shift of a gingham after all. The half-crown which is in his pocket to-night is already bespoken for to-morrow's dinner. As he listens to the account of the week's marketing, and knows that his wife and children have been living for three days out of seven upon little better than bread and dripping, he feels like an ogre as he thinks of the sevenpenny plate of meat that he consumed at one o'clock, because it was only "a makeshift" at home.

How is he to pay even the smallest premium to insure his life, when he is obliged to meet ordinary emergencies by a visit to the pawnbroker after dark?

Insure his life! Ah, the time may come when the hand of the bread-winner is still, when the little money left in the house is scarcely sufficient to pay for the "respectable funeral" which is the last effort of genteel poverty, when the red-eyed widow gathers her fatherless children about her, and wonders amidst her stupor of grief what is to become of the younger ones who yet so need her care that she will not be able to go forth to seek the means of living. To what evil influences may they be exposed while she is absent striving to earn their daily food?— the temptations of the streets for the boys: the certainty that the elder girls must either starve at home to mind the little ones, or must become drudges before they have learnt more than the mere rudiments of what they should be taught. It is then she feels that dread of degradation, which is amongst the sharpest pangs of the poverty which would fain hide itself from the world.

It may be that the children are left a parentless little flock, huddling together in the first dread and sorrow of the presence of death, and the sense of utter bereavement, and awaiting the intervention of those who are sent by the Father of the fatherless. Then, indeed, prompt and certain help is needed—help efficient and permanent—and such aid can seldom be secured except by organised institutions.

But let us see to what that Orphan Working School, established in 1758, has developed in 1874. We have but to take a short journey to the foot of Haverstock Hill, and there, in that pleasant locality named Maitland Park, part of which is the property of the Institution, we shall see the successor of the old house in Hogsden Fields, while its plain but large and lofty committee room is the modern representative of the parlour of the George Inn, Ironmonger Lane, where plans were first laid for the maintenance of forty orphan children.

This wide and lofty building, with its handsome front entrance and its less imposing side gate in the wing, is the home for nearly three hundred boys, and nearly two hundred girls, when its funds are sufficient to keep each of the long rows of neat beds in the great airy wards appropriated to a little sleeper.

I mention the dormitories first, because both on the girls' and on the boys' side of the building these are illustrative of the complete orderliness and excellent management of the Institution — illustrative of what should always be the first consideration, namely, to bring comfort to the child's nature, to join to necessary discipline a sense of real freedom and happy youthful confidence without dread of repression and the constant looking for of punishment.

As to the appliances that belong to the building, they are such as might almost raise a doubt in some prejudiced minds whether we are not doing too much for children in the present day, and thinking too constantly of their comfort. But, alas! it needs many compensations to make up for the loss of parents; and in any such an Institution where, 400 children form the great family, the arrangements must be on a large scale, so that it is only a matter of experienced forethought to combine a generous liberality with the truest economy. Thus, there are baths, and long well-ordered lavatories, to each wing, even to a large plunge bath for each side; and there is a great laundry, where the girls are taught to wash, clear-starch, and iron, not in the regular patent steam-heated troughs only, but in genuine homely tubs. There is a great handsome dining-hall, with a painted ceiling, wherein the vast troop of quiet, orderly, and happy-faced children sit down to well-cooked wholesome meals of meat and pudding. There are two great school-rooms, one divided into class-rooms for the girls, and another wherein the boys assemble to be taught, not in the narrow spirit of the first directors of the old building in the City Road, but with a full appreciation of the duty of giving these young minds and hearts full opportunity to expand. Next to the admirable evidences of *family* comfort, and bright *domestic* influences, which pervade this place, we may regard the efficient education of the children as the truest sign of its liberal and enlightened management. Not only the three R's to the extent of practised elocution, caligraphy worthy of the old minute books of the first scrivening secretaries, and the lower mathematics,—but history, geography, the elements of physical science, French, drawing, and vocal music, are among the subjects thoroughly studied. It only needs a perusal of the reports of the educational inspectors and examiners to see that the work of this great hive goes on healthily. The boys have already achieved a great position in taking Government prizes for drawing at South Kensington; and the girls are celebrated for their beautiful needlework. There is but little time to walk through all the departments of this great home—the kitchens with their spacious larders, and store-rooms, and mighty cooking apparatus; the great airy playgrounds; the large and handsome room used as a chapel (for those who do not go out to evening service), and containing its convenient reading desk, and sweet-toned organ. Let us not forget, however, that many of the things which add so vastly to the beauty and completeness of the building and its various departments are themselves gifts from loving and appreciative supporters of the Institution.

But we are due at that Lilliput village on the brow of Hornsey Rise—that series of cottage homes, where, on each lower and upper storey, with their exquisitely clean nursery cots and cradles, and their tiny furniture, a neat nurse is to be seen like a fairy godmother, with a family of chubby babies, or a more advanced charge of infants able to run like squirrels round the covered playground or to spend the regulation hours in that great glorious school-room, where learning is turned into recreation, and lessons are made vocal, gymnastic, zoological, picturesque, or even fictional, as the times and circumstances may dictate. "The Alexandra Orphanage for Infants" has become so well-known amidst the numerous institutions which have been established for the care of the orphans and the fatherless, that one might think it would be full of eager admirers who on visiting days go to see the two or three hundred. Why are not all the cottages full, and each little toy bedstead complete with its rosy, tiny sleeper, who, from earliest infancy to the maturer age of eight years form the assembly for which Mr. Soul set himself to provide by public appeal?

These, then, are the two institutions to which that modest little convalescent home in Harold Street, Margate, is a worthy appanage, and they may well find support among those whose maxim it is to do with all their might what their hands find wants doing.

WITH THEM THAT FAINT BY THE WAY.

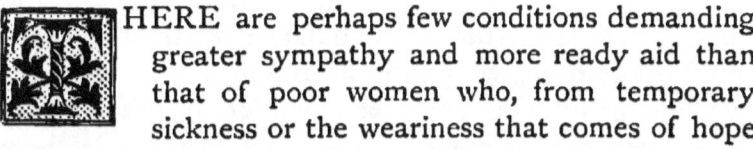HERE are perhaps few conditions demanding greater sympathy and more ready aid than that of poor women who, from temporary sickness or the weariness that comes of hope deferred, are unable to follow the employments, often precarious and yielding a bare subsistence, by which they strive to be independent of charitable aid. It is only those who know to what extremities of need they will submit for shame of making their poverty known, and what mental suffering they will endure as they find their scanty savings dwindling day by day, and their few household goods, or even their clothing, and the little family mementoes, which they can only part with as a last resource, going piece by piece, who can fully realise all that is meant by the genteel phrase, "very reduced circumstances," as applied to women of refined feelings, and frequently of gentle nurture, who find themselves without the means of obtaining necessary food and medical care when health and strength give way, and they can no longer work at those few callings by which they can earn enough to enable them to avoid a dreaded "application to friends."

Quite lately, the subject of some kind of provision for

poor governesses who are sick, or have to subsist during long holidays on the small balance of their quarterly wages, has occupied public attention, and it would be well indeed if means could be found for giving the healthy temporary employment, and the weakly a quiet home where their strength might be restored without the sacrifice of independence.

There are others, however, for which such help is equally needed—the dressmaker, or the shop-woman, on whom long hours of tedious and often of exhausting toil in an unhealthy atmosphere, has begun to tell too severely; the servant of good character and respectable habits, who is not so ill as to be admitted to a hospital, and yet is breaking down in strength, and regards with dread the necessity for going into some obscure lodging, where her surplusage of wages will barely pay for rent and food during two or three weeks enforced idleness; the girl who has learnt some ill-paid business, which affords her no more than a mere contribution to the family funds, and leaves no margin for extra food or medicine, or the fresh air that is as important as either.

Any careful observer standing at the door of a general hospital, and watching the throng of out-patients waiting wearily to see the doctor, will be able to distinguish a score of cases for which a temporary rest with wholesome food and the sympathy and loving-kindness that refresh the soul would bring true healing.

No large establishment in the nature of a hospital or a refuge affords the kind of help for such distress as theirs. They cannot be dealt with as occupants of wards; for they have either recovered from the actual crisis of some serious disorder, or are pining in a depressed condition to which no definite name can be given to classify it for admission to any public establishment for the cure of disease. To many of them the idea of entering a large charitable refuge—and I know of none in London adapted to such needs as theirs—would be repulsive, as suggesting that horror with which persons even of a lower grade regard the union workhouse; what they need is a temporary home, and if ever the time should come when a well-supported scheme for such a provision should be adopted, it will have to take the form of what is now known as the "cottage system." Indeed, in hospitals, as well as in other large charitable institutions, the defects of the old plan of maintaining a great number of adult persons in one vast building have been recognised. The immense ward with its long rows of beds, the divided and necessarily confusing duties of attendants, the ill-served meals at a great dinner-table where there is no possibility of escaping from a too rigid routine, the depressing, not to say degrading, influence, resulting from the loss of individuality, would make any vast institution for convalescents or invalids far less effectual in its operation. I make this reference only with regard to the probable inauguration of homes for invalid women in or near London, and because I have just visited one, which, although it is not on the cottage system, but is established in a rare old mansion of the period of Queen Anne, has yet the happy characteristic of being a family whose scanty means is largely increased by loving gifts, instead of an institution every corner of which bears a reminder that it is "supported by charity."

In the pleasant airy High Street of Stoke Newington, and within a stone's throw of the famous Cedar Walk of Abney Park—that locality made famous by the prolonged visit of Dr. Watts, who went to spend a week with Sir

Thomas Abney, and remained for the rest of his long blameless life the honoured guest of the family—is the house I speak of, "The Invalid Asylum for Respectable Females in London and its Vicinity," superintended by a ladies' committee, and with weekly visitors, and a matron to carry on the practical work of the executive.

There is nothing remarkably picturesque, nothing very striking about this home for thirty respectable invalid women employed in dependent situations, to whom it affords a temporary asylum, widely differing from the crowded receptacles for the sick in the metropolis. One of its peculiarities is, that the purity of the family circle is maintained, by the fact that no patient is admitted without a certificate of conduct signed by two housekeepers or by an employer, while her case is also recommended by an annual subscriber or life governor; and there is a sense of repose and quiet confidence about the inmates which is particularly suggestive of the care taken to recognise their individual claims, and the interest which is manifested in them during the time of their sojourn.

This very quietude and sense of rest, and gradual renewal of health and strength in a serene retreat is, in fact, the feature which attracts my attention. It is not too much to say that I am ready to attribute much of such influences to the fact that the institution was originally established by ladies representing the unobtrusive beneficent work of the "Society of Friends," and that the order and peace which is its delightful characteristic, may in a great measure be traced to that foundation. At any rate, these qualifications so identify it that I feel justified in regarding it to some extent as a worthy example of the method to be adopted in any institution, which, without being altogether a free "charity," takes only such a small sum from the patient or her friends as suffices to keep away the degrading feeling of pauperism, or of utter dependence on the bounty of strangers. It is true that the principal life-governorships include the privilege of sending entirely gratuitous patients, but in ordinary cases the annual subscriber of a guinea recommends the case, and when the patient is admitted, the sum of twenty shillings is received for the month's medical attendance, lodging, and full board, "including tea and sugar," for a time not exeeding one month, after which, should the case require a longer stay, the ticket must be renewed by the same or another subscriber, on the further payment of twenty shillings. If the patient be in the employment of the subscriber, the payment of this sum will suffice, without the renewal ticket, an arrangement which should commend the institution to every benevolent employer of female labour.

It need hardly be said that no cases of infectious disease are admitted, and that every applicant is examined by the medical attendant. No patient is admitted who is not above ten years of age; and neither "private cookery," nor the introduction of spirituous liquors by visitors, is permitted, any more than gratuities to servants of the Institution.

It may be remarked that though a large number of cases are received during each year, the very fact of contributions being made by the patients themselves, who are thus relieved from the sense of utter dependence, appears to have prevented the Institution from receiving as large a degree of public support as it might command if it were an ordinary charity. This is to be lamented, for the Institution is, after all, less a hospital than a temporary home, and it appeals on behalf of a peculiar form of distress, the claims of which are of a specific and none the less of a very urgent character. But in order to realise the kind of work that is most needed, and is here being accomplished, let us pay a visit to the house itself. We have been hitherto standing on the broad flight of steps inside the tall iron gates, and have hesitated to sully their hearthstone purity, for it is Saturday, and we may well have an inconvenient sense that the short hand of the clock is already close to the dinner-time of the institution.

With a long experience of paying unexpected visits, I am prepared to encounter remonstrance, even though it only take the form of a critical glance at my boots as a means of possible maculation of the newly-cleaned hall and passages. Conscious of having judiciously employed a member of the shoe-black brigade, I can endure this scrutiny, and, with a few words of explanation, am conducted, by the matron herself, over the grand old house, whose broad staircase and elaborately carved balusters of black oak at once attest not only its antiquity but also its aristocracy. I have already said that there is nothing here on which to found a "picturesque description," and yet the air of repose, the sense of almost spotless cleanliness, the freshness of the large lofty rooms containing from three to five or six comfortable beds with their snowy counterpanes, the general order and pleasant seclusion, are remarkably suggestive of the intention of the place. Two of the patients, to whom I make my respects, are not yet sufficiently recovered to join the daily dinner-party in the neat dining-room. One of them, an elderly lady, who has only just been brought here, is slowly recovering from very severe illness, and cannot even sit up in the bed, whence she regards me with an expression which seems to intimate that she has reached a haven of rest. Her companion, a young woman—also in bed in the same room—is sitting very upright, cheerfully engaged in some problem of needlework, and responds with a hopeful smile to the declaration of the matron, that they "mean to make a woman of her if she is good."

Close to this room is the neat lavatory with its bath, supplied with hot and cold water, and on the landing I note another bath, on wheels, for use in any part of the house where it may be required. All the accessories are home-like; and in the invalid sitting-room, on an upper storey, where two convalescents, not yet able to get downstairs, greet me from a pair of easy chairs, there is the same pervading influence which distinguishes the house from those large institutions where everything is characterised by a depressing mechanical dead level. The library—a pleasant cheerful room—is in course of refurnishing; and I am glad to learn that our best known periodicals find a place there, while the stock of books, either gifts or loans, are likely soon to be replenished, a matter wherein extra aid would be appreciated, and could readily be afforded by those who have volumes to spare.

Already the cloth is laid in the dining-room, and dinner itself consists of hot meat with the usual accessories every day, except on Sundays, when there is a cold dinner, while, of course, the invalids who are ordered medical diet have fish, custards, or other delicate fare specially provided. Each patient has a pint of ale or beer daily, and wine as a remedial stimulant, according to the doctor's orders.

There is just time before dinner is served to walk through the room into the grand old garden which extends from a pleasant sheltered lawn and flower-garden, with a glorious fig-tree in full leaf and fruit against the sunny wall, to a great kitchen-garden and orchard, with a wealth of fruit and vegetables (and notably a venerable and prolific mulberry tree), and extending in a pleasant vista of autumn leaves. On the other side of the high wall is the Cedar Walk already mentioned; and the whole place is so still and balmy on this autumnal day, that we may go away with a very distinct appreciation of the rest and peace which, with regular nutritious food, rest, and medicine, may bring restoration to the physical health, just as the hopeful ministrations of good and pious women who visit the home daily may bring a sense of peace and comfort to many a weary spirit and burdened heart.

"IN THE VALLEY OF THE SHADOW OF DEATH."

THERE are some of whom we might be ready to say, they dwell in that valley;—that the shadow of death lies darkling before them, constantly enwrapping them,—enshrouding them in gloom. We are accustomed to think so of persons suffering from what we call incurable diseases, some of which are painful, occasionally agonising, others susceptible of relief from the suffering that attends them.

We are so apt to forget that we are every one of us incurable. Though we may not at present be aware of the disease that will bear us farther and farther into that valley, where the wings of the great angel, so seeming dark as to overshadow all things, may yet be revealed to us as glowing with the brightness of the light which our unaccustomed eyes cannot behold, we are none the less certain to succumb to it. It may be that some of us will live to be conscious of no other than the most fatal of all diseases—because no mortal cure has been or ever will be found for it—incurable old age. There have been those who lived long enough to look calmly at the slowly lengthening shadow in the valley, and almost to wonder if Death had forgotten and were departing from them, leaving only the black trail behind; but the time at last came, perhaps when they had learnt to see more than shadow, to catch the glint of the heavenly glory beyond.

It is a happy thought that many poor afflicted children of God have seen this too, and continue to see it daily, although, like St. Paul, they also die daily. It is comforting to believe that many who know what their disease is—who are pronounced to be "hopelessly incurable" in a rather different sense to that in which we may all be declared to be hopelessly incurable also—do not dwell perpetually in the Valley of the Shadow. Christ has come to them and taken them out of it, that even in this life, where He is they may be also, secure in the love of the Father, having already, if one may so speak, overcome death through Him who is the Resurrection and the Life. The great, the essential difference between these sufferers and the rest of mankind is that they are almost always conscious of the disease which is incurable because of its accompanying pain, and that they are disqualified for many of the ordinary uses, and also most of the ordinary enjoyments of life. Perhaps the chief poignant sense of their condition is that they are no longer capable of fulfilling the ordinary duties of life either. They must be dependent always ; and to many souls the suspicion that they may live only to be a burden on others, to take instead of giving, to lean upon instead of supporting, is itself almost intolerable, until they learn to look higher, and acknowledge that not only all the things of the world, but we ourselves, they and theirs, belong to God, and that life and death, height and depth, principalities and powers, are but His creatures, incapable of separating us from His love. The same reflection, coupled with that of our own incurability and our own constant liability to be stricken down with hopeless and painful malady, should surely lead us to recognise the duty of helping some among the thousands who have not only lost health, but with it the means of maintaining life, and, more sadly still, the hope of restoration to former strength, or even temporary recovery.

I have already spoken of the work done by convalescent homes and hospitals; but there are those who, being sick unto death, yet do not soon die—those who must be discharged from hospitals uncured, in order to make room for the curable, and who, unable to work, unaccustomed to beg, and almost ready to meet death itself rather than sink into sordid abject pauperism, know not whither to turn in their dire necessity. It was to aid these that an appeal was written twenty years ago, asking for funds to establish an institution for the reception of those suffering from hopeless disease. It is to see what has been the result of that appeal that I visit the Royal Hospital for Incurables at Putney Heath to-day.

It was in 1854 that Doctor Andrew Reed—to whose indicating hand we are indebted for the installation of many of our noblest charities—made an urgent appeal on behalf of those who, being discharged as incurable from various hospitals, were left helpless, and often destitute, since, amidst all the institutions which beneficence had founded, there was none to which they could prefer a claim.

Let us see what has been done in twenty years to alleviate what might seem to be almost hopeless suffering.

Let us, coming face to face with the mystery of pain, and looking as it were from afar on that dark shadow which yet always lies so near to every one of us, note how in the heart of the mystery there is hidden a joyful hope for humanity, how in the very shadow of death there is a light that never yet has shone on land or sea.

It is a still autumnal day, and, as we turn up the wooded lane on the left of the hill leading from the Putney Railway Station to Wimbledon, a tender gleam in the grey clouds betokens coming rainfall. A light, hanging drift descends upon the distant hills, and breaks into pale vaporous shapes amidst the wooded slopes and valleys. The yellow leaves that strew the ground lie motionless, as though they waited for their late companions to fall gently from the branches overhead and join their silent company.

Coming into a broader roadway, and passing through the gate of a lodge, we come almost suddenly upon a glorious sloping lawn, adorned with goodly trees, worthy of the great building—meant for a ducal residence, and now put to nobler uses—which, for all its stately look, has about it a home-likeness that is full of promise. Even the matchless landscape lying around it—the expanse of wood and dale, the soft slopes of Surrey hills, the deep-embowered glades where the bronze-and-gold of moving tree-tops takes a changeful sheen from slowly-drifting clouds, or reflects strange gleams of colour from the glistening silver of the rain—will not hold us from the nearer glow of windows bright with flowers, which give a festal look to the place, although it is so quiet that we stand and imagine for a moment what it is that we have come to see. For this great mansion, with its long rows of windows and wide-spreading wings, is the home of a hundred and fifty-four men and women, some of whom have been suddenly stricken down, others having slowly fallen day by day into a condition of incurable disease, and, in many cases, also into a condition of utter bodily helplessness. They, and the attendants whose constant kindly services are essential for their relief, constitute the family of what is known, plainly enough, as "The Royal Hospital for Incurables." There are no distinctions among its members, though in their previous lives they have belonged to various grades—no distinctions, at least, except those which arise from personal qualifications.

The claim for election to the benefits of the charity is the necessity which is implied in the name of the institution itself: and once within its sheltering walls the patients, whose failing eyes brighten, and whose wan cheeks flush with every loving mention of it as their home, are all alike sharers in its benefits.

Not only the 154 at present within its walls, however, but 327 of those who, having family and friends with whom to dwell, receive pensions of £20 a year each, and so cease to be a heavy burden to others.

Do you think at first sight, and from the external appearance of the building, that charity here has gone beyond precedent in providing such a place—a palatial pile standing amidst scenery that one might well come far to see? Remember what is the need of those who have to be lifted out of the dark, hopeless depths of what is almost despair; of those who, finding themselves banished from hospital wards, unable to earn their bread, feeling themselves a burden upon those for whom they would almost consent to die rather than live upon their poverty; of those who, in the midst of hourly pain, have the mental anguish of knowing that the long calendar of darkening days may find them utterly dependent on the toil of others most dear to them, and whose few expedients can bring little ease, and will not serve to hide the ever-present sense of disappointment and distress.

Think how much wealth is wasted daily in the world, and what a small part of it suffices to lighten by every available means the burden of such lives as these; the sorrow of those who, in the dreadful deprivation of what to us seems almost all that makes life dear, have no resource between that provided for them in such a place as this and the infirmary-ward of a workhouse, amidst sordid surroundings and the hard, mechanical, unfeeling officialism which in such cases is little more than organised neglect.

There are people who would reduce all charitable institutions—yes, even such as this, of which living personal interest and the care that comes of more than merely casual benevolence are the very foundation and corner-stone—to a dead level of official rule, in which benevolence should be represented by a mechanical department, and the sentiment of charity by a self-elected board of control, dealing with public subscriptions as though they were a poor-rate, and recognising neither individual interest nor the right of contributors to give it expression. Such a system would lack the very qualification most needed here, and to be found only in that voluntary personal interest that brings to the recipients of bounty more than the mere bounty itself, the heart-throb of sympathy, the feeling that the gift means more than the cold official recognition of a national duty, that it is the expression of loving-kindness ever active and living; and so making for the helpless, the destitute, and the dying, not a mere asylum, but a home.

The entrance into the hall of a cheerful, genial gentleman, with a kindly, brisk manner, and a reassuring expression of deliberation and repose in his observant face and easy bearing, rouses us from melancholy fancies, and with a few words of courteous welcome we are at once conducted to the door that is to open to us the first scene in this wonderful visit.

A spacious assembly room—let us call it by the good old name of " parlour," for there is much quietly animated talk going on—talk, and needlework of all kinds, from the knitting of a warm woollen shawl to the manipulation of delicate lace, and the deft handling of implements for making those exquisite tortures of society known as antimacassars. With ever so wide an experience of halls, salons, suites, or drawing-rooms, the visitor can see nothing resembling this wonderful parlour elsewhere. A room of noble proportions, one end of which is occupied by an organ; the great windows reaching almost from floor to ceiling, and overlooking a broad expanse of lawn, with a glorious view of hill and woodland beyond; on the tables flowers, books, ornaments; in every kind of couch and chair—many of which are comfortable beds on wheels and springs—a company of women, with bright, cheerful, intelligent faces, full of a recent interest, and, even in cases where some paroxysm of pain is passing, with a certain serene satisfaction which it is infinitely good to see.

There has been a morning service, conducted by a visiting clergyman, and there is a general expression of approval which, if the reverend gentleman himself were present to witness it, would surely prove highly gratifying. The congregation has settled down to easy talk, and has resumed its occupation of plain and fancy needlework. Here is an old lady whose silver hair adds to her natural grace and dignity, who is busy with wool-knitting, and at the same time engages in a discriminating criticism of the address to one of the many visitors who sit and spend an hour of their afternoon in agreeable chat.

There is a pretty but rather sad-eyed *mignon* lady, whose excellently-fitting silk dress, delicate hands, and general " niceness " of appearance, quite prepare us to see the beautiful examples of all kinds of fancy work of which she never seems to tire. Every year, in June, they hold a grand bazaar at the hospital, so that those who are skilful and capable are able to earn enough money to clothe themselves as they please—everything except clothing being found by the charity, except to two or three inmates who are able to pay for their own maintenance. Now we hear the low tones of cheerful talk, the pleasant ripple of laughter—note the brightening glance, the quick smile, the feeble but earnest finger-clasp which greets the cheerful salutation of the house governor, Mr. Darbyshire, or the presence of his wife, the lady matron of this great happy family of incurables, we begin to wonder at our gloomy estimate of the place before this visit.

Nor is the revelation of cheerfulness, of light in shadow, less remarkable in the dormitories themselves. But then what rooms they are! Each bed is, as it were, set in an alcove of its own snow-white hangings, relieved by bits of colour which would delight an artist's eye—pieces of embroidery, framed illuminated texts, bright flecks of Berlin woolwork, or glistening designs in beads, or deep glowing knick-knacks wrought in silk and lace. Each little bedside table, though it may hold medicine and diet—drink and requisites for the sick—is decked with flowers and little framed pictures, gaily-bound books, and bright-hued toys and trifles, that make it look like a miniature stand at a fancy fair. In some cases the sense of combined purity and glow of colour is so great, that it is difficult to realise that we are in one or other of a series of sick-rooms. Everything is so spotless, so exquisitely clean and orderly, that nothing less than perfect nursing could explain it—for be it remembered that the place is open to visitors every day—and amidst some of the most terrible afflictions from which humanity can suffer there is nothing revolting. Expressions of pain and of utter prostration and weakness there are, of course; but even these are only alternative with the general placid contentment and thankfulness that is the prevailing characteristic.

Even in two severe cases of cancer the terrible effects of the malady are less notable, because of the surrounding conditions. A sprightly and engaging girl, with features and social life alike marred and obliterated by this dreadful malady, is surely one of the saddest of all the sad sights in such an institution; but here the brightness and genial influence of the place, and of those who are its ministrants, have had their effect, and even the half-obliterated features gain a grateful, loving, cheerful expression; the poor eyes beam with pleasure as the governor starts some reminiscence of that pleasant summer water-party of his, in which one of the two sufferers had to be carried to the boat in his arms, and both of them, deeply veiled, were rowed by those same guarding arms for a glorious voyage on the river, where the summer's sunshine and gladness stole into the hearts of the sufferers, and left a halo of remembrance that is not perhaps so very far from the anticipations of that stream which maketh glad the children of God.

Here are rooms wherein only two or three beds are placed, while few of them contain more than six, but all of them are bright, airy, lofty, full of space, and with the same sense of purity. And from every window some fresh and lovely view of the surrounding landscape, with all its changeful aspects, may be seen—the beds being so placed that every patient has her own special expanse of territory to solace her waking hours, even though she be unable to go down to the assembly-room. Here, in a room particularly bright and cheerful, lies a young woman with a wealth of dark hair on the pillow where her intelligent face beams with a certain courage, although her body and limbs have been for years immovable—only one arm, for an inch or two, and three fingers of the right hand, can be stirred—and yet, as we stand and talk with her, some small simple jest about her own condition causes her to laugh till the bed shakes. She has learnt to write by holding a pencil in her mouth, and inscribes neat and legible letters on paper placed on a rest just in front of her face. She is not only cheerful, but actually hopeful, though she has been for years in this condition; and her relations, great and small, visit her, to find her always heartily determined to look on the bright side. At the foot of her bed, near the window, is a swing looking-glass on a pedestal, and in this she sees reflected the distant prospect of autumn wood and field, extending miles away. Judging from her nobly equable and smiling face, she must be the life of the room of which she has been so long an occupant. In another apartment a poor schoolmistress suffering from hemorrhage of the lungs lies reading for many hours a day, her face bearing a painful expression, her manner eager, her constant craving to work on, by the study of books concerning the problems of this earthly life and the sciences that strive to demonstrate them and yet only bring us to the barrier of the eternal world. She yearns for one more day amidst her classes, and for the opportunity of testing the results of sick-bed thoughts on a method of education which should adapt itself to the individual temperament and mental peculiarity of each child. Amidst a troubled tide of thoughts that are perhaps sometimes too much for the weary brain, she may learn to recognise the rest that comes after hearing the Divine voice say, "Peace! be still;" and so a great spiritual calm may fall upon her, and give her rest.

Yet another visit, and we find a girl who, from an accidental fall, is as immovable as a statue, her dark questioning eyes and mobile face alone excepted. Yet she is sometimes lifted into a wheel-chair that stands stabled by her bedside, and joins the company in the great parlour downstairs. There is another little parlour, with quite a select coterie, under the presidency of an elderly gentlewoman, who is busily knitting at a table, while her friends recline at the windows, on their special couches; and in several of the dormitories patients are sitting up, reading, working, or looking at the fitful aspect of earth and sky on this October afternoon. Sufferers from heart-disease, with that anxious contracted expression so indicative of their malady, are numerous; but the larger number of the patients seem to suffer from rheumatism, or paralysis—among them one lady, with silvered hair, and yet with bright expressive eyes, and still bonny face, who was once a a well-known singer in London. She is unable to rise from couch or bed, but the readiness of repartee, the bright inquiring look, the quick appreciation and retort, remain, as do a certain swift expressive action of head and hands, which is marvellously suggestive of dramatic gesture; for, happily, her hands and arms are still capable of movement, and she has several periodicals on the coverlet—among them the latest monthly part of a magazine, in one of the stories in which she is evidently interested. She, with two or three others, are inmates of the hospital at their own charges.

We have but little time to devote to the men's side of this great institution; but its dormitories and furniture, its large day-room, where daughters sit talking in low voice to fathers, sisters to brothers, wives to husbands —its pleasant out-door contingent, who have just returned from slowly perambulating the grounds in wheel-chairs, or sit basking outside in the latest gleam of sunshine— its club in the rustic hut especially appointed for this purpose—all might bear comment. Here is a sturdy youth, who, falling from a tree, and alighting on his heels, incurably injured his spine, and now lies all day, mostly out of doors, and without a coat, frequently engaged in knitting. There is a poor gentleman, who has for sixteen years been almost immovable, from rheumatism, even his jaw being so fixed that he takes food through an aperture in the teeth. He has been through two or three hospitals, and under the care of the most eminent surgeons, and has come here now as to an ark of refuge, where he can read and talk, and be wheeled about the neighbourhood on occasional visits. Only one case of all those that we witness is startling in its melancholy sense of terrible loss and incurability; that rigid, grimly-set face, in the ward where the corner bed in which the grizzled head lies is the only one occupied this afternoon. The body belonging to that face is almost immovable— the ears are deaf, the tongue is mute, the eyes are nearly sealed—not by sudden calamity, but by gradual yielding to decay or disease. He has been an inmate several years, and is the one case here before which we may almost quail in our solemn sense of affliction; and yet and yet, to the touch of certain loving hands that dead face kindles; that mind, seemingly locked in stupor, wakes to life; that intelligence, encased in a casket iron-bound and motionless, can understand the signs that are made upon his own hands or forehead, and interpret them so as to give some kind of grateful answer. It needs the touch of the lady nurse to bring out this strange music from an instrument so unstrung; but that it should be done at all is an evidence of the hold that loving sympathy and some subtle influence almost beyond mere bodily capacity of expression has taken in these dear souls of the sick and the afflicted. That is where the shadow lifts, even in the darkness of the valley; that is how the Spirit of Christ may abound; and the soul, in recognizing the work of the disciple, may recognise the Lord therein, and remember the Living Word—"Though I walk through the valley of the shadow of death, I will fear no evil, for Thou art with me."

"WITH THE HALT AND THE LAME."

SUPPOSE there are few people in England, who are at all accustomed to keep Christmas amidst a loving family circle, who have not during the sacred festivities of the season, and all the household sentiments with which they are inseparably associated, made some reference to the "Christmas Carol," that famous story of the great novelist whose presence in the spirit of his books has brightened so many a Christmas hearth, and moved so many gentle hearts to kindly thoughts and words of loving cheer.

Amongst all the well-known characters to which Mr. Dickens introduced thousands of readers—characters who, to many of us, became realities, and were spoken of as though they were living and among our ordinary acquaintances—there have been none, except perhaps little Nell, who have evoked more sympathetic recognition than Tiny Tim, the poor crippled child of Bob Cratchit—the child, the sound of whose little crutch upon the stair was listened for with loving expectation—the shadow of whose vacant chair in the "Vision of Christmas," gave to the humbled usurer as keen a pang as any sight that he saw afterwards in that strange dream of what might come to pass. So completely do we share the anxiety of Scrooge in this respect, that we can all remember giving a sigh of relief when, at the end of the story, we learn that the poor crippled boy remains to bless the fireside where even his afflictions were felt to be a hallowing influence to soften animosities, and to draw close the bonds of family love.

"Somehow he gets thoughtful, sitting by himself" (says Bob Cratchit), "and thinks the strangest things you ever heard. He told me, coming home, that he hoped the people saw him in the church, because he was a cripple, and it might be pleasant to them to remember upon Christmas-day who made lame beggars walk and blind men see."

If I needed an excuse for so long an allusion to that pathetic story, which has stirred so many hearts throughout England, I might find it in the passage I have just quoted; but I seek none. I refer to the "Christmas Carol," because in it the figure of the crippled boy, occupying so small a space, yet is such a living, touching influence as to be one of the household fancies that associate themselves with our thoughts of Christmas-tide in poor homes; because there are so many little crutches the sounds of which are heard—though fewer than there used to be before *orthopædic* surgery became a special branch of study, and hospitals were founded for its practice; because, though Tiny Tim may represent so many crippled children who are the helpless members of poor families, where they are tended with as kindly care as working fathers and mothers can find time for—there are hundreds of other deformed or maimed lads whose lot is made the harder because of the want of sympathy and ready aid that would lift them out of utter helplessness, or give them such light labour to perform as would diminish their sense of dependence. Finally, because I desire you to bear me company to one place in London where this last need is recognised, and where forty crippled boys, suffering from various incurable deformities, which yet have left them the use of their hands, are not only taught a trade, but are encouraged, fed, and nurtured for the three years during which they are inmates of the home—"The National Industrial Home for Crippled Boys."

Alighting from the railway carriage which conveys us from Mansion House Station to the pleasant old High Street of Kensington, we are close to the place that we have come to see, for the building itself—a quaint old house, with a central doorway between two projecting deep bay-windowed fronts, and built of the reddest of red brick—stands at the end of Wright's Lane, looking us full in the face as we approach it to read the style and title plainly painted across its upper storey.

The house has good reason for looking the world thus bluffly in the face, for it is an independent building, bought and paid for: hearth-stone, roof tree, and chimney, freehold, and without debt or mortgage. Till this was done, all thought of considerable extension was put aside. The question was how to provide, out of voluntary subscriptions and contributions, for the fifty inmates who could be admitted within those sheltering walls. It must be premised, however, that ten pounds a year has to be paid for each boy who is accepted, during the three years that he remains there, to be taught in the evening school and in the workshop, not only how to read and write and cipher, but to become a good workman at tailoring, carpentering, or die-engraving and colour-stamping.

These are at present the only three trades taught in

this truly industrial home, but they appear to be very admirably suited to the cases of those who are deformed or crippled in various ways; and they are taught well, as an inspection of the work accomplished will prove. For the workshops are real workshops, where the boys do not play at work, but are taught their trades in a way that will enable them when they leave the institution to gain a decent livelihood, or even, if they can save a little money, to go into business for themselves.

This has been lately done, in fact, by two youths, who, having thoroughly learnt the relief-stamping process, have contrived to buy a press and the materials for their trade, and are now in partnership in a country town, and earning a respectable maintenance. Of sixteen lads who left during the year, twelve were doing well as journeymen at the industries they had learnt; one had set up in business for himself (the relief-stamping gives the greatest facility for this); and two had returned to their friends because of ill health, while one had not reported himself, But during the same period forty of the former inmates had been to visit the old home, and gave a very encouraging account of themselves. Let us add, in a whisper, that amongst these visitors were a " team" of old boys who had come to accept the challenge of a "team" of the new boys, to play a match at cricket. Yes, and that these teams of cripples have, over and over again, carried off their bats against opponents who, if they expected an easy victory, found themselves to have been most amazingly mistaken. I don't think this is mentioned in the Report, but it is well to know it, because it serves to prove how truly beneficent a work is being done here, in removing boys from a too often almost "hopeless" condition to one of useful, intelligent, skilled labour, and to healthy self-forgetfulness and association in the ordinary duties and recreations of their fellows. It must be remembered that every boy there is, in a certain sense, incurable. After having been nominated by the person willing to contribute the annual payment of £10, the medical officers of the institution (or if in the country, some qualified practitioner) examine the candidate, who must be above twelve and less than eighteen years of age, and neither blind, deaf and dumb, nor without the use of his hands. The name of the candidate is then added to the list of those waiting for admission—of whom there are now, unfortunately, above seventy—and when there is a vacancy, and funds are sufficient to maintain the full number of inmates, these candidates are taken in succession, without voting, by order of the Committee of Management, of whom the President is the Earl of Shaftesbury, and the Honorary Secretary Mr. S. H. Bibby, of Green Street, Grosvenor Square. There is also an efficient Ladies' Committee for the household management and for advising as to the education of the boys, the visits of the friends of the inmates, and the domestic affairs of the Home generally. There are some severe cases of deformity here—club-foot, spinal curvature, and various distortions of the legs—and in many cases instruments are worn, but the Institution does not profess to provide these. Frequently they are procured by special contributions, and among the latest gifts of this kind is a serviceable wooden leg or two, which have had the happy effect of relieving their recipients from the necessity of using crutches; but it is distinctly insisted on that the Home is not a hospital, and is only curative in the sense of improving the condition of those who, having been pronounced incurable, are yet capable of greatly increased activity and strength by means of nourishing and regular food, interesting occupation, and healthy exercise with companions who themselves are to be numbered among the halt and the lame, and yet are, in a very certain sense, made to walk and to leap and to praise God. For see, at the very moment that I am speaking, a little figure darts out of the passage yonder and scampers across the large open green space at the back of the house on his way to the new range of workshops that are now nearly completed, and are also paid for. Is it possible to apply the term cripple to such an elf, who is out of reach before one can ask his name? Yes; that very elf-like look is the result of a deformity which stops growth, though it leaves the limbs as active as you see them. But come up-stairs to the first of the present workshops, and you may note among the colour-stampers, sitting on their high stools before the dies and presses, cases of more decided deformity or of crippling by accident. These boys follow an artistic, pretty business, and visitors may do worse than give a small or a large order for notepaper and envelopes, stamped with crest, motto, or quaint design. So well is the work executed, that the Home has orders constantly in hand for the trade, and some of the dies are really beautiful examples of engraving. I think that in this long pleasant upper room, with its high bench running along the window, fitted with the presses and implements for the work, there are more severe cases of deformity than will be seen in either in the tailors' department on the same floor, or the carpenters' shop below. One reflects on the numerous accidents to which the children of the poor are liable, such as falls down flights of stairs; to the inhuman neglect of old women who are paid as "minders' by mothers compelled to go out to work in neighbourhoods where no infant crèche, no babies' cradle home, has yet been established, or in country towns where such institutions have scarcely been heard of. One remembers with pity the scores of poor little creatures who have to nurse and tend children almost as big as themselves, so that they and their charges too often become deformed together, the nurse with lateral curvature of the spine and the baby with vertical curvature or with deformities of the feet or legs. One thinks, in short, of the many perils to healthy life and well-formed limb that beset the children of the poor, and then coming back to the figures of this *National* Home, which yet, with careful management and due economy, can only receive forty or fifty crippled boys—wonders how long it is to be before the ruddy old house in Wright's Lane will expand its broad bosom and stretch out long arms on either side to embrace three-score more lads, taken from present neglect and want and probable ill-usage, to be fed and taught and nurtured for three years, during which the whole future will be changed for them, and their lives redeemed from the degradation that had threatened them just as their bodies expand with renewed health and strange developments of unsuspected strength, and their souls are lighted with hope and the sympathy of loving words and hearty manly encouragement.

A beginning has been made already; for that munificent anonymous benefactor, whose thousand-pound cheques have helped so many of our deserving charities, showed his usual nice discrimination by taking a walk in the direction of Wright's Lane. The result of this has been the erection of those long workshops which extend across one side of the wide green area, with its ornamental trees, at the back of the building—an area which is a good part of the acre on which the property stands, and forms a capital recreation-ground, without quite leaving out of sight the pleasant kitchen-garden beyond, or the little building in the further corner, which is intended as a cottage-infirmary in cases of sickness. There are the workshops, quite ready for another contingent of lads, such as are now busily at work in the tailoring department, where they are sitting on the board in the proper tailor-fashion, sewing away at one or other of the many private orders for gentlemen's clothes, or "juvenile suits," which are the better appreciated because they *are* hand-sewn, instead of being made with that machine, at the end of the room, to learn the working of which is, however, a necessary part of the modern tailor's trade. Quite ready, also, for our friends the relief-stampers, and for an additional crew of young carpenters to join those who are now busy below amidst a fine odour of fresh deal and the cheery sound of hammer, chisel, and plane. One of our young friends of the wooden legs— a strapping fellow of seventeen—is just deftly finishing off a very attractive chest of drawers, which will only need to be taken to the painting and varnishing rooms that form a part of the new building to be a very capital example of the workmanship of the establishment. For it cannot be too strongly insisted on that the customers of the Industrial Cripples get value for their money, whether it be in ornamental stationery, in plain furniture, packing cases, boxes, and general carpentry, or in "superfine suits" to order, or "own materials made up and repairs neatly executed." It is no sham industrial school, but a real practical working establishment, and when the new buildings are quite completed, and the dwelling-house has that other wing added to it, in order to provide proper dormitories and a school-room, dining-room, and lavatory, at all in proportion to the number of boys who are waiting anxiously for admission——

Ah! but the question is, When shall this be? Not till another £5,000 is added to the funds, I am told—about as much money as is sometimes spent in some public display which lasts three or four hours, and going to look at which probably half a dozen men, women, or children are lamed and crippled in the crowd. Judging from the present arrangements, with very little room to spare, and a not very conveniently-adaptable space, the money would be carefully spent; for there is no tendency to undue luxury, and the present household staff would still be sufficient for providing meals and looking after the family needs of these robust and independent young cripples. That it would be a work all the more beneficial, because of this very independence with which it is associated, it needs few arguments to prove; but, should reasons be asked for, let us take three cases for which the benefits of the Home are earnestly sought, and they will speak in suggestive accents of the need of that extension for which an appeal is being made. I need not tell you the names either of those who nominate the cases or the boys themselves; but be assured that the former would be sufficient guarantee of the need which it is sought to relieve :—

No. 1.—"The father is paralysed, and can do no work. The mother is not a very satisfactory person. Family consist of—
   1. The eldest, a boy of twenty, who does odd jobs.
   2. The cripple.
   3. Boy, works, and gets 5s.
   4. Boy, sells lights in the City.
       There are four little girls at home besides.

The cripple is in a very wretched state from want of food, but he has the use of his hands."

No. 2 (EDINBURGH).—"Was never at school more than a year in his life, and never attended regularly two months together. He can neither read nor write, and has been neglected and often half-starved by his dissipated parents. His mother pawns everything she can get to buy drink, and the boy has little benefit from the wages he makes, which are about 5s. per week. Their house is miserably dirty, Mrs. —— (the mother) being always drunk or incapable on the Saturday and Sunday. The boy works at Mr. B——'s Pottery, P——. He is honest and industrious. He is more miserable at home of late since he is left alone with his mother. It would be a great advantage to the boy if he could be admitted to the Industrial Home at Kensington, where he would be well trained, and where he would be quite beyond his mother's reach."

No. 3 (recommended by a Clergyman).—"Has been very regular at our school, and has been attentive and got on very well. His mother, a widow, lives with her sons, all of whom she has brought up well. She is an industrious, honest woman, and receives no help from the Board of Guardians excepting an allowance made for the maintenance of the cripple, and which, in case of his being accepted at the Home, they have promised to continue to pay for his maintenance. I may add that the Board, when he was called before them the other day, gave great praise to his mother for the cleanliness and respectability of his appearance."

Poor, depressed, starved, neglected, hopeless crippled boys, how long will it be before they come here for shelter, for hope, and renewal of life? I should ask the question—though the answer could only be a guess—but I am suddenly diverted by the tremendous ringing of a hand-bell, on which one vigorous young cripple is ringing a peal, which is almost loud enough to announce to all Kensington that it is "tea-time." The sound has the effect of bringing all the forty from their work—a contingent of young carpenters staying behind for a little while to dispose of some waste shavings which have been swept out of some corner where they may have been in the way. Then they come trooping into the big room, where they present so strange a variety of height and appearance, and also so remarkable a diversity of twist and lameness and distortion, that we are impressed at once with the melancholy fact that every boy there is in reality a cripple, and yet with the cheering reflection, inspired by some of the lively smiling faces, that there are vast mitigations of such afflictions—mitigations that come so near to cures as to make our neglect of them a very serious evil, when the means lie near at hand.

In this big room, which is neither dining-room, nor kitchen, nor refectory, but a homely combination of all three, there is no ornament, no sign of luxury, or of unnecessary expenditure—plain deal forms or stools at plain deal tables, on which are arranged a regiment of full-sized mugs of good sound tea, and plates, each containing a substantial half-pound slice of bread from a homely two-pound loaf, spread with butter or dripping. For breakfast the same quantity is provided, with the substitution of coffee for tea; and dinner consists of a half-pound of roast or boiled meat, with plenty of vegetables, and dumplings, pies, or puddings; while bread and cheese, or bread and butter, is served for supper. For it must be remembered that these are working lads, and that they require to be substantially, and, from the nature of their bodily affliction, even generously fed, so that these supplies of pure plain diet are not by any means excessive; and they are such as one very ordinary kitchen can supply—a kitchen, by the bye, which will probably be superseded by a more convenient one when the new wing shall be finished. Yet there is something in these unadorned, bare, almost too plainly appointed places, which brings with it a reassuring conviction that the institution has never been pampered. The dining-room, which has to do duty for a school-room also—the play-room, which is a rather dim kind of retreat on this November evening—and the plain, rather bare, but still clean and airy dormitories (especially those in the big bay-windowed front rooms of the old red brick house), are evidences that the place does not belie its name; that it is really a home, but essentially an industrial home, where work goes on as part of each day's blessing, and the title to play freely and with a light heart is thereby ensured.

WITH THEM WHO HAVE NOT WHERE TO LAY THEIR HEADS.

HERE is a degree of poverty which, while it is not absolute pauperism, often has deeper needs than those which are alleviated by parochial relief—a destitution which is none the less bitter because those who suffer it cannot stoop to actual mendicancy, and shrink from the degradation of the casual ward and its contaminating influences.

Those of us who at this season of the year are surrounded with comforts, and can meet together to enjoy them, should feel that there is no sadder phase of the life of this great city than that to which our attention is called by the statistics of those same casual wards, and the accompanying certainty that every night there are men, women, and children, who, amidst surrounding luxury and splendour, have not where to lay their heads, and for whom the repellent door of the nearest union workhouse is closed, even if they could summon such courage as comes of desperation, and dared to enter.

Happily, the numbers of those who seek what is called casual relief have diminished in proportion to the general abatement of pauperism; and it is perhaps encouraging to know that the applicants for nightly shelter at Refuges for the homeless and destitute are fewer than they were three or four years ago. This is a fact which should be made public, because some of these Refuges have been accused of offering inducements to casual paupers to seek food and shelter provided by charitable subscriptions, instead of betaking themselves to the night-wards provided for them at metropolitan workhouses. The complaint was made on altogether insufficient grounds, at a time when, during a hard winter, and with a fearful amount of distress among the poorest class of the community, the workhouse night-wards themselves were frequently inadequate to the demands made upon them; while, apart from the persons who were known as casual paupers, there were hundreds of unfortunates suffering from temporary starvation and the want of a place in which to find a night's lodging, who yet were altogether removed from what is known as pauperism, and dreaded the abject hopelessness which they associated with "the Union."

It should not be forgotten, either, that the task which is, and was then, imposed upon the pauper on the morning following his night's lodging and its previous dole of gruel and bread, renders it almost impossible for the recipient to obtain work. Before his job of stone-breaking or oakum-picking is accomplished, the hour for commencing ordinary labour outside the workhouse walls has passed, and his hope of resuming independent employment, and the wages that will provide food and lodging for the next four-and-twenty hours, has passed also. This alone is always sufficient to make a very marked distinction between the regular casual pauper and the temporarily unfortunate man or woman who, having failed to get work, and seeking only the aid that may give rest and strength for a renewed effort, might look in vain for succour but for the existence of places like that admirable Institution to which I wish to take you to-night.

The shameful spectacle of groups, and, in many instances, of crowds, of houseless, starving, and half-naked creatures huddled about the doors of casual wards, to which they had been refused admission in direct defiance of legislation, led to the establishment of Night Refuges. There was then no time to dispute. While boards and committees were squabbling and vilifying each other, the poor were perishing. But even now that a better system prevails, and pauperism has so considerably diminished, there is much necessity for the continuance of these institutions and their adaptation to the relief of that kind of distress which is all the more poignant because it is at present only temporary, but would receive the brand and stamp of permanence if it could find no other mitigation than that secured by an appeal to workhouse officials, the shelter of the casual shed, the union dole, and the daily task required in return.

At the time that Night Refuges were first founded, in consequence of the failure of the Houseless Poor Act, there were one or two institutions which went on the plan of offering no inducement whatever to those who sought shelter within their walls. The provisions were barer, the beds harder, the reception little less cold and un-sympathetic than they would receive at any metropolitan union.

Those of my readers who remember the Refuge for the Houseless Poor which once stood in Playhouse Yard, close to that foul tangle of courts that still exists between Barbican and St. Luke's, and is known as " The

Chequers," will understand me when I say that there were no alluring inducements for the houseless and the destitute to seek its aid.

I have seldom seen a more painfully suggestive crowd than that which waited outside the blank door of that hideous building on a cold drizzly evening when I paid the place a visit, only a short time before it was finally closed. I cannot deny, however, that the applicants for admission consisted of those persons for whom the institution seemed to be especially designed. The very lowest class of poverty, the representatives of sheer destitution, made up the 350 men and the 150 women who were to occupy the bare wooden bunks in the two departments of the building that night, and to accept, as a stay against starvation, the half-pound of dry bread and the drink of water. What I would call emphatic attention to, is the fact that this place was filled nightly at that time, because the inmates could leave early in the morning to seek a day's work, and so rise out of that depth of destitution which was represented by the nightly return to the casual ward. But let us remember that, though this Institution could scarcely be characterised by the warm name of "charity," it received all applicants who were not suffering from infectious diseases, and therefore its policy was deterrent. In order to separate itself from the idle casual, it made its provisions little short of penal, and, indeed, very far short of those common comforts that are to be found in prison.

But the Refuge in Newport Market was one of those which had been founded on a different principle. It was never intended as a supplement to the casual ward, or as having any relation to poor-law relief; though, during the terrible distress that overtook the houseless in that severe winter when our poor-law arrangements broke down utterly, it was impossible for any place founded in the name of Christian love and charity to be very particular in excluding famishing and frozen men and women on the suspicion that they had already somehow obtained parochial relief the night before.

This "Refuge" was originally established by the influence and the personal exertions of Mrs. Gladstone, and a few ladies and gentlemen who, knowing of the extreme distress that prevailed in all that poverty-stricken neighbourhood about Seven Dials, around the alien-haunted district of Soho, and in the purlieux of Drury Lane, and the courts of Long Acre, set about providing some remedy for the misery that homeless, destitute men, women, and children had to suffer during the bitter nights of winter. First, a regular mission was established in an ordinary room, and, after a time, space was secured to make a Refuge—first for six, then for ten, and afterwards for twenty of the most destitute cases which came under the notice of the mission-woman. This went on till the funds were sufficient to warrant a very earnest desire to obtain larger premises, and at last to make a bid for that queer ramshackle old slaughter-house, which was the rather too indicative feature of the locality. The landlords of this place were fully alive to the value of any property rising in proportion to the anxiety of somebody to become its tenant, and they demanded a high rent accordingly. Still, the work had to be done, and the slaughter-house—cleansed, repaired, whitewashed, and divided into several queer, irregular-shaped wards and rooms, which were reached by strange flights of steps and zig-zag entries—was opened with cheerful confidence and hope, under the earnest superintendence of the Rev. J. Williams, who was at that time incumbent of the parish of St. Mary, Soho. It was at that period that I first made acquaintance with the Institution, and with the quiet, undemonstrative work of charity which was carried on there, and is continued to this day, though it is less arduous now that the neighbourhood itself has felt the influence of such an organization—not so much in the diminution of actual poverty, as in the humanising and constantly suggestive presence of men and women who have brought a gospel to those who were hopeless, and seemed to have none to care for them.

The need to receive numbers every night to the utmost limits of the Institution has passed now, except occasionally during very severe weather; and though the cases admitted are still those where deep, and sometimes apparently almost fatal, misfortune is the claim, there is no longer the urgency which forbade a too discriminating selection, and the regular casual stands no chance under the quick and experienced eye of the superintendent, Mr. Ramsden, whose military tone and manner are, by the way, modulated so as to carry the sense of detection to the pretender, and to support and give courage to the weak and faint-hearted.

The same complete, quiet method of receiving applicants who await admission enables me to repeat the impression which I received during the time that the demands upon the night Refuge were more urgent. The experienced visitor who stands at the gate of this rehabilitated building that was once the old slaughter-house, and who watches the people go in one by one, and listens to their low-voiced pleas for food and shelter, cannot mistake them for casual ward cases. Just as, in some other Institutions, the pain of the spectacle is the degraded poverty of those who seek aid, the most affecting element here is utter destitution, without that *accustomed* debasement which would find a fitting resource at the workhouse door, leading to the night shed.

These are broken-down men and women; old men beaten in the battle of life, and full of present sorrow; young men who have fought and failed, or who have eaten of the husks, and seek occasion to rise to a better mind; middle-aged men not altogether crushed or hopeless, but in sore want, and needing the sound of a kindly voice, the touch of a friendly hand; women who have lost youth and worldly hope together—women who, more weak than wicked, and without resource, need some stay alike for fainting bodies and for wandering souls; women worn and hungry, because of the lack even of ill-paid work, and asking for rest and food till they can seek employment: some who will go forth in the morning and set out afresh; others who, if they can secure two or three nights' lodging, with a mouthful of food and drink morning and evening, have a good hope of doing better in the future.

To those who know how the demand for certain kinds of labour varies, and frequently slackens towards the winter months, when need is sorest, this latter most merciful provision comes with a sense of truest charity. Tickets of admission are issued to friends and visitors of the Institution (and any one may be a visitor who chooses to ring at the bell of the old slaughter-house), entitling the holder to admission after the regular evening hour of half-past five to six, so that in bestowing one of these the judicious subscriber (not necessarily, but surely from sympathy a subscriber) can [be a true benefactor. For these tickets will admit the really deserving nightly for a week, with supper of bread and coffee or cocoa, or occasional savoury soup, and breakfast of bread and coffee. And even this time is occasionally extended, if there be a reasonable prospect of obtaining work. Not only ticket-holders, but every applicant, may have the same privilege, if it can be shown that he or she is really likely to obtain employment. But there is more than this. There are men here—truest of gentlemen, beyond that social stamp of rank which rightfully belongs to them—who, with a real, manly instinct, know how to take poverty by the hand without offensive patronage or untimely preaching. There are ladies who, in their true womanhood, can see the contrition in faces bowed down —the shame that is caused, not by evil doings, but by the feeling of dismay which comes of having to ask for charity — can sympathise with broken fortunes, with gentle nurture—cast upon a hard, relentless world, with that poverty which is "above the common."

More still. Among the supporters and the constant visitors are those who can use special influence for cases that need it most, and obtain for them admission to hospitals and other asylums, or introduce to situations those who by sudden calamity have been deprived of the means of living.

Yes, even in their deepest need, poor, wandering, homeless women may come here and find help, for in that large, lofty, yet warm and well-lighted room, the women's dormitory—one side of which is composed of a series of niches where the comfortable beds are placed—there are to be seen a row of doors, which seem to belong to a series of cabins, as, indeed, they do. Each door opens into a small bed-room—small, but with room for a chair, a tiny table, and the neat bed. They are the lodgings set apart for women, who, in the midst of their poverty and destitution, are looking forward fearfully to the time when children will be born to them, and so to a period of weakness, and of the sad mingling of maternal pity and desponding sorrow. Let me say, in one line from the Report, that last year eight young women were received into the Refuge some time before their confinement, were passed on to Queen Charlotte's Hospital, and were helped until such time as they were able to help themselves.

I think the knowledge of this is so cheerful an instance of the value of this most representative Refuge, that even the sight of the bright, warm, glowing kitchen, with its great boiler of hot coffee, and its noble kettle of soup occupying the jolly range, scarcely imparts an extra beam to the picture; while the long rows of white mugs, the pleasant, clean, fragrant loaves, the big milk-cans, the courteous *chef*, who has a true and pardonable pride in his surroundings—no, not even the cosy, rug-covered berths and bunks in the dormitories, nor the quaint little corner-room to which I have to climb a crooked staircase to shake hands with the sister who is in charge, nor the equally quaint and cornery, not to say inconvenient, sitting-room of Mr. and Mrs. Ramsden, who have left their tea unfinished to do the honours of the Institution—can suggest to me a better word to say than that which is suggested by the picture of the poor wandering, weary, fainting women, who, almost in despair, not only for a real, but for an expected life, come here to find rest and peace.

Stay; one word more. Who are the class of people for whom the Refuge doors are ordinarily open? Let us see what were the most numerous cases among the inmates who during the year received 6,669 nights' lodgings and 16,889 suppers and breakfasts. Among the men "labourers," of course, are most numerous; then discharged soldiers—poor fellows who have perhaps foolishly snatched at liberty when offered, and foregone the advantages of re-engagement and a pension; next in numerical order come *clerks*—a very painfully suggestive fact, especially when read by the light of the advertisement-columns of our newspapers, and the sad story of genteel poverty in that great suburban ring which encircles the wealthiest city in the world. Of house-painters there were 24; of servants, 21; of tailors, 13; of seamen, 8; and other callings were represented in remarkable variety, including 1 actor, 6 cooks, 1 schoolmaster, 2 surveyors, and 1 tutor. Among the women, 199 servants—show sadly enough the truth of the old adage, "Service is no inheritance;" while in numerical succession there were, 55 charwomen, 41 laundresses, 37 needlewomen, 31 tailoresses, 27 dressmakers, 26 machinists (alas! how many women still utterly depend on "the needle" for a subsistence!), 24 cooks, 20 ironers, 16 field-labourers. There were 4 governesses, 1 actress, 1 mission-woman, and 1 staymaker, the rest being variously described.

From among these, 94 men and 193 women obtained employment, 77 women having been sent to Penitentiaries and Homes, while 18 were supported in the Refuge or elsewhere by needlework, 13 were sent to their friends, 60 obtained permanent work, and 14 girls of good character were sent to Servants' Homes.

But I have left out one thing now. Among this great representative company of refugees were 60 children, of whom 37 were sent to nurse or to school, while those who were old enough——— Well, just listen to that burst of military music in a distant upper-room of the old slaughter-house. I must tell you something about the Newport Market boys in another chapter.

TAKING IN STRANGERS.

ES; listen to that startling clangour of military music coming from an upper room. We are standing, you know, in the cheerful kitchen of that Refuge for the Homeless in the renovated old slaughter-house in Newport Market, and I want you to come with me to see the boys' school, which occupies a very considerable portion of that weatherproof but ramshackle building.

Only those who are acquainted with the poverty and the crime of this great metropolis can estimate the deep and urgent need that still exists for refuges in which homeless, destitute, and neglected children can be received for shelter, food, and clothing. Only the practical student of the effect of our present administration of the Education Act can calculate how vast a necessity is likely to exist for the reception and instruction of the children of the poorest, even when all the machinery of the present School Board is put in motion for vindicating the compulsory clause.

Let that clause be interpreted in the most liberal manner—which would be in effect to provide State education without cost to the parents—and the Act will still leave untouched a vast number of children for whom nothing can be done until their physical necessities are provided for — children who are perishing with cold, starving for want of food. A visit to some of the big buildings recently erected by the London School Board will reveal the fact that there are many such children now in attendance; neglected, barefoot, half-clothed, hungry, and with that wistful eager look, sometimes followed by a kind of stupefaction, which may be observed in the poor little outcasts of the streets. There is no reasonable hope of doing much with these little creatures till the "soup-kitchen" and the "free breakfast" are among the appliances of education, where the necessity is most pressing, and the children perish for lack of bread as well as for lack of knowledge.

As it is—I need not refer again to the escape which is always open from the streets to the prison. The few Government industrial-schools to which magistrates occasionally consign young culprits brought before them are intended only for those who come within the cognisance of the law.

The operations of these reformatory-schools are successful so far as they go. They represent seventy-five per cent. of successful reformatory training as applied to juvenile transgressors committed by magistrates to their supervision.

Perhaps, when we are fully impressed with the meaning of the statistics which are published each year in the Report of the Inspectors of Certified Schools in Great Britain, we shall begin to consider how it will be possible to regard destitute children in relation to the guardianship of the state *before* they qualify themselves for Government interposition by the expedient of committing what the law calls a crime.

The last Report states distinctly that the sooner criminal children are taken in hand, the more complete is their reformation. There are fewer "criminals" of less than ten years of age than there are hardened offenders of from twelve to sixteen. This is, so far, satisfactory; but when we consider that (including Roman Catholic establishments) there are but fifty-three reformatories in England, and twelve in Scotland (thirty-seven of those in England and eight in Scotland being for boys, and sixteen in England and four in Scotland for girls), and that in 1873, when the Report was issued, the sum-total of children in all these institutions was but 5,622, of whom one-fourth were in the Roman Catholic schools—we cease to wonder at the vast number of homeless, neglected, and destitute children in London alone—a number which, notwithstanding the efforts of philanthropy and the activity of School Board beadles, exceeds the total of all the inmates of the State reformatories throughout the kingdom.

This refuge at Newport Market had included destitute and starving boys among those who were brought to its shelter from the cruel streets, the dark arches of railways and of bridges, and the miserable corners where the houseless huddle together at night, long before its supporters could make provision for maintaining any of the poor little fellows in an industrial-school. But the work grew, and the means were found, first for retaining some of the juvenile lodgers who came only for a night's food, and warmth, and shelter, and afterwards for receiving them as inmates.

Some of these are sent to the Refuge by persons who are furnished with printed forms of application, or by mothers who can afford evident testimony that they can scarcely live on the few shillings they are able to earn by casual work as charwomen, or by the no less casual employments where the wages are totally inadequate to support a family; while a few lads have themselves applied for admission because they were orphans, or utterly destitute and abandoned by those on whom they might be supposed to have a claim.

A portion of the old building, which has been adapted to the purpose, and has been added as the need for increased space became pressing, is now devoted to the dormitories, play-room, and school-room of some fifty to sixty of this contingent of the great army of friendless children; and at the time of the last Report fourteen had but just left to be enlisted in military bands; two had become military tailors; situations had been found for others; while one had been regularly apprenticed to a tailor in London.

There are frequently several boys ready for such apprenticeship, for tailoring is the only regular trade taught, the time of the lads being occupied in learning to read, write, and cipher, to acquire the outlines of history and geography, and to take a place in the military band which is at this moment making the cranky old building resound with its performance on clarinets, hautboys, cornets, "deep bassoons," and all kinds of wind instruments, under the direction of an able bandmaster, who keeps the music up to the mark with a spirit which bespeaks confidence in the intelligence of his pupils.

This confidence is not misplaced, for during the past year eleven youthful recruits have been drafted from among these boys into the bands of various regiments, while there are above ninety applications still on the books for more musicians who have chosen this branch of the military service. It is a matter of choice, of course; and there are some who prefer to become sailors, or to go into situations and learn the trade of tailoring, that their instructors may be able to recommend them to respectable masters as apprentices.

But let us walk through the kitchen, and ascend the short zig-zag stairs which lead us by a passage to the school-room, where most of the boys are at work with their slates. Very few of the little fellows are more than thirteen years old, and some of them have been but a short time at school; but even those who came here totally uninstructed have made admirable progress, and some of the writing-books containing lessons from dictation are well worth looking at for their clean and excellent penmanship and fair spelling; while in arithmetic the boys who have been longest under tuition have advanced as far as "practice." There is nothing superfluous in school-room, work-room, or play-room—indeed, one might almost say that they are unfurnished, except for desks and forms and plain deal tables. The play-room is a lower portion of the old slaughter-house, with a high ceiling, to a beam in which is fixed a pair of ropes terminating in two large wooden rings by which the youthful gymnasts swing and perform all kinds of evolutions, while a set of parallel bars are among the few accessories.

It is evident that nothing is spent in mere ornament, and that the expenditure is carefully considered, though recreation, and healthy recreation too, is a part of the daily duty, which is regulated in a fashion befitting the rather military associations of the place. Even now, as the cheery superintendent, Mr. Ramsden, who was lately quartermaster-sergeant of the 16th Regiment, calls "Attention!" every boy is quickly on his feet and ready to greet us; and what is more, the boys seem to like this kind of discipline, for it is kind in its prompt demand for obedience, and the regularity and order includes a kind of self-reliance, which is a very essential part of education for lads who must necessarily be taught what they have to learn in a comparatively short time, and are then sent out where order and promptitude are of the utmost service to them. Economy is studied, but the recollection of the cheery kitchen suggests that there is no griping hard endeavour to curtail the rations necessary to support health and strength. In fact, the boys are sufficiently fed, warmly clothed, and are encouraged both to work and play heartily. Breakfast consists of bread and coffee; dinner of meat and vegetables three days in the week, fish on one day (Wednesday), pudding on Monday, soup on Friday, meat and cheese on Saturday; tea or coffee with bread and dripping, while on Sundays butter is an additional luxury both at breakfast and tea; and on Thursdays and Sundays tea is substituted for coffee at the evening meal. All the boys are decently and warmly clothed, and though only some of their number "take to music" as a profession, and choose to go into the military bands, they all receive instruction. They are taught to keep their own bunks and dormitories neat, and, in fact, do their own household work; while, morning and afternoon, personal trimness is promoted by the military "inspection" which is part of the discipline. There is half an hour's play after breakfast, another quarter of hour before dinner, three-quarters of an hour for "washing and play" after dinner, a quarter of an hour before tea, and from an hour and a half to two hours for boot-cleaning and play before bed-time, besides out-door exercise daily, except in wet weather, when drill and gymnastics take its place. They also go to Primrose Hill on Tuesday and Saturday afternoons, there to run in the fresh air and disport themselves in cricket, or such games as they can find the toys for, by the kindness of the committee or generous visitors. Even with these recreations, however, they find time to go through a very respectable amount of work in the fourteen hours between rising and bed-time; and the letters received from lads who have left the school are an evidence that they remember with pleasure and with gratitude the Refuge that became a home, and to which they attribute their ability to take a place which would have been denied to them without the aid which grew out of pity for their neglected childhood.

Here is a short epistle from one of the juvenile band, at Shorncliffe Camp, written a year or two ago :—

"I now take the pleasure of writing these few lines and I hope all the boys are all well, and all in the school and please Mr. Ramsden will you send me the parcel up that I took into the school it was laying in the bookcase in the school-room and I hope that all the boys are all getting on with their instruments and the snips with their work and I should like you to read it to the boys and I wish that you would let ―――― answer it and I am getting on with my instrument very well, and I will be able to come and see you on Cristamas season."

This is a characteristic schoolboy letter, which shows how much boys are alike in all grades. The following is another letter from Shorncliffe :—

"Dear Sir,

"I received your kind and welcome letter along with mothers, and I wrote back to tell you we have all been enlisted and sworn in, and we expect to get our clothes next week and we all feel it our duty to express our deeply felt gratitude to you Mr. Dust and the

TAKING IN STRANGERS.

Committee, and we are all very happy at present please give our respects to Mrs. Ramsden Sister Zillah Mr. McDerby Mr. Mason Mr. Goodwin Miss Cheesman and please remember us to all the boys. Leary is on sick furlough since the 15th of Decr. and has not returned yet and Brenan, Lloyd Graham McCarthy Henderson and all the others are very jolly at present and been out all the afternoon amongst the snow. So I conclude with kind thanks to one and all and believe me to be Dear Sir

"Your late pupil———

"Band———Regt."

The following will show how the memory of the old slaughter-house and the school in Newport Market remains after the boys have left and have entered on a career. It is addressed from Warley Barracks:—

"Dear Sir

"I now take the opportunity of writing to you hoping you and all the rest of the school and the sister also. It is a long time since I left the school now and I dont suppose you would know me if I was to come and see you I was apprenticed out off the school along of J———R———to Mr W———in 1869 I think it was as a Tailor. I should like you to write and tell me if you know what rigment J——— H——— belong to his school number was 34 and mine was 35 me and him was great friends when we were in the school and I should like to know very much were he is. When I left the School Mr. L———was Supperintendant and I dont suppose I should know you sir if I was to see you I shall try to come down and see the School if I can on Christmas for I shall be on pass to London for seven days and I should like to know where J——— H——— is so as I should be able to see him. I have a few more words to say that is the school was the making of me and I am very thankful to the school for it so with kind love to you all

"I remain your humble servant,

"Band———Regiment,

"Warley Barracks, Essex.

"J——— H———number was 34 and mine was 35.

"Excuse me addressing this Letter to you as I dont know anything about you sir."

There is something pleasant indeed in letters like

these; and I for one am not surprised that the boys should go to their musical practice with a will.

They are just preparing to play something for our especial delight now, and so burst out, in a grand triumphant blast, with "Let the Hills Resound," after which we will take our leave, and, we hope, not without melody in our hearts. Just one word as we go through this kitchen again. Two West End clubs supply the Newport Market Refuge with the remnants of their well-stocked larders. Did it ever occur to you how many hungry children and poor men and women could be fed on the actual waste that goes on in hotels, clubs, inns, dining-rooms, and large and ordinary households every day? M. Alexis Soyer used to say that he could feed ten thousand people with the food that was wasted in London every day; and I am inclined to think he was not far wrong. At all events, an enormous salvage of humanity might be effected if only the one meal daily which might be made of "refuse" pieces of meat and bread, bones, cuttings of vegetables, cold potatoes, and general pieces—was secured to the thousands to whom "enough" would often indeed be "as good as a feast." To people who know how much that is really good for food—not the plate-scrapings and leavings, but sound and useful reversions of meat and bread and vegetables, bones, and unsightly corners of joints—is either suffered to spoil or is thrown at once into the waste-tub, both in hotels and private houses, the additional knowledge that there are hungry children in every district in London to whom a bowl of nourishing soup or a plate of minced meat and vegetables would be a boon, may easily be a pain, because of the inability to suggest how to organise the means of utilising what one is tempted to call undeserved plenty.

FEEDING THE MULTITUDE.

SUPPOSE there are people still to be found who have but a vague notion of what it is to be really hungry. They may be conscious of possessing a good appetite now and then, and having the means of obtaining food, and to a certain extent of choosing what they will eat, regard being rather "sharp set" as a luxury which gives additional zest to a dinner, enabling them to take off the edge of their craving with a plate of warm soup, and to consider what they would like "to follow."

Of course we most of us read in the papers of the distress of the poor during the winter, of the number of children for whom appeals are made that they may have a meal of meat and vegetables once or twice a week, of the aggregate of casual paupers during a given period, and of cases where "death accelerated by want and exposure" is the verdict of a coroner's jury; but we do not very easily realise what it is to be famished; have perhaps never experienced that stage beyond hunger—beyond even the faintness and giddiness that makes us doubt whether we could swallow anything solid, and would cause us to turn hopelessly from dry bread. There is no need here to detail the sufferings that come of starvation.

They are dreadful enough; but if our charity needs the stimulus of such descriptions we are in a bad way, and are ourselves in danger of perishing for want of moral sustenance.

Those who need assurance of the hunger of hundreds of their poor neighbours need not go very far to obtain it. A quarter of an hour at the window of any common cook-shop in a "low neighbourhood," at about seven o'clock in the evening, when the steam of unctuous puddings is blurring the glass, and the odour of leg-of-beef soup and pease-pudding comes in gusts to the chilly street, should suffice. There is pretty sure to be a group of poor little eager-eyed pinch-nosed boys and girls peering wistfully in to watch the fortunate possessor of two-pence who comes out with something smoking hot on a cabbage-leaf, and begins to bite at it furtively before he crosses the threshold.

Of course, according to modern social political economy, it would be encouraging mendicity, and sapping the foundations of an independent character, to distribute sixpenny pieces amongst the juvenile committee of taste who are muttering what they would buy if only somebody could be found to advance "a copper." But it is to be hoped or feared (which?) that a good many people yet live who would instinctively feel in their pockets for a stray coin to expend on a warm greasy slab of baked or boiled, or on half a dozen squares of that peculiarly dense pie-crust which is sold in ha'porths. This is a vulgar detail; but somehow poverty and hunger *are* vulgar, and we should find it difficult to get away from them if we tried ever so hard. Even School Boards, peeping out upon the children perishing for lack of knowledge, find themselves in a difficulty, because there is no provision under the compulsory or any other clause for the children who are also perishing for lack of food. The Board beadle does not at present go about with soup-tickets in his pockets; and for the poor shivering shoeless urchins who are mustered in the big brick-built room where they assemble according to law there is no free breakfast-class.

It must one day become a question how they are to learn till they are filled. Grown people find it hard enough to fix their attention on the best advice or the most saving doctrine while they suffer involuntary hunger. The multitude must mostly be fed before they are taught. Even disciples have had a revelation of the Bread of Life in the breaking of bread that perishes. Do we still need a miracle to teach us that?

Happily, efforts are made to give meat to the hungry. During the winter weather food is distributed in various ways amidst some of those poverty-stricken neighbourhoods to which I am obliged to take you during our excursions; but the demand far exceeds the supply, and people suffer hunger at all seasons, though most of all in the time of bleak winds and searching cold.

I want you to come to-day to a kitchen which is open all the year round—the only kitchen of the kind in London which does not close its doors even when the springtide brings buds of promise on the shrubs in Leicester Square, and the London sparrow comes out from roofs and eaves, and preens his dingy plumage in the summer sun, as though Great Windmill Street had something in common with its name, and sweet country odours came from the region of the Haymarket.

For, you know, we are still in the district of Soho. I have but just now brought you out of Newport Market, and now we are in a very curious part of this vast strange city. The streets are dim and dingy, but not so squalid as you might have imagined. They are still and silent, too, as of a neighbourhood that has seen better days, and even in its poverty has a sense of gentility which is neither boisterous nor obtrusive.

You will remember that I referred to this neighbourhood of Soho when I spoke of those old French refugees who came and made industrial colonies in London after the revocation of the Edict of Nantes. This is the only really foreign quarter of London which has lasted until to-day; but that is to be accounted for by the fact that it became representative of no particular industry, and that, probably from the fact of many of the patrons of literature and art having then town houses about Leicester and Soho Squares, the more artistic refugees took up their abode in the adjacent streets.

From the time when William Hogarth painted his picture of the Calais Gate till only a short time ago, when refugees fled from besieged Paris to find some poor and wretched lodging in the purlieus of Cranbourne Street, where they might live in peace and hear their native tongue, this has been the resort of poor foreigners in London. It almost reminds one of some of the smaller streets of a continental city; and as we look at the queer shabby restaurants, and the shops with strange names painted above them in long yellow letters, we almost expect to find the pavement change to cobble-stones, and to see some queer wooden sign dangle overhead, so like is the place to the small *bourgeois* quarter that in our earlier days lay behind the Madeleine and the Porte St. Denis.

For here is an actual *crêmerie*—a queer compound of

cook-shop and milkseller's—with a couple of bright dairy cans outside the door, and a long loaf or two amidst the cups and plates and sausages in the dingy window. Over the way you see "*Blanchisseuse*" in large letters; and next door is a *laiterie*, which differs from a *crêmerie* as a *café* alone differs from a *café restaurant* with its "*commerce de vins*" painted in big capitals in front of a long row of sour-looking bottles and a green calico curtain. It is a quaint jumble, all the way to Dean Street, and till we reach the edge of the Haymarket—a jumble of Brown and Lebrun, of Jones and Jean, of Robin *(fils)* and Robinson; but for all the little musty-smelling *cafés*, the blank bare-windowed *restaurants*, the *crêmeries*, and the *boulangeries*, there is nothing of a well fed look about the district, especially just at this corner, leading as it seems to a stable-yard or the entrance to a range of packers' warehouses. There is one open front here—is it a farrier's or a blacksmith's shop?—where they appear to be doing a stroke of business, however, for there is a clinking, and a fire, and a steam; but the steam has a fragrant odour of vegetables—of celery and turnips, of haricots and gravy—the clink is that of basins and spoons getting ready, and the fire is that of the boiler which simmers two mighty cauldrons.

Step to the front, and you will see in big white letters right across the house, "Mont St. Bernard Hospice." You may well rub your eyes, for you are in the heart of London, and stand in Ham Yard, Leicester Square, before the soup-kitchen that is open all the year.

There is something very appetising in the steam that arises from both these huge cauldrons, one of which is the stock-pot, containing bones, remnants of joints (*not* plate-clearings), and reversions of cold meat, &c., from two West End clubs. To this are added vegetables—celery, haricot beans, or barley—making it a fresh palatable stock, not remarkable for meatiness, but still excellent in flavour, as you may find for yourself if you join me in a luncheon here. But the real strengthening gravy has yet to be added, and the cauldron on the left hand is full of it—real, genuine gravy soup, made from raw meat and bones purchased for this purpose. As soon as this has simmered till it is thoroughly ready, the contents of the two cauldrons are mixed, and the result is a delicious stew, which is ready to be turned out into these yellow pint basins, for the hungry applicants, who will sit down at one of these two deal tables, each of which has its rough clean form, or to be dispensed to those who bring jugs, bowls, cans, saucepans, kettles, pipkins—any and almost every receptacle in which they can carry it steaming away to their families.

Let us stand here and see them come in. Here is a poor famishing fellow, who looks with eager eyes at the savoury mess. He has evidently seen better days. There is an unmistakable air of education about him, and as he sits down with his basin and spoon, and the handful of broken bread, which is added to the soup from one of a series of clean sacks emptied for the purpose, the superintendent, Mr. Stevens, scans him with a quick eye, and will probably speak to him before he leaves. There is a foreigner—an Italian, by the look of his oval olive face—who takes his place very quietly, and as quietly begins to eat; and yonder a famished-looking, rough fellow, who has already devoured the basinful with his eyes, and is evidently in sore need. Men, women, and children, or, at all events, boys and girls, come and present their tickets, and receive this immediate relief, against which surely not the most rigorous opponent to mendicancy can protest. The cadger and the professional beggar do not go to the soup-kitchen where nothing is charged, for they do not need food, and will only see a ticket where it is likely to be accompanied by the penny which will buy a quart. Be sure that there are few cases here which are not so necessitous that they are not far from starvation; and many of them represent actually desperate want.

The tickets for obtaining this prompt relief—often only just in time to save some poor creature from utter destitution and crime, and as often administered when a family is without food, and yet clings to the hope of finding work to prevent that separation which they must submit to by becoming paupers—are placed in the hands of clergymen, doctors, district visitors, Bible-women, and those who know the poor, and can feel for them when in hard times they pawn furniture, tools, and clothes, and suffer the extremity of want, before they will apply for parochial relief, and have offered to them the alternative of "going into the house."

The annals of the poor, from which extracts occasionally appear in the newspapers in the accounts of coroners' inquests, prove to what dreadful sufferings many decent but destitute people will submit rather than become recognised paupers; and no system of charitable relief outside the workhouse walls will be effectual or useful which does not recognise and respect this feeling. Who would let the possible accident of some unworthy person getting a gratuitous pint of soup stand in the way of a work such as we see going on here, where one year's beneficent action includes above ten thousand persons relieved?— a large number of whom are temporarily taken into the Hospice, as we shall see presently, while a great contingent is represented by the family tickets, which enable poor working men and women from various districts in London to carry away a gallon of strong nourishing soup, and an apronful of bread to their hungry little ones. You see that great heap of pieces of fine bread—slices, hunches, remnants of big loaves, dry toast, French bread, brown bread, and rolls—all placed in a clean wooden bin, they also come from the two great West End clubs before mentioned, and are so appreciated by the applicants for relief (they being usually good judges of quality) that you may note a look of disappointment if the stock of club bread has been exhausted, and a portion of one of the common loaves bought for the purpose is substituted. The small broken bread in those clean sacks is club bread also—the crumbs from rich men's tables, but clean, and thoroughly good, fit for immediate addition to the soup, which a hungry company of diners consume in a painfully short space of time.

They are not inhabitants of this district, either; comparatively few come from the immediate neighbourhood, though, of course, some poor families of the adjacent streets and alleys, and occasionally foreign workmen—many of them adepts in artistic employments, who are in the land of the stranger and in want—come here and have not only the help of a meal, but the kind inquiry, the further aid that will sustain hope, and enable them to look for work, and find the means of living. Londoners from Kentish Town, Lambeth, Shoreditch, and Chelsea —poor hungry men and women from all parts of the great city—find their way here to obtain a dinner; and it is extremely unlikely that they would leave even the least profitable employment and walk so far for the sake of a basin of soup. Food alone is offered, not money, and there is little probability of imposition when there is so little to be gained by the attempt. But while the great cauldrons are being emptied, let us hear what they do at this "Mont St. Bernard Hospice" at the Christmas season.

Here is a list of good things that were sent at Christmas-tide for a special purpose :—A noble earl sent a sheep, if not more than one, and other generous givers in kind—many of them manufacturers of or dealers in the articles they contributed—forwarded loaves, biscuits, hams, rice, flour, currants, raisins, ale, porter, cocoa, peas, and other comfortable meats and drinks, so that there was a glorious distribution to the poor on Christmas Eve, when 936 families were provided with a Christmas dinner, consisting of 4 lbs. of beef, 3 lbs. of pudding, bread, tea, and sugar, together with such other seasonable and most acceptable gifts as were apportioned to them in accordance with the number of their children and the quantity of miscellanous eatables and drinkables available for the purpose.

But we have not quite done with it yet, for it is a hospice in fact, as well as in name. Just as in the Newport Market Refuge, the houseless and destitute are received with little question—the homeless and friendless are here taken in after little inquiry, even the subscriber's ticket for admission being occasionally dispensed with, when Mr. Stevens, the superintendent, sees an obviously worthy case among the applicants who come to ask for a meal. It must be remembered, however, that an experienced eye can detect the casual very readily, and that Mr. Stevens, who served with his friend Mr. Ramsden, of Newport Market, when they were both in the army, is as smart a detective as that shrewd and compassionate officer. It is so much the better for those who are really deserving—so much the better even for those who, being ashamed to dig, are not ashamed to beg —the ne'er-do-weels who, even in the degradation of poverty brought about by idleness and dissipation, come down to solicit food and shelter, and find both, together with ready help, if they will mend their ways. There are some such, but not many : more often a man of education, broken by misfortune, and perhaps by the loss of a situation through failure or accident beyond his control, finds himself starving and desolate. Such men have come here, and found, first, food, then a lavatory, then a bed in a good-sized room, where only seven or eight persons are received to sleep, then a confidential talk, advice, the introduction to people willing and able to help them among the committee and subscribers of the Institution.

It may be a French tutor destitute in London, but with his character and ability beyond doubt ; it may be, it *has* been, a young foreign artist ; a skilled labourer from the country, who has come to London to find work and finds want instead ; a poor school-teacher who, having lost an appointment, and being unable to work at any other calling, is in despair, and knows not where to turn ; an honest fellow, ready and willing to turn his hand to anything, but finding nothing to which he can turn his hand without an introduction. Such are the cases which are received at this hospice in Ham Yard, where they are permitted to remain for a day or two, or even for a week or two, till they find work, or till somebody can make inquiries about them and help them to what they seek.

About seven men and eight women can be received within the walls, but there are seldom the full number there, because it is necessary to discriminate carefully. The object is to relieve immediate and painful distress, and to give that timely aid which averts starvation by the gift of food, and prevents the degradation of pauperism by means of advice, assistance, and just so much support as will give the stricken and friendless men or women time to recover from the first stupor of hopelessness or the dread of perishing, and at the same time afford the opportunity of proving that they are ready and willing to begin anew, with the consciousness that they have not been left desolate.

GIVING REST TO THE WEARY.

E have not yet done with this wonderful district of Soho. It is one of those attractive quarters of London, which is interesting alike for its historical associations and for memorable houses that were once inhabited by famous men. In essays, letters, fiction—all through that period which has been called the Augustan age of English literature—we find allusions to it; and after that time it continued to be the favourite resort of artists, men of letters, wealthy merchants, and not a few statesmen and eminent politicians. In Leicester Square, Hogarth laughed, moralised, and painted. The house of Sir Joshua Reynolds stands yet in that now renovated space, and a well-known artist has a studio there to-day. But the tide of fashion has receded since powdered wigs and sedan chairs disappeared. The tall stately houses are many of them dismantled, or are converted into manufactories and workshops. The great iron extinguishers which still adorn the iron railings by the doorsteps have nearly rusted away. It must be a century since the flambeaux carried by running footmen were last thrust into them, when great rumbling, creaking coaches drew up and landed visitors before the dimly-

lighted portals. Silence and decay are the characteristics of many a once goodly mansion; and the houses themselves are not unfrequently associated with the relief of that poverty which is everywhere so apparent as to appeal to almost every form of charity. Before one such house we are standing now, its quietly opening door revealing a broad lofty hall, from which a great staircase, with heavy baluster of black oak and panelled walls leads to the spacious rooms above. This mansion is historical, too, in its way, for we are at the corner of Soho Square, in Greek Street, and are about to enter what was once the London residence of the famous Alderman Beckford, and his equally famous son—the man who inherited the mysterious and gorgeously furnished palace at Fonthill, the author of "Vathek," the half-recluse who bought Gibbon's extensive library at Lausanne, that he might have "something to amuse him when he went that way," and afterwards went that way, read himself nearly blind, and then made a friend a present of all the books, sold Fonthill, went abroad, and set about building another mysterious castle in a strange land.

In that big committee-room on the first floor, which we shall visit presently, there was to be seen, four or five years ago, a stupendous chimney-piece of oak, elaborately carved, and said to have been a masterpiece of Grinling Gibbons. It was taken down and sold for a handsome sum of money, to augment the funds of the Institution which now occupies the old mansion, for the door at which we enter receives other guests than those who once thronged it—suffering, depressed, poverty-stricken, weary men and women, who come here to seek the rest that is offered to them in the quiet rooms—the restoration of meat and drink and refreshing sleep, the

comfort of hopeful words and friendly aid. It is named
"The House of Charity," and the work that its supporters have set themselves to do is carried on so
silently—I had almost said so secretly—that the stillness you observe within the building, as we stand here
waiting for the lady who superintends the household,
is suggestive alike of the repose which is essential to
the place, and of a severe earnestness not very easy to
define.

Members of the same committee, whose earnest hearty
work is apparent at Newport Market and at the Soup
Kitchen in Ham Yard, are helping this House of Charity,
which has the Archbishop of Canterbury for its patron
and the Bishop of London for its visitor.

Here, in the two large sitting-rooms opening from the
hall, we may see part of what is being done, in giving
rest to the weary and upholding them who are ready to
faint. One is for men, the other for women, who have
been received as inmates, for periods extending from a
fortnight to a longer time, according to the necessities of
each case, and the probability of obtaining suitable employment. Of course the aid is intended to be only
temporary—though in some peculiar cases it is continued
till the applicant recovers from weakness following either
uninfectious illness or want. There can be, of course,
no actual sick-nursing here; but in a warm and comfortable upper room, near the dormitory, which we shall see
presently—a room which is the day-nursery of a few
children who are also admitted—I have seen young
women, one who was suffering from a consumptive
cough, another an out-patient at an hospital for disease
of the hip, and wearing an instrument till she could be
admitted as a regular case. They were both sitting

cosily at their tea, and were employed at needlework, as most of the women are who find here a temporary home. For it is one of the beneficent results of an influential committee, that a number of cases are sent to hospitals or to convalescent homes, and so are restored; but till this can be done they are fed and tended—fed with food more delicate than that of the ordinary meal—and are allowed to rest in peace and to regain strength.

But we are still in the men's sitting-room, where several poor fellows are looking at the lists of advertisements in the newspapers for some announcement of a vacant situation. A supply of books is also provided both for men and women, and the latter are just now engaged in mending or making their clothes.]

Between thirty and forty inmates can be received at one time, and those who are in search of employment, or who require to go out during the day, may leave the house after breakfast, and return either to dinner or to tea. There are, indeed, few restrictions when once preliminary inquiries and the recommendation of a member of the committee result in the admission of an applicant; and it is easy to see how deeply and thankfully many of these poor depressed men and women, beaten in the battle of life, with little hope of regaining a foothold, weak, dispirited, destitute, and with no strength left to struggle under the burden that weighs them down, find help and healing, food and sleep, advice, and very often a recommendation which places them once more in a position of comfort and independence. A large proportion of those who are admitted are provided with situations either permanently or for a period long enough to enable them to turn round the difficult corner from poverty and dependence to useful and appropriate employment. Some are sent to Homes, hospitals, or orphanages, and many return to their own homes. From those homes they have wandered, hoping to find the world easier than it has proved to be, and in going back to them they have fallen by the wayside.

There are sometimes remarkable varieties here—emigrants waiting for ships to sail that will bear them to another land; men of education, such as tutors, engineers, engravers, and professional men, who have been unsuccessful, or have lost their position, often through no immediate fault of their own. Of course, the large class of genteel poverty is largely represented in the five or six hundred cases which make the average number of yearly inmates. Clerks, shopmen, and travellers are about as numerous as servants, porters, and pages. Poor women, many of whom are ladies by birth or previous position and education, find the House of Charity a refuge indeed, and feel that the person who has charge of the household arrangements, as well as those who have charge of the inmates, the accounts and correspondence, may be appealed to with an assurance of true sympathy. Here, beside the two sitting-rooms, is a large room which we will call the refectory; it is plainly furnished, with separate tables for men and women, and the quantity and description of the food supplied is such as would be provided in a respectable and well-ordered family—tea or coffee and plenty of good bread-and-butter morning and evening, meat, bread and vegetables, for dinner, and a supper of bread and cheese. There are no "rations," nor any special limit as to quantity, and if one could forget the distress which brings them hither, the family might be regarded as belonging to some comfortable business establishment, with good plain meals and club-room on each side the dining-hall for meeting in after working hours.

Let us go upstairs, and look at the dormitories, which occupy respectively the right and left side of the building, and we shall see that they are so arranged as to secure that privacy, the want of which would be most repulsive to persons of superior condition. Each long and lofty room is divided into a series of enclosures or cabins by substantial partitions about eight feet high, and in each of these separate rooms—all of which are lighted by several windows or by gas-branches in the main apartment—there is a neat comfortable bed and bedstead, with space for a box, a seat, and a small table or shelf.

A resident chaplain or warden conducts morning and evening prayer in the chapel, which is built on part of the open area at the back of the building; and I would have you consider, not only that to many of these weary souls this sacred spot may come to be associated with that outcome to renewed life for which their presence in the Institution gives them reason to hope, but that it is most desirable for the invalids, who frequently form so large a portion of the congregation, to be able to attend worship without practically leaving the house.

Not only because of the sick and the physically feeble, however, does the House of Charity represent a work that needs vast extension.

The case-book would reveal a series of stories none the less affecting because they are entered plainly, briefly, and without waste of words. They need few touches of art to make them painfully interesting. They tell of ladies, wives of professional men, brought to widowhood and sudden poverty; of men of education cast adrift through failure or false friendship, and not knowing where to seek bread; of children left destitute or deserted under peculiar circumstances; of women removed from persecution, and girls from the tainted atmosphere of vice; of weary wanderers who, in despair of finding such a shelter, and dreading the common lodging-house, have spent nights in the parks; of foreigners stranded on the shore of a strange city; of ministers of the gospel brought low; of friendless servant-girls, ill-treated, defrauded of their wages, or discharged almost penniless, and cast loose amidst the whirlpool of London streets.

But, as I have already intimated, it is not alone for its temporary aid in affording a home that the House of Charity is distinguished; it affords a good hope also, by seeking to obtain situations, for cases where peculiar circumstances make such a search difficult—for bereaved and impoverished ladies, and for educated men, as well as for domestic servants and ordinary employés. Its supporters give their special aid to the work, and, as they number amongst them many ladies and gentlemen of considerable social influence, employment is frequently found for those whose misfortunes would otherwise be almost irretrievable.

WITH THE POOR AND NEEDY.

"ALL hope abandon, ye who enter here," would, as we might fancy, be an appropriate inscription for many a wretched court and alley in the greatest and most opulent city in the world—a city distinguished for its claims to be regarded as the centre of civilisation; as the exemplar of benevolence, and of active Christianity. It is one of the marvellous results of the vast extent of this metropolis of England that there are whole districts of foul dwellings crowded with a poverty-stricken population, which yet are almost ignored, so far as public recognition of their existence is concerned. Legislation itself does not reach them, in the sense of compelling the strict observance of Acts of Parliament framed and presumably enforced for the purpose of maintaining sanitary conditions; philanthropy almost stands appalled at the difficulty of dealing with a chronic necessity so widely spread, a misery and ignorance so deep and apparently impregnable; sentimentalism sighs and turns away with a shiver, or is touched to the extent of relieving its overcharged susceptibilities by the comfortable expedient of the smallest subscription to some association in the neighbourhood. True, active, practical religion alone, of all the agencies that have operated in these places, gains ground inch by inch, and at last exercises a definite and beneficial influence, by taking hold of the hearts and consciences of the people themselves, and working from within the area of vice and misery, till the law of love, beginning to operate where the law of force had no influence, a change, gradual but sure, here a little and there a little, is effected.

We are continually hearing of the "dwellings of the poor;" and can scarcely take up a newspaper without noting the phrase, "one of the worst neighbourhoods in London," connected with some report of crime, outrage, or suffering; yet how few of us are really familiar with the actual abodes of the more degraded and miserable of our fellow-citizens! how quickly, how gladly, we dismiss from our memory the account of an inquest where the evidence of the cause of death of some unfortunate man, woman, or child, without a natural share of light, air, food, and water, reveals hideous details of want and wretchedness, which we might witness only a few streets off, and yet are unconscious of their nearness to us in mere physical yards and furlongs, because they are so far from us spiritually, in our lack of sympathy and compassion.

Even at the time that these lines are being written I have before me a report of an examination by the coroner into the circumstances attending the death of a woman seventy years of age, who obtained a miserable and precarious living by stay-making, and who was found dead in the back kitchen of a house. Her death was alleged to have been brought about by the unhealthiness of the house in which she lived, although the landlord was a medical officer of health for one of the metropolitan districts.

In this case the alleged landlord, who was actually a medical officer of health, answered the charge made against him by the statement that he had only just come into possession of the property, and had at once set about putting it in repair. It is to be hoped that this was the case, and, indeed, the evidence of the sanitary inspector went to show that it was so; but the question remains: How is it that dwellings are permitted to be thus overcrowded, and to become actual centres of pestilence in the midst of entire neighbourhoods, where, for one foul tenement to have an infamous reputation amidst such general filth and dilapidation, it must indeed be, as one member of the jury said this place was, "so bad, that no gentleman would keep his dog there?"

Keep his dog indeed! Why I know whole rows and congeries of intersecting courts and alleys where a country squire would no more think of kennelling his hounds than he would dream of stabling his horses! There has during the past few years been a tolerably determined stand made against the introduction of pigsties into the back-yards of some of the hovels about Mile End and Bethnal Green; and though cow-sheds are not altogether abolished everywhere in close and overbuilt localities, there are some precautions taken to diminish the sale of infected milk by an inspection of the laystalls, and the enforcement of lime-whiting and ventilation in the sheds. Costermongers' donkeys are the only animals besides dogs and cats which are commonly to be found in London slums now, and as these can be stowed in any shanty just outside the back door, or can be littered down in a spare corner of a cellar, they remain, in costermongering districts, without much opposition on the part of the local authorities. For, after all, what can these authorities do? Under the 35th section of the Sanitary Act, power was given to them to register all houses let out by non-resident landlords, who were under a penalty of forty shillings for not keeping their houses in repair, well supplied with water, drainage clear, &c. To those who have an intimate acquaintance with the density of population in whole acreages of London slums, there is something almost ludicrous in these words, especially when they are read in the light of the fact that the landlords of such places are frequently parochial magnates or officials who know how to make things pleasant with subordinate sanitary inspectors.

What may be the ultimate result of an Act of Parliament "for improving the dwellings of the poor" it is not at present easy to say; but assuredly any plan which commences by a general and imperfectly discriminative destruction of existing houses, hovels though they may be, will only have the effect of crowding more closely the already fœtid and swarming tenements where, for half-a crown a week, eight or ten people eat, live, and sleep in a single apartment. It was only the other day, in a district of which I shall presently speak more definitely, that a "mission woman" was called in to the aid of a family, consisting of a man, his wife, his wife's brother—who was there as a lodger—and five or six children, all of whom occupied one room, where the poor woman had just given birth to an infant. The place was almost destitute of furniture; beds of straw and shavings, coverlets of old coats and such ragged clothing as could be spared; little fire and little food. Such destitution demanded that the "maternity box," or a suddenly-extemporised bag of baby-clothing and blankets, should be fetched at once; and though the mission there is a poor one, with terrible needs to mitigate, a constant demand for personal work and noble self-sacrifice, such cases are every-day events, such demands always to be answered by some kind of helpful sympathy, even though the amount of relief afforded is necessarily small and temporary in character.

Not in one quarter of London alone, but dotted here and there throughout its vastly-extending length and breadth —from St. Pancras, and further away northward, to Bethnal Green and all that great series of poverty-stricken townships and colonies of casual labour, on the east; from the terrible purlieux of Southwark, the districts where long rows of silent houses, in interminable streets, chill the unaccustomed wayfarer with vague apprehensions, where "Little Hell" and the knots and tangles of that "Thief-London" which has found a deplorable Alsatia in the purlieux of the Borough and of Bermondsey; and so round the metropolitan circle, westward to the neighbourhood of aristocratic mansions and quiet suburban retreats, where the garotter skulks and the burglar finds refuge; further towards the centre of the town, in Westminster, not a stone's-throw from the great legislative assembly, which, while it debates in St. Stephen's on sanitation and the improvement of dwellings, scarcely remembers all that may be seen in St. Peter's, about Pye Street, and remembers Seven Dials and St Giles's only as traditional places, where "modern improvements" have made a clean sweep, just as the Holborn Viaduct and the metropolitan Railway swept away Field Lane, and the new meat market at Smithfield put an end for ever to the horrible selvage of Cloth Fair—and only left the legends of Jonathan Wild's rookery and the "blood-bowl house."

But the very mention of these places brings the reflection that not in outlying districts, but in the very heart of

London, in the core of the great city itself, the canker of misery, poverty, and vice is festering still. What is the use of eviction, when the law punishes houselessness, and the *Poor* Law cannot meet any sudden demand, nor maintain any continuous claim on the part of the houseless? Summarily to thrust a score or so of wretched families into the streets is to make them either criminals or paupers. They must find some place of shelter; and if they are to live *by* their labour, they must live *near* their labour, the wages of which are, at best, only just sufficient to procure for them necessary food and covering for their bodies.

In the neighbourhood to which I have already referred, four thousand evictions have taken place, or, at any rate, the population has diminished from 22,000 to 18,000, because of a small section of a large puzzle map of courts and alleys having been taken down in order to build great blocks of warehouses. The consequence is, that in the remaining tangle of slums the people herd closer, and that a large number of poor lodgers have gone to crowd other tenements not far distant, and which were already peopled beyond legal measure.

For this acreage of vice and wretchedness of which I speak is close to the great city thoroughfares—almost within sound of Bow Bells. It is about a quarter of a mile in extent each way, lying between the Charterhouse and St. Luke's, close to the new meat market at Smithfield on one side, and Finsbury Square on the other. One entrance to it is directly through Golden Lane, Barbican; the other close to Bunhill Fields burial ground, along a passage which bears the significant name of "Chequer Alley." It is a maze of intersecting and interlocking courts, streets, and alleys, some of them without any thoroughfare, some reached by ascending or descending steps, many of them mere tanks, the walls of which are represented by hovels inhabited by costermongers, French-polishers, dock-labourers, chair-makers, workers at all kinds of underpaid labour and poor handicrafts. Many of the women go out to work at factories, or at charing, and the children are—or at least were—left to the evil influences of the streets, till another and a more powerful influence began to operate, slowly, but with the impetus of faith and love, to touch even this neglected and miserable quarter of London with "the light that lighteth every man."

In this square quarter of a mile—which, starting from the edge of Aldersgate, stretches to the further main thoroughfare abutting on the pleasant border of the City Road, and includes the northern end of Whitecross Street—there are eighty public-houses and beer-shops!

I tell you this much, as we stand here at the entrance of Golden Lane, but I have no intention just now to take you on a casual visit either to the dens of wretchedness and infamy, or to the homes where poverty abides. I must try to let you see what has been done, and is still doing, to bring to both that Gospel which is alone efficient to change the conditions, by changing the hearts and motives of men. I may well avoid any description of the places which lie on either hand, for, in fact, there is nothing picturesque in such misery, nothing specially sensational in such crime. It is all of a sordid miserable sort; all on a dreary dead-level of wretchedness and poverty, full of poor shifts and expedients, or of mean brutality and indifference. There is no show-place to which you could be taken, as it is said curious gentlemen were at one time conducted to the dens of the mendicants, thieves, and highwaymen of old London. Even in the tramps' kitchen the orgies, if there are any, are of so low a kind that they would be depressing in their monotonous degradation.

Let us go farther, and enter this strange wilderness by its fitting passage of Chequer Alley, so that we may, as it were, see the beginning of the work that has been going on with more or less power for more than thirty years.

I think I have some acquaintance with what are the worst neighbourhoods of London. I have made many a journey down East; have studied some of the strange varieties of life on the shore amidst the water-side population; have lived amidst the slums of Spitalfields, and passed nights "Whitechapel way;" but never in any unbroken area of such extent have I seen so much that is suggestive of utter poverty, so much privation of the ordinary means of health and decency, as on a journey about this district which I long ago named "The Chequers." Each court and blind alley has the same characteristics—the same look of utter poverty, the same want of air and light, the same blank aspect of dingy wall and sunken doorsteps, the same square areas surrounded by hovels with clothes'-lines stretched from house to house, almost unstirred by any breeze that blows, shut in as they are in close caverns, only to be entered by narrow passages between blank walls. It is the extent of this one solid district, almost in the very centre of City life, that is so bewildering, and wherein lies its terrible distraction.

The labour of reformation has begun, but the labourers are few. For more than thirty years some efforts have been going on to redeem this neglected and unnoticed neighbourhood, which lies so near to, and yet so far from London's heart.

Let it be noted that this moral effort had gone on for nearly twenty-nine years before any very definite attempt was made to improve the physical condition of the place.

In 1841 a tract distributor, Miss Macarthy, began an organised endeavour to teach the depraved inhabitants of Chequer Alley. In 1869, a sanitary surveyor, reporting on *one* of the courts of this foul district, recommended that the premises there should be demolished under the "Artisans' and Labourers' Dwellings Act," because the floors and ceilings were considerably out of level, some of the walls saturated with filth and water, the others broken and falling down, doors, window-sashes and frames rotten, stairs dilapidated and dangerous, roof leaky and admitting the rain, no provisions for decency, and a foul and failing water supply.

The "pulling-down" remedy, without any simultaneous building up, has been extended since then in a locality where a model lodging-house, which has been erected, has stood for years almost unoccupied, because like all model lodging-houses in such neighbourhoods, neither the provisions nor the rentals are adapted to meet the wants and the means of the poorest, of whom, as I have already said, a whole family cannot afford to pay more than the rental for a single room, or two rooms at the utmost.

But we are wandering away from the work that we came to see. Look at that wistful young native, standing there quite close to the mouth of Chequer Alley. Ask him what is that sound of children's voices from a casually-opened doorway, and he will tell you "It's our school; yer kin go in, sir, if yer like—anybody kin." As the name of the institution is "Hope Schools for All," his invitation is doubtless authorised, and we may well feel that we have made a mistake in thinking of the Italian poet's hopeless line, for out of the doorway there comes a sound of singing, and inside the doorway is a room containing fifty or sixty "infants," seated on low forms, and many of them such bright, rosy—yes, rosy—clean—yes, comparatively, if not superlatively clean—little creatures, that hope itself springs to fresh life in their presence. It is thirty-four years since Miss Macarthy, with an earnest desire to initiate some work of charity and mercy, resolved to become a distributor of tracts, and the district she chose was this same foul tangle to which I have asked you to accompany me. Bad as the whole neighbourhood is now, it was worse then. It was never what is called a thief-quarter, but many juvenile thieves haunted it; and the men were as ruffianly and abusive, the women as violent and evil-tongued as any who could be found in all London. Instead of being paved, and partially and insufficiently drained, it was a fœtid swamp, with here and there a pool where ducks swam, while the foul odours of the place were suffocating. No constable dare enter far into the maze without a companion. But the tract distributor ventured. In the midst of an epidemic of typhus, or what is known as "poverty" fever, she went about among the people, and strove to fix their attention on the message that she carried. The religious services commenced in a rat-catcher's "front parlour," and at first the congregation broke into the hymns with scraps and choruses of songs. The crowd which collected outside not only interrupted the proceedings, but threatened those who conducted them with personal violence, and even assaulted them, and heaped insult upon them; but the lady who had put her hand to the plough would not turn back. In the midst of her patient and difficult work she herself was stricken down with fever. She had visited and tended those who were suffering. When the question was asked what had become of her, the barbarous people learnt that she was like to die. Perhaps this touched the hearts of some of them, for she had begun to live down the brutal opposition of those who could not believe in unselfish endeavours to benefit them. She recovered, however; and supported by others, who gave both money and personal effort, the beneficent work went on.

In this large room where the children are singing we have an example of what has been effected. Some of the little creatures are pale, and have that wistful look that goes to the heart; but there are few of them that have not clean faces, and who do not show in the scanty little dresses some attempt at decent preparation for meeting "the guv'ness."

There is a school for elder children also; and in the ramshackle old house where the classes are held there are appliances which mark the wide application of the beneficent effort that has grown slowly but surely, not only in scope, but in its quiet influence upon the people amidst whom it was inaugurated. Yonder, in a kind of covered yard, is a huge copper, the honoured source of those "penny dinners," and those quarts and gallons of soup which have been such a boon to the neighbourhood, where food is scarce, and dear. Then there was the Christmas dinner, at which some hundreds of little guests were supplied with roast meat and pudding, evidences of how much may be effected within a very small space. Indeed, this Hope School, with its two or three rooms, is at work day and night; for not only are the children taught—children not eligible for those Board schools which, unless the board itself mitigates its technical demands, will shut up this and similar institutions before any provision is made for transferring the children to the care of a Government department — but there are "mothers' meetings," sewing classes, where poor women can obtain materials at cost price, and be taught to make them into articles of clothing. There are also adult classes, and Sunday evening services for those who would never appear at church or chapel but for such an easy transition from their poor homes to the plain neighbourly congregation assembled there. There are evenings, too, when lectures, dissolving views, social teas, and pleasant friendly meetings bring the people together with humanising influences. It becomes a very serious question for the London School Board to consider whether, by demanding that ragged schools such as this shall be closed if they do not show a certain technical standard of teaching, the means of partially feeding and clothing, which are in such cases inseparable from instructing, shall be destroyed.

But here is a youthful guide—a shambling, shock-headed lad, with only three-quarters of a pair of shoes, and without a cap, who is to be our guide to another great work, on the Golden Lane side of this great zigzag, to the "Costermongers' Mission," in fact. You may follow him with confidence, for he is a Hope School-boy —and that means something, even in Chequer Alley.

Still threading our way through those dim alleys, where each one looks like a *cul-de-sac*, but yet may be the devious entrance to another more foul and forbidding, we leave the "Hope-for-All" Mission Room resounding with infant voices, all murmuring the simple lessons of the day. That room is seldom empty, because of the evening school where a large class of older pupils are taught, reading, writing, and arithmetic; the adult class, and the "mothers' meeting," to which poor women are invited that they may be assisted to make garments for themselves and their children from materials furnished for them at a cheap rate in such quantities as their poor savings can purchase. The visiting "Bible woman" is the chief agent in these works of mercy, since she brings parents and children to the school, and reports cases of severe distress to be relieved when there are funds for the purpose. Not only by teaching and sewing, however, are the hopeful influences of the place supported, for, as I have said already, in this big room the people of the district are invited to assemble to listen to lectures, readings, and music, to see dissolving views; and in the summer, when fields are in their beauty and the hedge-rows are full of glory, there is an excursion into the country for the poor, little, pallid children, while, strangest sight of all, a real "flower show" is, or was, held in Chequer Alley. One could almost pity the flowers, if we had any pity to spare from the stunted buds and blossoms of humanity who grow pale and sicken and so often die in this foul neighbourhood.

But we have strange sights yet to see, so let us continue our excursion in and out, and round and round, not without some feeling of giddiness and sickness of heart, through the "Pigeons"—a tavern, the passage of which is itself a connecting link between two suspicious-looking courts—round by beershops. all blank and beetling, and silent; past low-browed doorways and dim-curtained windows of tramps' kitchens, and the abodes of more poverty, misery, and it may be crime, than you will find within a similar space in any neighbourhood in London, or out of it, except perhaps in about five streets "down East," or in certain dens of Liverpool and Manchester.

One moment. You see where a great sudden gap appears to have been made on one side of Golden Lane. That gap represents houses pulled down to erect great blocks of building for warehouses or factories, and it also represents the space in which above 4,000 people lived when the population of this square quarter of mile of poverty and dirt was 22,000 souls. This will give you some idea of the consequences of making what are called "clean sweeps," by demolishing whole neighbourhoods before other dwellings are provided for the evicted tenants. One result of this method of improving the dwellings of the poor is that the people crowd closer, either in their own or in some adjacent neighbourhood, where rents are low and landlords are not particular how many inmates lodge in a single room. Remember that whole families can only earn just enough to keep them from starving, and cannot afford to pay more than half-a-crown or three-and-sixpence a week for rent. They must live near their work, or they lose time, and time means pence, and pence represent the difference between eating and fasting.

"The model lodging-house!" See, there is one, and it is nearly empty. How should it be otherwise? The proprietors of such places, whether they be philanthropists or speculators—and they are not likely to be the latter—can never see a return of any profitable percentage on their outlay while they enforce necessary sanitary laws. The top-rooms are half-a-crown a week each, and the lower "sets" range from about six shillings for two to eight-and-sixpence for three rooms. The consequence is that the few tenants in this particular building are frequently changing their quarters. Some of them try it, and fall into arrear, and are ejected, or want to introduce whole families into a single room, as they do in these surrounding courts and alleys, and this, of course, is not permitted. Imagine one vast building crowded at the same rate as some of these two-storeyed houses are! Ask the missionary, whose duty takes her up scores of creaking staircases, to places where eight or ten human beings eat, drink, sleep, and even work, in one small room — where father, mother, children, and sometimes also a brother or sister-in-law, herd together, that they may live on the common earnings; places where children are born, and men, women, and children die; and the new-born babe must be clothed by the aid of the "maternity box," and the dead must be buried by the help of money advanced to pay for the plainest decent funeral.

I do not propose to take you to any of these sights. You could do little good unless you became familiar with them, and entered into the work of visitation. Even in the published reports of the organisation to which we are now going, the "cases" are not dwelt upon, only one or two are given from the experiences of the missionary, and she speaks of them simply as examples of the kind of destitution which characterises a district where deplorable poverty is the result sometimes of drink, or what, for want of a word applicable to the saving of pence, is termed improvidence; but frequently also, because of sickness, and the want even of poorly-paid employment. "In such cases," says the report, "almost everything is parted with to procure food and shelter *outside* the workhouse."

One of the two "ordinary" cases referred to was that of a poor woman who was "found lying on a sack of shavings on the floor, with an infant two days old; also a child lying dead from fever, and two other children crying for food. None had more than a solitary garment on. The smell of the room was such that the missionary was quite overcome until she had opened the window. Clean linen was obtained, and their temporal and spiritual wants at once looked after." This was in the Report of above a year ago; but cases only just less distressing occur daily still. This foul and neglected district, which lies like an ulcer upon the great opulent city, the centre of civilization and benevolence, seems to be as far from us as though it were a part of some savage or semi-heathen land under British influence. Indeed, in the latter case, there would be a probability of more earnest effort on behalf of the benighted people, on whose behalf meetings would perhaps be held, and a committee of inquiry and distribution appointed. Still, let us be thankful that something is done. Twenty-nine poor mothers have had the benefit of the maternity fund and clothing, the Report tells us. "They are very grateful for this assistance in their terrible need. Frequently the distress is so great that two changes of clothing are given to mother and babe, or they would be almost entirely denuded when the time arrived for returning the boxes. Our lady subscribers at a distance may be glad to know that blankets, sheets, flannel petticoats, warm shawls, and babies' clothing will always be acceptable." Thus writes Mrs. Orsman on the subject, for the mission is known as the Golden Lane Mission, and more popularly as "Mr. Orsman's Mission to the Costermongers." Perhaps these words scarcely denote the scope of the work; but costermongers must be taken as a representative term in a district where, in an area of a square quarter of a mile, there are, or recently were, eighty public-houses and beershops, and a dense mass of inhabitants, including street-traders or hucksters, labourers, charwomen, road-sweepers, drovers, French polishers, artificial flower-makers, toy-makers, with what is now a compact and really representative body of costermongers, working earnestly enough to keep to the right way, and, as they always did, forming a somewhat distinctive part of the population.

Sixteen years ago, Mr. Orsman began the work of endeavouring to carry the gospel to the rough-and-ready savages of this benighted field for missionary enterprise. He held an official appointment, and this was his business "after office hours." About the results of his own labour he and his Reports are modestly reticent, but at all events it began to bear fruit. Others joined in it; a regular mission was established, and, with vigorous growth, shot out several branches, so wisely uniting what may be called the secular or temporal with the spiritual and religious interest, that the Bread of Life was not altogether separated from that need for the bread which perishes. These branches are full of sap to-day, and one of them is also full of promising buds and blossoms, if we are to judge of the rows of ragged—but not unhappy—urchins who fill this large room or hall of the Mission-house.

It is only the first-floor of two ordinary houses knocked into one, but a great work is going on. The parochial school was once held here, and now the room is full of children who might still be untaught but for the effort which made the Ragged School a first consideration in an endeavour to redeem the whole social life of the disdrict. Wisely enough, the School Board accepted the aid which this free day-school for ragged and nearly destitute children affords to a class which the Education Act has not yet taught us how to teach.

In four years, out of ninety-five boys and girls who entered situations from this school, only one was dismissed for dishonesty, and it was afterwards found that he was the dupe of the foreman of the place at which he worked.

Well may Mr. Harwood, the school superintendent, be glad in the labour that he has learnt to love in spite of all the sordid surroundings. There is life in the midst of these dim courts—a ragged-school and a church, which is poor, but not, strictly speaking, ragged. In fact, "the patching class" for ragged boys, which meets on Thursdays, from five to seven in the afternoon, remedies even the tattered garments of the poor little fellows, who, having only one suit, must take off their habiliments in order to mend them. Occasional gifts of second-hand clothes are amongst the most useful stock of the schoolmaster, as anybody may believe who sees the long rows of children, many of them, like our juvenile guide, with two odd boots, which are mere flaps of leather, and attire which it would be exaggeration to call a jacket and trousers.

The school-room is also the church and the lecture-hall. It will hold 300 people; and the Sunday-evening congregation fills it thoroughly, while, on week-nights, special services, and frequently lectures, entertainments, and attractive social gatherings bring the costers and their friends in great force.

The chief of the costermongers is the Earl of Shaftesbury; and here, standing as it were at livery in a quiet corner of a shanty close to the coal-shed, is the earl's barrow, emblazoned with his crest. This remarkable vehicle, and a donkey complimentarily named the "Earl," which took a prize at a Golden Lane donkey show, designate his lordship as president of the "Barrow Club," a flourishing institution, intended to supersede the usurious barrow-lenders, who once let out these necessary adjuncts to the costermongering business at a tremendous hire. Now the proprietors of the barrows, going on the hire and ultimate purchase-system, are prospering greatly. There are free evening classes, mothers' meetings, a free lending library, a free singing class, a penny savings bank, dinners to destitute children, numbering more than 10,000 a year, a soup-kitchen, tea-meetings, and other agencies, all of which are kept going morning, noon, and night, within the narrow limits of these two houses made into one. It is here, too, that the annual meeting is held, an account of which every year filters through the newspapers to the outer world—"The Costermongers' Annual Tea-Party." The records of this united and earnest assembly have been so recently given to the public, that I need not repeat them to you as we stand here in the lower rooms, whence the big cakes, the basins of tea, the huge sandwiches of bread and beef, were conveyed to the 200 guests. But as we depart, after shaking Mr. Harwood by the hand, let me remind you that it has been by the hearty, human, living influence of religion that these results have been effected. The stones of scientific or secular controversy have not been offered instead of food spiritual and temporal. The mission-hall has been made the centre; and from it has spread various healing, purifying, ameliorating influences. From this we may well take a lesson for the benefit of another organised effort which appeals to us for help—that of the London City Mission. This institution is trying to effect for various districts and several classes of the poor and ignorant in and about London that introduction of religious teaching which Mr. Orsman began with amongst the costermongers and others in the benighted locality where now a clear light has begun to shine.

At a recent meeting of the promoters of the City Mission work, held at the Mansion House, it was stated that the 427 missionaries then employed by the society were chosen without distinction, except that of fitness for the office, from Churchmen, Presbyterians, Congregationalists, Wesleyans, and Baptists, while the examining and appointing committee were composed of thirteen clergymen of the Established Church and thirteen Dissenting ministers.

Anybody who is accustomed to visit the worst neighbourhoods of London will know that these missionaries go where the regular clergy cannot easily penetrate, and where even the parish doctor seldom lingers. Every missionary visits once a month about 500 families, or 2,000 persons. They read the Scriptures, exhort their listeners, hold prayer and Bible meetings, distribute copies of the Scriptures, see that children go to school, address the poor in rooms when they cannot persuade them to go to church, visit and pray with the dying, lend books, hold open-air services, endeavour to reclaim drunkards (1,546 were so restored during the last year), admonish and frequently reclaim the vicious, raise the fallen, and place them in asylums or induce them to return to their homes, and work constantly for the great harvest of God to which they are appointed.

Then there are special missionaries appointed to visit bakers, cabmen, drovers, omnibus men, soldiers, sailors, and foreigners of various countries. They also go to tanneries, the docks, workhouses, hospitals, and other places; and there is a vast harvest yet, without a sickle to reap even a single sheaf. When will the time come, that, to the means for carrying the sustaining comfort of the Word to men's souls, will be added some means of helping them to realise it by such temporal aid as will raise them from the want which paralyses and the degradation which benumbs?

GIVING THE FEEBLE STRENGTH.

HAVE had occasion lately to take you with me to some of the worst "parts of London." The phrase has become so common, that there is some difficulty in deciding what it means; and we are obliged to come to the conclusion, that in every quarter of this great metropolis, large and lofty buildings, splendid mansions, gorgeous shops, and even stately palaces, are but symbols of the partial and imperfect development of true national greatness, and can scarcely be regarded as complete evidences of genuine civilisation, if by that word we are to mean more than was expressed by it in heathen times, and amidst pagan people. Perhaps there is no more terrible reflection, amidst all the pomp and magnificence, the vast commercial enterprise and constantly accumulating wealth of this mighty city, than that here we may also find the extremes of want and misery, of vice and poverty, of ignorance and suffering. Side by side with all that makes material greatness—riches, learning, luxury, extravagance—are examples of the deepest necessity and degradation. "The rich and the poor" do indeed "meet together" in a very sad sense. It would be well

if the former would complete the text for themselves, and take its meaning deep into their hearts.

There is reason for devout thankfulness, however, that here and there amidst the abodes of rich and poor alike, some building with special characteristics may be seen; that not only the church but the charity which represents practical religion does make vigorous protest against the merely selfish heaping-up of riches without regard to the cry of the poor. There are few neighbourhoods in which a Refuge for the homeless, a soup-kitchen, a ragged-school, a "servants home," an orphanage, a hospital or some asylum for the sick and suffering, does not relieve that sense of neglect and indifference which is the first painful impression of the thoughtful visitor to those "worst quarters," which yet lie close behind the grand thoroughfares and splendid edifices that distinguish aristocratic and commercial London.

I have said enough for the present about those poverty-haunted districts of Shoreditch, Spitalfields, and Bethnal Green, to warrant me in taking you through them without further comment than suffices to call your attention to the poorly-paid industries, the want and suffering, and the too frequent neglect of the means of health and cleanliness which unhappily distinguish them and the surrounding neighbourhoods lying eastward. The weaver's colony can now scarcely be said to survive the changes wrought by the removal of an entire industry from Spitalfields to provincial manufactories, and the vast importations of foreign silks, and yet there is in this part of London a great population of workers at callings which are scarcely better paid than silk weaving had come to be, previous to its comparative disappearance.

Marvellous changes have been effected in the way of

buildings and improvements during the last thirty years, but much of the poverty and sickness that belonged to these neighbourhoods remain. The looms may be silent in the upper workshops with their wide leaden casements, but the labour by which the people live seldom brings higher wages than suffice for mere subsistence. The great building in which treasures of art and science are collected is suggestive of some kind of recognition of the need of the inhabitants for rational recreation and instruction, and what is perhaps more to the purpose, it is also a recognition of their desire for both ; but it cannot be denied that the recognition has come late, and has not been completely accompanied by those provisions for personal comfort, health, and decency, which a stringent application of existing laws might long ago have ensured in neighbourhoods that for years were suffered to remain centres of pestilence.

The greatest change ever effected in this quarter of London was that which followed the formation of Victoria Park. That magnificent area, with its lakes and islands, its glorious flower-beds and plantations, its cricket-ground and great expanse of open field, made Bethnal Green famous. There had always been a fine stretch of open country beyond what was known as " the Green," on which the building of the Museum now stands. A roadway between banks and hedges skirting wide fields led to the open space where a queer old mansion could be seen amidst a few tall trees, while beyond this again, across the canal bridge, were certain country hostelries, one of them with what was, in that day, a famous "tea-garden;" and, farther on, a few farms and some large old-fashioned private residences stood amidst meadows, gardens, and cattle pastures, on either side of the winding road leading away to the Hackney Marshes and the low-lying fields beyond the old village of Homerton. It was on a large portion of this rural area that Victoria Park was founded. Tavern and farmhouse disappeared; the canal bridge was made ornamental; and just beyond the queer old mansion that stood by the roadway, the great stone and iron gates of " the people's pleasure-ground " were erected.

Now, the mansion, to which I have already twice referred, was in fact one of the few romantic buildings of the district, for it was what remained of the house of the persecuting Bishop Bonner, and the four most prominent of the tall trees—those having an oblong or pit excavation of the soil at the foot of each—were traditionally the landmarks of the martyrdom of four sisters who were there burnt at the stake and buried in graves indicated by the hollows in the ground, which popular superstition had declared could never be filled up.

That they have been filled up long ago, and that on the site of the ancient house itself another great building has been erected, you may see to-day as we stand at the end of the long road leading to the entrance of " the people's park."

The abode of cruelty and bigotry has been replaced by one of the most truly representative of all our benevolent institutions. The graves of the martyred sisters might well take a new meaning if the spot could now be discovered in the broad and beautifully planted garden, where feeble men and women sun themselves into returning life and strength amidst the gentle summer air blowing straight across from the broad woods of Epping and Hainault miles away.

The people's playground is fitly consummated by the

people's hospital. That the City of London Hospital for Diseases of the Chest, Victoria Park, might well be called "the people's," is shown, not because it is supported by state aid or by charitable endowment, on the contrary, it depends entirely on those voluntary contributions and subscriptions which have hitherto enabled it successfully to carry on a noble work, but yet have only just sufficed to supply its needs, "from hand to mouth." Yet it is essentially devoted to patients who belong to the working population. Like the park itself it attracts crowds of visitors, not only from the City, from Bethnal Green, Mile End, Poplar, Islington, Camden Town, and other parts of London, but even from distant places whence excursionists come to see and to enjoy it. This hospital receives patients from every part of London, and even from distant country places. There were seven inmates from York last year, as well as some from Somerset, Hereford, Derby, Lincolnshire, Lancashire, Norfolk, Suffolk, Huntingdon, Northampton, Wiltshire, and other counties; so that in fact the districts of Bethnal Green, Spitalfields, and Shoreditch, represented only a very small proportion of the 781 in-patients and the 13,937 out-patients, who were admitted to medical treatment during the twelve months. More than this, however, amongst the contributions which are made for the support of this hospital, there must be reckoned those collected by working men of the district in their clubs and associations, in token of the appreciation of benefits bestowed by such an institution to failing men and women, wives and shopmates and relatives, who being threatened or actually stricken down with one of those diseases which sap the life and leave the body prostrate, require prompt skill and medical aid, even if they are not in absolute need of nourishing food and alleviating rest.

Standing here, in front of this broad noble building, with its many windows, its picturesque front of red brick and white stone, its central tower, its sheltered garden-walks, and pleasant lawn, we may well feel glad to hear that the work done within its wards is known and recognised. What a work it is can only be estimated by those who remember how fell is the disease from which so many of the patients suffer, and how great a thing it has been, even where cures could not be effected, usefully to prolong the lives of hundreds of those who must have died but for timely aid. Nay, even at the least, the alleviation of suffering to those on whom death had already laid his hand has been no small thing; and when we know that of 240,000 out-patients who have received advice and medicines, and 10,400 in-patients whose cases have warranted their admission to the wards, a large number of actual cures have been effected since the establishment of this hospital, we are entitled to regard the institution as one of the most useful that we have ever visited together.

Let us enter, not by the handsome broad portico in the centre of the building, but at the out-patients' door, in order that we may see the two waiting-rooms, where men and women bring their letters of admission, or attend to see one of the three consulting physicians. Of these three gentlemen the senior is Dr. Peacock, of whom it may be said that he is the organiser of the hospital, the efficiency of which is mainly due to his direction. This is no small praise, I am aware, but there are so many evidences of thorough unity and completeness in all the details of management that, considering how great a variety of cases are included under "diseases of the chest," from the slow insidious but fatal ravages of consumption to the sudden pang and deadly spasm of heart disease, and the various affections of throat and lungs, it may easily be seen how much depends upon the adoption of a system initiated by long study and experience. The perfect arrangements which distinguish this hospital are doubtless rendered easier by ample space and admirable appliances. Plenty of room and plenty of air (air, however, which has been warmed to one even temperature before it enters the wards and corridors where the patients eat and drink, sleep and walk) are the first characteristics of the place, while a certain chaste simplicity of ornament, and yet an avoidance of mere utilitarian bareness, is to be observed in all that portion of the structure where decoration may naturally be expected.

The board-room, the secretary's room, and the various apartments devoted to the resident officers on the ground-floor, are plain enough, however, though they are of good size and proportions, the only really ornamental article of furniture in the board-room being a handsome semi-grand piano, the gift of one of the committee. This is a real boon to such of the patients as can come to practise choral singing, as well as to those who can listen delightedly to the amateur concerts that are periodically performed, either in the hospital itself or in one of the wards. For they have cheerful entertainments in this resort of the feeble, where, to tell the truth, food is often the best physic, and sympathy and encouragement the most potent alleviations.

As to the actual physic—the employment of medicines—it is only in some of the large endowed hospitals that we can see such a dispensary as this spacious room, with its surrounding rows of bottles and drawers, its two open windows, one communicating with the men's and the other with the women's waiting room, its slabs, and scales and measures, on a central counter, where 380 prescriptions will have to be made up to-day before the alert and intelligent gentleman and his assistants who have the control of this department, will be able to replace the current stock out of the medical stores.

These small cisterns, each with its tap, occupying so prominent a place on the counter, represent the staple medicine of the establishment, pure cod-liver oil, of which 1,200 gallons are used every year, and they are constantly replenished from three large cylinders, or vats, containing 800 gallons, which occupy a room of their own adjoining the dispensary and the compounding room, the latter being the place where drugs are prepared, and the great art of pill-making is practised on a remarkable scale.

Continuing our walk round the hospital, we come to the consulting-rooms, where the physicians attend daily at two o'clock, each to see his own patients, and the reception-room, where an officer takes the letters of introduction, and exchanges them for attendance cards. This is the door of the museum; and though we shall be admitted, if you choose to accompany me, it is, like other surgical museums, of professional more than general interest, and not a public portion of the hospital. Turning into the great main corridor, with its peculiar honey-combed red-brick ceiling and pleasant sense of light and air, we will ascend the broad staircase to the wards, those of the women being on the first floor, while the men occupy a precisely similar ward on the second. These wards consist of a series of rooms of from two to six, eight, and twelve beds each, so as to afford opportunity for the proper classification of the cases. A day-room is also provided for each set of wards, so that those patients who are well enough to leave their beds may take their meals there, or may read, play at chess, draughts, or bagatelle, or occupy themselves with needlework. These wards and their day-rooms all open into a light cheerful corridor, with large windows, where the inmates may walk and talk, or read and rest, sitting or reclining upon the couches and settees that are placed at intervals along the wall. All through these rooms and corridors the air is kept at a medium temperature of from fifty-five to sixty degrees, by means of hot-air or hot-water apparatus, the latter being in use as well as the former. You noticed, as we stood in the grounds, a large square structure of a monumental character;—that was in fact the chamber through the sides of which draughts of air are carried to channels beneath the building, there they are drawn around a furnace, to be heated, and to escape through pipes that are grouped about the entire building. In order to ensure the necessary comfort of patients requiring a higher temperature, each ward is provided with an open fire-place.

It is now just dinner-time. The ample rations of meat and vegetables, fish and milk, and the various "special diets," are coming up on the lift from the kitchens, and in the women's day-room a very comfortable party is just sitting down to the mid-day meal. Here, as elsewhere, greater patience and more genuine cheerfulness are to be observed among the women, than is as a rule displayed by the men, and there are not wanting signs of pleasant progress towards recovery, of grateful appreciation of the benefits received, and of a hopeful trusting spirit, which goes far to aid the doctor and the nurse. There are, of course, some sad sights. Looking into the wards, we may see more than one woman for whom only a few hours of this mortal life remain; more than one child whose emaciated form and face looks as though death itself could bring no great change. Yet it must be remembered that cases likely soon to terminate fatally are not admitted. The severity of the diseases and their frequently fatal character under any condition will account for the large proportion of sickness unto death which finds here alleviation but not absolute cure; though, of course, the sufferers from heart disease, who are on the whole the most cheerful, as well as those whose affections of the lungs can be sensibly arrested, if not altogether healed, are frequently restored to many years of useful work in the world. On this second storey, in the men's ward, there are some very serious cases, and some sights that have a heartache in them; yet they are full of significance, for many of them include the spectacle of God's sweet gift of trust and patience—the mighty courage of a quiet mind. Yonder is a courageous fellow, who, suffering from a terrible aneurism, had to cease his daily labour, and now lies on his back, hopeful of cure, with a set still face and a determined yet wistful look at the resident medical officer, or the nurse who adjusts the india-rubber ice-bag on his chest. Here, near the door, is that which should make us bow our heads low before the greatest mystery of mortal life. Not the mystery of death, but the mystery of meeting death and awaiting it. A brave, patient, noble man is sitting up in that bed, his high forehead, fair falling hair, long tawny beard, and steady placid eye, reminding one of some picture of Norseman or Viking. Lean and gaunt enough in frame, his long thin hand is little but skin and bone, but it is clasped gently by the sorrowing wife, who sits beside him, and glances at us through tearful eyes as we enter. One can almost believe that the sick man who is going on the great journey whither he cannot yet take the wife who loves him, has been speaking of it calmly, there is such an inscrutable look of absolute repose in that face. He is a Dane, and the doctor tells us has borne his illness and great pain with a quiet courage that has challenged the admiration of those about him—a courage born of simple faith, let us believe, a calm resting on an eternal foundation of peace. Here, in the corridor, is a party, some of its members still very weak and languid, who, having just dined, are about to take the afternoon lounge, with book or newspaper, and, leaving them, we will conclude our visit by descending to the basement, whence the chief medicine comes in the shape of wholesome nourishing food, of meat and fish, of pure farina, of wine, and milk, and fresh eggs, of clean pure linen, and even of ice, for ice is a large ingredient here, and several tons are consumed every year. The domestic staff have their apartments in this basement portion of the building, another division of which is occupied by the kitchens and storerooms, while lifts for coal and daily meals and every other requisite, ascend to the upper wards, and shoots or wells from the upper floors convey linen and bedding that require washing, as well as the dust and refuse of the wards, to special receptacles.

The kitchen itself is a sight worth seeing with its wide open range, where prime joints are roasting, or have been roasted, and are now being cut into great platefuls for the ordinary full-diet patients. In the great boilers and ovens, vegetables and boiled meats, farinaceous puddings, rice, tapioca, fish, and a dozen other articles of pure diet are being prepared, while a reservoir of strong beef-tea represents the nourishment of those feeble ones to whom liquid, representing either meat or milk, is all that can be permitted. We have little time to remain in the separate rooms, which are cool tile-lined larders, where bread and milk and meat are kept, but among the records of donations and contributions to the hospital it is very pleasant to read of the multifarious gifts of food and other comforts sent from time to time by benevolent friends. They consist of baskets of game, fruits, rice, tea, flour, books, warm clothing for poor patients leaving the hospital, prints, pictures, fern-cases, all kinds of useful articles, showing how thoughtful the donors are, of what will be a solace and a comfort to the patients, while not the least practically valuable remittances are bundles of old linen. Still more touching, however, are the records of gifts brought by patients themselves, or by their friends.

"I was a patient here four years ago," says a man who has made his way to the secretary's room, "and I made up my mind that if ever I could scrape a guinea together I should bring it, and now I have, and here it is, if you'll be so good as to take it, for I want to show I'm truly grateful."

"If you'll please accept it from us; my husband and I have put by fifteen shillings, and want to give it to the hospital for your kindness to our son, who was here before he died."

These are the chronicles that show this to be a people's hospital indeed, and that should open the hearts of those who can take pounds instead of shillings. In such cases the secretary has ventured to remind the grateful donors that they may be unable to afford to leave their savings, but the evident pain, even of the hint of refusal, was reason for accepting the poor offering. Poor, did I say? nay, rich—rich in all that can really give value to such gifts, the wealth of the heart that must be satisfied by giving.

There is one more adjunct to this great human conservatory which we must see before we leave. Down four shallow stone steps from the corridor, and along a cheerful quiet sub-corridor, is the chapel. A very beautiful building, with no stained glass or sumptuous detail of ornament, and yet so admirable in its simple architectural decoration and perfect proportions, that it is an example of what such a place should be. It is capable of seating three or four hundred persons, and visitors are freely admitted to the Sunday services when there is room, though of course seats are reserved for the patients, who have "elbows" provided in their pews, that they may be able to lean without undue fatigue. The chapel itself was a gift of a beneficent friend, and was presented anonymously. One day an architect waited on the committee, and simply said that if they would permit a chapel to be erected on a vacant space in their grounds, close to the main building, he had plans for such a structure with him, and the whole cost would be defrayed by a client of his, who, however, would not make known his name. The gift was accepted, and the benevolent contract nobly fulfilled. I should be glad to hear that some other charitable donor had sent in like manner an offer of funds to fill those two great vacant wards, which, waiting for patients, are among the saddest sights in this hospital.

HEALING THE SICK.

MIDST the numerous great charities which distinguish this vast metropolis, hospitals must always hold a prominent if not pre-eminent place. Helpless infancy, the weakness and infirmity of old age, and prostration by sudden accident, or the ravages of disease, are the conditions that necessarily appeal to humanity. The latter especially is so probable an occurrence to any of us, that we are at once impressed by the necessity for providing some means for its alleviation. Helpless childhood has passed, old age may seem to be in too dim a future to challenge our immediate attention; but sickness, sudden disaster, who shall be able to guard against these, in a world where the strongest are often smitten down in the full tide of apparent health; where, in the streets alone, fatal accidents are reckoned monthly as a special item in Registrars' returns, and injuries amount annually to hundreds?

The great endowed hospitals, therefore, those magnificent monuments of charity which have distinguished London for so many years, and the value of which in extending the science of medicine can scarcely be overrated, are regarded by us all with veneration. At the same time we ought to feel a certain thrill of pleasure, a satisfaction not far removed from keen emotion, when we see inscribed on the front of some building, large or small, where the work of healing is being carried on, the words, " Supported by Voluntary Contributions." One other condition, too, seems necessary to the complete recognition of such a charity as having attained to the full measure of a truly beneficent work—admission to it should be free : free not only from any demand for money payments, but untrammelled by the necessity for seeking, often with much suffering and delay, a governor's order or letter, by which alone a patient can be received in many of our otherwise admirable and useful institutions for the sick. It should be remembered that immediate aid is of the utmost importance in the effort to heal the sick, and that delays, proverbially dangerous, are in such cases cruel, often fatal, always damaging to the sense of true beneficence, of the extension of help because of the *need* rather than for the sake of any particular influence. It would seem that we have no right to hesitate, or to insist on the observance of certain forms, before succouring the grievously sick and wounded, any more than we have to withhold food from the starving till ceremonial inquiries are answered, and certificates of character obtained. There are cases of poverty, and even of suffering, where inquiry before ultimate and continued relief may be useful, and personal influence may be necessary, but extreme hunger and nakedness, cold and houselessness, sudden injury or maiming, the pain of disease, the deep and touching need of the sick and helpless, are not such. Prompt and effectual measures for relief, and, if necessary, admission to the place where that relief can alone be afforded, will be the only means of completely meeting these wants. Free hospitals, freer even than workhouses, are what we need, and I am about to visit one of them to-day which rejoices in its name, "The Royal Free Hospital," now in its forty-seventh year of useful and, I am glad to say, of vigorous life.

To anyone acquainted with that strange neighbourhood which is represented by Gray's Inn Lane and all the queer jumble of courts and alleys that seem to shrink behind the shelter of the broad thoroughfare of Holborn, there is something consistent in the establishment of such a noble charity as this hospital in Gray's Inn Road. Its very position seems to indicate the nature and extent of its duties. Near the homes of poverty, the streets where people live who cannot go far to seek aid in their extremest need, it receives those who, breaking down through sudden disease, or requiring medical and surgical skill to relieve the pain and weakness of recurrent malady, have no resource but this to enable them to fulfil their one great desire "to get back to work." The causes of much of the sickness which sends patients thither may be preventable: they may be found in foul dwellings, impure water, insufficient clothing, want of proper food, alternate hunger and intemperance; but whatever may be its occasion, a remedy must be found for it. Till all that is preventable *is* prevented, the consequences will have to be mitigated, the fatal results averted where it is possible; and when boards of health and sanitary measures have done, there will still be sick men to heal, failing children to strengthen, weak and wasting women to restore.

It is well, then, that this Institution should stand as a landmark of that free charity which takes help where it is needed most; and this qualification is the more obvious when we turn from the sick wards to the accident wards, and remember that three great railway termini are close at hand, and others not far off; that all round that teeming neighbourhood men, women, and even children, are working at poor handicrafts, which render them liable to frequent injuries, and that in the crowded streets themselves—from the great busy thoroughfare of Holborn, to the bustle and confusion of the approaches to the stations at King's Cross—there is constant peril to life and limb.

There is something so remarkable in the external appearance of the building, such a military look about its bold front, such a suggestion of a cavalry yard about the broad open area behind this tall wooden entrance gate, that you begin to wonder how such a style of architecture should have been adopted for a hospital. The truth is that like many—nay, like most of our noblest work—this great provision for healing the sick began by not waiting for full-blown opportunities. The need was there, and the means that came to hand were used to meet it. This building was originally the barracks of that loyal and efficient regiment, the "Light Horse Volunteers," and so excellently had those gallant defenders of king and constitution provided for their own comfort and security, that when in 1842 the premises were vacant, and the lease for sale, the governors of the Royal Free Hospital became the purchasers, the long rooms were easily turned into ample, cheerful, and well-ventilated wards, and the various outbuildings and offices were quickly adapted to the reception of patients.

But the hospital had at that date been working quietly and effectually for above fourteen years. Fourteen

years before its inauguration in Gray's Inn Road, this
"free" hospital, which was not then "royal," had been
commenced in Greville Street, Hatton Garden, and the
immediate incident which led to its foundation is so
suggestive, so inseparable from the recollection of the
want which it was designed to alleviate, and from its
own generous recognition of the unfailing freedom of
true charity, that it might well be the subject of a memorial picture. Alas! it would be a tragic reminder of
those days before any provision was made for extending
medical aid to sufferers who had no credentials save
humanity and their own deep necessity. It would be a
grim reminder to us, also, that some of our great charities established for the relief of the sick are still tram-
melled with those restrictions which demand recom-
mendations, to obtain which the applicant is often condemned to delay and disappointment. It would show
us that our hospitals are not yet free.

Those of my readers who can remember the entrance
to the broad highway of Holborn nearly fifty years ago
—stay, that is going back beyond probable acknowledg-
ment,—let me say those of us who knew Smithfield when
it was a cattle market, who had heard of "Cow Cross,"
and been told of the terrible purlieux of Field Lane;
who had occasionally caught a glimpse of that foul
wilderness of courts that clustered about the Fleet Ditch;
had read of Mr. Fagin, when "Oliver Twist" was first
appearing in chapters, and had dim recollections of
nursery tales about Bartlemy fair and "hanging morning" at the Old Bailey; those of us who remember the
cries of drovers, and the lowing and bleating of herds
and flocks in the streets on Sunday nights; the terrible
descent of Snow Hill; the confusion and dismay of

passengers and vehicles on the steep incline of Holborn Hill; the reek of all that maze of houses and hovels that lay in the valley; those of us, in short, who can carry our memories back for a few years beyond the time when the new cattle market was built at Islington, the pens and lairs of Smithfield demolished, the whole Holborn valley dismantled, only a remnant, a mere corner, of Field Lane being left standing after the great viaduct was built—can imagine what the church of St. Andrew was like when, with its dark and dreary churchyard, it stood on the slope of Holborn Hill, instead of being as it now is in a kind of subway. That churchyard, with its iron gate, was reached by stone steps, which were receptacles for winter rain and summer dust, the straw from waggons, the shreds and sweepings from adjacent shops, the dirt and refuse of the streets.

On those steps a young girl was seen lying one night, in the winter of 1827—lying helpless, lonely, perishing of disease and famine.

The clocks of St. Andrew, St. Sepulchre, St. Paul, had clanged and boomed amidst the hurry and the turmoil of the throng of passengers; had clanged and boomed till their notes might be heard above the subsiding roar of vehicles, and the shuffling of feet, till silence crept over the great city, and more distant chimes struck through the murky air, tolling midnight. Still that figure lay upon the cruel stones, under the rusty gate of the churchyard, as though, unfriended and unpitied by the world, she waited for admission to the only place in which she might make a claim in death, if not in life.

Not more than eighteen years old, she had wandered wearily from some distant place where fatal instalments of the wages of sin had done their work. She had come to London unknown, unnoted, to die. That she had come from afar is but a surmise; she may have been a dweller in this great city, lost amidst the stony desert of its streets, friendless with the friendlessness of the outcast or the wretched, to whom the acquaintances of to-day have little care or opportunity to become the solacers of to-morrow; she may have crept to that dark corner by the churchyard gate, amongst the rack and refuse of the street, as a place in which she, the unconsidered waste and refuse of our boasted civilisation, could most fitly huddle from the cold. She was not left actually to die there, but two days afterwards she passed out of the world where she had been unrecognised. Not without result, however.

Among those who had witnessed the distressing occurrence was a surgeon, Mr. William Marsden, who for some time before had repeatedly seen cause to lament, that with all our endowed hospitals, our great medical schools, and the advance of scientific knowledge, the sick poor could only obtain relief by means of letters of recommendation and other delay, until the appointed days for admission. The sight that he had witnessed awoke him to fresh energy. He determined to establish a medical charity, where destitution or great poverty and disease should be the only necessary credentials for obtaining free and *immediate* relief. His honest benevolent purpose did not cool; in February in the following year (1828), the house in Greville Street was open as a free hospital, and it was taken under the royal patronage of George IV., the Duke of Gloucester becoming its president.

King William IV. succeeded George IV. as the patron

of this free hospital, and one of the earliest manifestations of the interest of our Queen in public charitable institutions was the expressed desire of her Majesty to maintain the support which it had hitherto received, and to confer upon it the name of the *Royal* Free Hospital.

It need scarcely be said that the late Duke of Sussex took a very strong interest in this charity, and at his death it was determined to erect a new wing, to be called "the Sussex" wing. This work was completed in 1856; and in 1863, by the aid of a zealous and indefatigable chairman of the committee, above £5,000 was raised by special appeal for the purposes of buying the freehold of the entire building, so that it is now, in every sense, a free hospital, with a noble history of suffering relieved, of the sick healed, the deserted reclaimed, the sinful succoured, and those that were ready to perish snatched from the jaws of death.

Since the foundation of the modest house in Hatton Garden in 1828 above a million and a half of poor sick and destitute patients have obtained relief, and the average of poor patients received within its wards is now 1,500 annually, while 45,000 out-patients resort thither from all parts of London. The relief thus afforded costs some £8,000 a year, and this large sum has to be provided by appeals to the public for those contributions by which alone the continued effort can be sustained.

Standing here within the "Moore" ward, so called after the energetic chairman before referred to, I cannot think of any appeal that should be more successful in securing public sympathy than these two statements— First, that many of the inmates have been immediately received on their own application; and secondly, that, bearing in mind the sad story which is, as it were, the story of the foundation of the hospital, this ward is occupied by women. Many of them are persons of education and refinement, who yet would have no asylum if they had not been received within these sheltering walls, others may be poor, ignorant, and perhaps even degraded, but divine charity is large enough to recognise in these the very need which such an effort is intended to alleviate. Here at least is a peaceful retreat, where in quiet reflection, in grateful recognition of mercies yet within reach, in the sound of pitying voices, and the touch of sympathetic hands, the weary may find rest, the throes of pain may be assuaged.

Here are the two fundamental rules of the hospital, and they form what one might call a double-barrelled appeal not to be easily turned aside :—

IN-DOOR PATIENTS.	OUT-DOOR PATIENTS.
Foreigners, strangers, and others, in sickness or disease, having neither friends nor homes, are admitted to the Wards of this Hospital on their own application, so far as the means of the charity will permit.	All sick and diseased persons, having no other means of obtaining relief, may attend at this Hospital every day at Two o'clock, when they will receive Medical and Surgical Advice and Medicine free.

Even while I read the latter announcement the out-patients are assembling in the waiting-room, on the right of the quadrangle; the dispenser, in his repository of drugs, surrounded by bottles, jars, drawers, and all the appliances for making up medicines, has set his assistants to work, and is himself ready to begin the afternoon's duty; the consulting-physician of the day has just taken his seat in one plain barely-furnished apartment, the consulting-surgeon in another, while the resident house-surgeon has completed his first inspection of in-patients, and is ready with particulars of new cases.

These rooms, where patients assemble, and doctors consult, are on the right of the pleasant quadrangle, with its large centre oval garden plot, containing a double ring of trees; and here also is the reception room for "accidents" and urgent cases—a very suggestive room, with styptics, immediate remedies, and prompt appliances ready to hand, but like all the rest of the official portion of the building, very plain and practical, with evidence of there being little time to regard mere ease or ornament, and of a disregard of anything which is not associated with the work that has to be done. It is the same with other apartments, where it is obvious that no unnecessary expenditure is incurred for mere official show.

The business of the place is to heal by means of food, of rest, and of medicine, and there, on the left of the quadrangle, a flight of steps leads downwards to a wide area, where, in the kitchens, the domestic servants are busy clearing up, after serving the eighty-eight rations which have been issued for dinner—rations of fish, flesh, and fowl, or those "special diets" which are taken under medical direction. There is something about this kitchen, the store-rooms, and offices, with the steps leading thereto, and the cat sitting blinking in the sun, which irresistibly reminds me of the heights of Dover and some portion of the barrack building there; the old military look of the place clings to this Gray's Inn Road establishment still, and the visitor misses the wonderful appliances and mechanical adaptations of some more modern institutions, not even lifts to convey the dinners to the wards being possible in such an edifice.

There is some compensating comfort in noting, however, that the nursing staff is so organised as to secure personal attention to the patients, and that the arrangements are touchingly homely, not only in regard to the simple furniture, the few pictures and engravings, and the little collection of books that are to be found in the wards, but also in the matter of sympathetic, motherly, and sisterly help, which is less ceremonious, but not less truly loving, than is to be found in some places of higher pretensions.

Here, on the ground floor, the twenty-two beds of the men's severe accident ward are always full, and some of the cases are pitiable, including maiming by machinery, railway accidents, or injury in the streets. The "Marsden Ward," adjoining is devoted to injuries of a less serious kind, so that there many of the patients can help themselves. In the women's accident ward there are three or four children, one of whom, a pretty chubby-faced little girl of five years old, has not yet got over her astonishment at having been run over by a cab the day before yesterday, picked up and brought into this great room where most of the people are in bed, only to hear that she is more frightened than hurt, and is to go home tomorrow. There are some other little creatures, however, suffering from very awkward accidents, and they seem to be petted and made much of, just as they are in the women's sick ward above, where a delicate-faced intelligent girl, herself improving greatly under prompt treatment for an early stage of phthisis, is delighted to have a little companion to tea with her at her bed-side, the child being allowed to sit up in a chair, and the pair of invalids being evidently on delightfully friendly terms. There is a lower ward, with half a dozen little beds devoted solely to children, who are, I think, all suffering from some form of disease of the joints. Alas! this class of disease comes of foul dwellings, of impure or stinted food, of want of fresh air and water; and it brings a pang to one's heart to note the smiling little faces, the bright beaming eyes, the pretty engaging grateful ways of some of these little ones, and yet to know how long a time it must be before the results of the evil conditions of their lives will be remedied at the present rate of procedure; how difficult a problem it is to provide decent dwellings for the poor, in a city where neighbourhoods such as that which we have just traversed have grown like fungi, and cannot be uprooted without pain and loss which social reformers shrink from inflicting. Thinking of this, and of all that I have seen in this Royal Free Hospital, I am glad to carry away from it the picture of this child's ward and its two young nurses, though I could wish that the walls of that and all the other wards were a little brighter with more pictures, that a fresh supply of books might soon be sent to replenish the library, and that the flowers, that are so eagerly accepted to deck the tables of those poor sick rooms, and carry thither a sense of freshness, colour, and beauty, may come from the gardens and greenhouses of those who can spare of their abundance. To keep the eighty-eight beds full requires constant dependence on public contributions, and yet when we think of the work that is going on here, not the eighty-eight only, but the whole number of 102 should be ready for applicants, who would, even then, be far too numerous to be received at once in a hospital which, with a royal freedom of well-doing, sets an example that might be hopefully followed by other and wealthier charities for healing the sick.

WITH THE PRISONER.

WHAT is the first greeting which a convict receives when he or she is discharged from prison?

Imagine, if you can, the shivering, shrinking, bewildered feeling of the man or woman who, after, undergoing a term of penal servitude, some of it passed in hours of solitary confinement, has all this great city suddenly opened again, with its wilderness of streets, its crowd of unfamiliar faces, its tremendous temptations, its few resources for the friendless and the suspected, its great broad thoroughfares, where on every side may be seen evidences of wealth and plenty; where the tavern and the gin-shop offer a temporary solace to the wretched; and where, also, in every neighbourhood, there are evil slums in which vice finds companionship, and the career of dishonesty and crime can be resumed without difficulty or delay.

Those who have stood outside the walls of Clerkenwell or Coldbath Fields prison, and have watched the opening of the gates whence prisoners emerge into a freedom which is almost paralysing in its first effects, will tell you how the appearance of these poor wretches is greeted in low muttered tones by silent slouching men and women who await their coming. How, after very few words of encouragement and welcome, they are taken off to some adjacent public-house, there to celebrate their liberation; and how, almost before a word is spoken, the male prisoner is provided with a ready-lighted pipe from the mouth of one of his former companions, in order that he may revive his sense of freedom by the long-unaccustomed indulgence in tobacco.

I should be very sorry to cavil at these marks of sympathy. They are eminently human. They do not always mean direct temptation — that is to say, they are not necessarily intended to induce the recipient to resume the evil course which has led to a long and severe punishment. That the result should be a gradual, if not an immediate, weakening of that remorse which is too frequently sorrow for having incurred the penalty rather than repentance of the sin that led to it, is obvious enough; but what else is to be expected? Not many men or women come out of gaol with a very robust morality. Without entering into the question how far our present system of prison discipline and management is calculated to influence the moral nature of culprits who are under punishments for various crimes, scarcely ever classified, and never regarded in relation to the particular circumstances under which they are committed or the character and disposition, the social status, or the mental and moral condition of the offender, it may be broadly and barely stated that our penal legislation is not effectual in promoting the reclamation of the criminal.

Even if some determination to begin life anew, to avoid associations that have led to infamy and disgrace to accept any labour anywhere in order to obtain an honest subsistence, has been working in the mind of a convict during the period of imprisonment, and under the advice and remonstrance of the chaplain and the governor, what is to sustain such half-formed resolutions? Supposing even that the discharged prisoner has been so amenable to the regulations of the gaol that he or she has had placed to the credit account that weekly "good-conduct money," which, when the term of punishment has ended, amounts to a sum sufficient to provide for immediate necessities, where is employment to be looked for? In what quarter is the owner of a few shillings—which may have to last a week or more—to seek a lodging and a meal, and that companionship which must be one of the keenest longings of the newly-released and yet solitary and half-dazed creature, who is ready to receive with grateful avidity any friendly greeting that promises relief from the long monotony of the gaol?

Surely, then, there can be few conditions which appeal more forcibly to Christian beneficence than that of the captive who is released after having undergone a sentence of penal servitude, part of which has been passed in solitary confinement. Whatever may have been the impressions made upon the mind during the period of punishment, and the influence exercised by instruction or exhortation, the very fact of regaining liberty, the excitement of freedom, and the uncertainty of the first steps a man or woman is to take outside the prison walls, will always involve a danger, before which a very large proportion of released convicts will succumb.

What, then, is being done in order to extend a helping hand to these, who are among the most destitute and unfortunate; who, even if they have relatives, may be ashamed to seek their aid, or are doubtful of the reception that awaits them, while the only companionship which they can claim at once, and without question, is that which will surround them with almost irresistible incentives to a lawless life?

In the very centre of this vast metropolis, at the point where its great highways converge, and yet in a modest quiet house standing a little back from the roar and turmoil of the main street, we shall find what we seek. Here, on the doorpost of No. 39, Charing Cross, is the name of "The Discharged Prisoners' Aid Society," and in two or three offices on the first floor—one of which is, in fact, a reception-room for the discharged prisoners themselves—the work for which there is such a constant and pressing need is steadily carried on, under the direction of a very distinguished committee, of whom the treasurer is the Hon. Arthur Kinnaird, and the first honorary secretary, Mr. W. Bayne Ranken, who is assisted by Mr. S. Whitbread and Mr. L. T. Cave. In looking at the names of the gentlemen who are concerned in this admirable effort, you will have noticed that some of them are also associated with other charitable organisations which we have visited together, and notably with those of that Soho district where we last joined in the musical diversions of the Newport Market Refuge. As we enter this front office at Charing Cross, we have a pleasant reminder of that occasion, for we are welcomed by the indefatigable performer on the cornet, who, when we last met him, was making "the hills resound" in the upper room of the old slaughter-house, and carrying all his juvenile military band with him in one resonant outburst of harmony that awoke the echoes as far as Seven Dials. To-day he is carrying out his ordinary secretarial and managerial duties, as officially representing the

Society, about which he can give us some information worth hearing.

But there are other visitors for whom preparation has already been made in the next room—men dressed decently, and yet having a certain furtive, unaccustomed bearing, as though they were not at the moment quite used to their clothes or to public observation. Some of them are not without a truculent half-defiant expression lurking beneath their subdued demeanour; others have an open, keen outlook; and a few others, again, both in the shape of their head and the peculiar shifty expression of eye and mouth, and one might also say of hand, would at once be characterised by the experienced observer of London life as men who had "been in trouble" more than once. On the table of the front office the object which has at once attracted our attention is a perfectly new carpenter's basket containing a decent set of tools, and the man for whom it is intended will be here for it by-and-by to take it away, just as the shoemaker who has just gone out has carried with him "a kit," with which, in addition to a little stock of money, he is about to begin the world afresh, under the auspices of his friends, one of whom—either a member of the committee, or the secretary, or one of the visiting agents—will keep him in view, and give him an occasional encouraging call while he remains in the metropolitan district. If a situation should be found for him in the provinces, either the clergyman of the district, or some other friend of the Society, is informed of his previous history, and has a sincere interest in his well-doing. In no case have the London police anything whatever to do with watching or inspecting discharged prisoners under the care of the

Society; and, on the other hand, it is a standing rule that where situations are found for these men and women, the employers are informed of their previous history, though any recommendation of the Society may be regarded as a strong inference that their *protégé* is trying to redeem lost character.

It must be remembered that a report of each of those who are under the care of the Society is made at the office once a month, either by the man or woman in person, or by one of the visiting agents or correspondents of the committee of management; and that, though the police are forbidden to interfere with them, except on strong suspicion that they are about to commit a crime, the most accurate and careful record of their mode of life and conduct is kept at the offices of the Society. Should they fail to observe the regulations which the Society demands, they are liable to police surveillance instead of friendly, encouraging, and confidential visitation; and it needs scarcely be said that this liability is often of itself sufficient to make them desire to retain the aid and protection which has been extended to them.

From a long and tolerably intimate observation of the lower strata of the London population, and of the results of various methods adopted to check the progress of crime, I am convinced that what is called police surveillance, as it is conducted in this country, is altogether mischievous in relation to any probable reformation of the offender. Even if it be denied (as it has been) that it is a practice of police-constables to give to persons employing a discharged prisoner, information conveyed in such a way as to lead to the loss of employment and despair of obtaining an honest living, it is quite certain that the constant dread of being branded as a returned felon, and the hopeless dogged temper which such a condition produces, must be enormous obstacles to true reclamation. The man who could really surmount them must, whatever may have been his casual crime, be possessed of a hardy and indomitable desire for virtue which should challenge our profound respect.

But, apart from what may be called legitimate surveillance of convicts by the police, it is unfortunately notorious that members of "the force," who occupy positions as detectives, or " active and intelligent officers," employ agents of their own to bring them information, and that these agents, being men of bad character—frequently thieves—are interested for their own safety's sake in providing "charges," or "putting up cases," by conveying information of suspected persons. This is according to the old evil traditions that have descended to constables from the time of Jonathan Wild, and probably earlier; but it is obvious that where such nefarious tools are employed for obtaining evidence which will suffice to sustain a charge and convict a prisoner, there is constant danger to those who, having been once sentenced for crime, are not only peculiarly liable to be drawn into fresh offences, but are, from their position, easily made the victims of cunningly-laid traps for their re-arrest, on a suspicion that is readily endorsed, because of their previous conviction and the knowledge of all their antecedents.

It is the removal of discharged prisoners from this probability, and from the kind of interposition that forbids their return to the paths of honesty, and so actually produces " a criminal class," that is, in my opinion, the best distinction of a Society like this.

Some of the volumes of interesting records which are preserved here would probably doubtless confirm this view. Let us refer to one only, where a nobleman residing in London had engaged a butler who went to him with a very excellent character, and in whom he had the greatest confidence. Happening to have occasion to employ a detective constable on some business, his lordship was dismayed at receiving from that astute officer the intelligence that his trusted servant had once been sentenced to five years' penal servitude for some dishonest act, but had been liberated on a ticket-of-leave. Puzzled how to proceed, the nobleman had the good sense to apply for advice to this Society, where it was discovered that the representation of the detective was true enough, and that the man had been recommended to a situation by the Society itself, an intimation of his antecedents being given to the employer. In that situation he had remained for several months, without the least fault being brought against him, and he then applied for and obtained the vacant and more lucrative appointment in the family of his lordship, who, though he acknowledged he should not have engaged him had he known of his previous fault and its punishment, kept his secret, and retained him in his service, where he remained at the time of the last report, respected by the household, and faithfully fulfilling his duties.

Probably this was one of those cases where, yielding to sudden temptation, a man incurs for a single crime punishment that awakens moral resolution; and it must be remembered that there are many convicts who, while in prison they are practically undistinguished from the habitual or the repeated criminal, or from the convict of brutalised, undeveloped, or feeble moral nature, are in danger of being utterly ruined because of a single and perhaps altogether unpremeditated offence, of which they may bitterly repent. The feeling of shame, of humiliation, of doubt as to any but a cold and deterrent reception by former friends, the dread of scorn, derision, or abhorrence, may lead such men or women to abandon as hopeless any expectation of resuming their former avocations, or even of once more attaining a respectable position. To such as these the Society offers such aid as may keep them from the despondency that destroys; and in every case, even in that of the wretch who has been convicted again and again, it holds out some hope of reformation. That there is some such hope may be learned from the fact, that even thieves— "habitual criminals"—do not, as a rule, bring their own children up to dishonesty, and are often careful to conceal from them the means by which they live. The ranks of crime are not so largely augmented from the children of dishonest parents (though, of course, evil example bears its dreadful results) as from the neglected children of our great towns.

But let us see what are the means adopted by the Society for helping discharged prisoners. Of course the procedure must begin with the prisoners themselves, in so far that they must express their willingness to accept the aid offered to them, and make known their decision to the governor of the prison where they are confined, and where the rules and provisions of the Society are displayed and explained.

This refers to the convict prisons, since only these are eligible, the prisoners from county gaols being assisted by other organisations; therefore, discharged convicts from Millbank, Pentonville, Portland, Portsmouth, Chatham, Parkhurst, Dartmoor, Woking, and Brixton, are able to seek help; and it is gratifying to know that, according to the prison returns, of 1,579 male prisoners discharged from these places in one year, 796 sought aid from this and local provincial societies having the same object, the number of applicants to the London Society being 524, or nearly two-thirds of the whole.

On any convict, male or female, accepting the offer of the Society, and making that decision known to the governor of the prison, the latter forwards to this office at Charing Cross a printed document, or recommendation, stating full particulars of the prisoner's age, date of conviction, number of previous convictions (if any), degree of education, religion, former trade or employment, ability to perform labour, and general character while in prison, together with the amount of good-conduct money which is to be allowed for work performed during the period of incarceration. This good-conduct money may amount to a maximum sum of £3, and the Society takes charge of it for the benefit of the prisoner, disbursing it only as it may be required, and supplementing it, when necessary, by a further grant of money, or even by advances or loans as may be deemed desirable in certain cases.

These reports from the prison governor reach the office about six weeks before the discharge of the convicts named in them, and following them come other papers, each of which contains a graphic personal description of the prisoner referred to, and a fairly-executed photograph, which is usually not without certain striking characteristics, though you will be surprised to find how often you fail to discover the lineaments which you have associated in fancy with lawlessness and crime. At the time of their discharge, the men and women are conducted hither by a plainly-clothed messenger from the prison, appointed for the purpose, and take their places in yonder back room, where they are immediately identified by means of the descriptions and photographs, and are then questioned as to their capabilities and the particular employment in which they desire to engage. It is manifestly impossible that the Society can provide them with employment in the particular trades which they may previously have followed, since there may be no openings in those industries, or they may be such as would be obviously unsuitable for persons who are still on probation.

Should the prisoner have friends or relatives able and willing to receive or assist him, they are communicated with, but should he be entirely dependent on personal exertion, the agent or secretary at once procures for him a decent outfit of clothes, and a lodging as far as possible from the scene of his former companions. A small sum of money is advanced for immediate subsistence, and he usually has employment provided for him, either in a situation, at manual labour, or by being set up in a small way at shoemaking, tailoring, or carpentering, either as journeyman, or, where possible, on his own account.

From six to twenty prisoners at a time are discharged from one or other of the convict establishments and brought to the Society's offices, and of the younger men a considerable proportion are assisted to go to sea, others —but, alas! too few—to emigrate, while a number obtain work as builders and contractors' labourers; and others again resume former occupations, as potmen, waiters, or employés in various situations, where the masters are always (if they take them on the recommendation of the Society) fully apprised of their position. A good many are set up again as costermongers, and in that case the agent of the Society quietly accompanies them to market, and advances the money for their first purchases; others go into the country and obtain work, and not a few of the better-educated or more skilled soon obtain engagements of various kinds, by personal application, and without reference to the Society, though they continue to report themselves, and to be kept in view by the agents, and, being separated from evil companionship, and feeling that they are not altogether friendless, retrieve their position and regain an honourable reputation.

Of 514 men and women who were received by the Society during the year, 180 obtained employment in London and are doing well; 156 were sent to places beyond the metropolitan district, and were placed under the supervision of the local police; 32 were sent to relatives and friends abroad; 57 obtained berths on board ship; 50 had failed to report and notify their change of address as required by Act of Parliament; 23 had been re-convicted; 6 were not satisfactorily reported on; one had died; and 9, who had been recently discharged at the end of the year, were waiting for employment at the time of the Report. To read the Report Book, recording the visits of the agents or secretary to men employed in various avocations, and to their friends or relatives, is very encouraging, for it shows that of a large proportion, say seventy per cent., there is a good hope of reclamation by their long continuance in industrious efforts to retain their situations and to work honestly in various callings; while the reports of country cases by clergymen in the provinces is equally satisfactory, especially as they frequently record the return of the former convict to his family and friends, amidst whom he earns an honourable subsistence.

The female convicts, who are also received at the office, are, if they cannot be sent to relatives and friends, mostly taken to a Refuge, which has been established by the Society at Streatham, where they find a home until situations can be obtained for them; and it is to the credit of some earnest ladies who are willing to engage these discharged prisoners as domestic servants that the result is often most favourable. A very large proportion of the women return to friends, however. Of 53 who left the Refuge at Streatham last year, 30 were received by friends, 18 obtained situations, 3 returned to Millbank Penitentiary, 1 emigrated, and 1 died, 25 remaining at the Refuge at the time of the report.

In the case of these discharged female prisoners, as well as for the sake of those men who would eagerly seize an opportunity of beginning life anew in a new country, it would be most desirable if greater facilities existed for promoting and assisting the emigration of such as gave satisfactory evidence of reformation of character. The Society finds its own funds, supported by contributions from the public, barely sufficient to maintain, and insufficient largely to extend its useful work. One of the committee, a resident in Canada, has rendered invaluable assistance to emigrants recommended to his notice by the Society. The governor of Dartmoor Prison in his Report, says :—

"I cannot too strongly again express my conviction that an emigration scheme connected with the Aid Societies would be an invaluable aid to the restoration of many casual criminals to a position of respectability and honesty. It would be especially appreciated by those (unfortunately a too numerous class) who had incurred the shorter sentences of penal servitude as punishments for breaches of trust of various kinds. These men are often cast off by their respectable friends, and, from the shortness of their sentences, are unable to earn the additional gratuity. With no lasting means of subsistence, and an overstocked market for their labour, it is not to be wondered at if such men speedily add a second conviction to their criminal career." Let us trust that practical steps will be taken to remove this difficulty.

THE END.

BILLING AND SONS, PRINTERS, GUILDFORD, SURREY.

January, 1876.

AN ALPHABETICAL LIST

OF

HENRY S. KING & CO.'S

PUBLICATIONS.

65 Cornhill, and 12 Paternoster Row, London,
January, 1876.

A LIST OF

HENRY S. KING & CO.'S PUBLICATIONS.

ABBEY (Henry).
 BALLADS OF GOOD DEEDS, AND OTHER VERSES. Fcap. 8vo. Cloth gilt. 5s.

ADAMS (A. L.), M.A.
 FIELD AND FOREST RAMBLES OF A NATURALIST IN NEW BRUNSWICK. With Notes and Observations on the Natural History of Eastern Canada. 8vo., cloth. Illustrated. 14s.

ADAMS (F. O.), H.B.M.'s Secretary of Embassy at Paris, formerly H.B.M.'s Chargé d'Affaires, and Secretary of Legation at Yedo.
 THE HISTORY OF JAPAN. From the Earliest Period to the Present Time. New Edition, revised. Demy 8vo. In 2 vols. With Maps and Plans. 21s. each.

ADAMS (W. Davenport, Jun.)
 LYRICS OF LOVE, from Shakespeare to Tennyson. Selected and arranged by. Fcap. 8vo., cloth extra, gilt edges, 3s. 6d.

ADON.
 THROUGH STORM AND SUNSHINE. Illustrated by M. E. Edwards, A. T. H. Paterson, and the Author. 1 vol. Crown 8vo. Price 7s. 6d.

A. K. H. B.
 A SCOTCH COMMUNION SUNDAY, to which are added Certain Discourses from a University City. By the Author of "The Recreations of a Country Parson." Second Edition. Crown 8vo. 5s.

ALLEN (Rev. R.), M.A.
> ABRAHAM: HIS LIFE, TIMES, AND TRAVELS, as told by a Contemporary 3800 years ago. Post 8vo., with Map. Cloth. Price 10s. 6d.

AMOS (Professor Sheldon).
> THE SCIENCE OF LAW. Second Edition. Crown 8vo. 5s. Vol. X. of the International Scientific Series.

ANDERSON (Rev. Charles), M.A.
> CHURCH THOUGHT AND CHURCH WORK. Edited by. Containing articles by the Revs. J. M. Capes, Professor Cheetham, J. Ll. Davis, Harry Jones, Brooke, Lambert, A. J. Ross, the Editor, and others. Second Edition. Demy 8vo. 7s. 6d.
>
> WORDS AND WORKS IN A LONDON PARISH. Edited by. Second Edition. Demy 8vo. 6s.
>
> THE CURATE OF SHYRE. Second Edition. 8vo. 7s. 6d.
>
> NEW READINGS OF OLD PARABLES. Demy 8vo. 4s. 6d.

ANDERSON (Colonel R. P.)
> VICTORIES AND DEFEATS. An Attempt to explain the Causes which have led to them. An Officer's Manual. Demy 8vo. 14s.

ANSON (Lieut.-Col. The Hon. A.), V.C., M.P.
> THE ABOLITION OF PURCHASE AND THE ARMY REGULATION BILL OF 1871. Crown 8vo. 1s.
>
> ARMY RESERVES AND MILITIA REFORMS. Crown 8vo. 1s.
>
> THE STORY OF THE SUPERSESSIONS. Crown 8vo. 6d.

ARGYLE (Duke of).
> SPEECHES ON THE SECOND READING OF THE CHURCH PATRONAGE (SCOTLAND) BILL IN THE HOUSE OF LORDS, June 2, 1874; and Earl of Camperdown's Amendment, June 9, 1874, placing the Election of Ministers in the hands of Ratepayers. Crown 8vo. Sewed. 1s.

ARMY OF THE NORTH GERMAN CONFEDERATION.
> A Brief Description of its Organization, of the Different Branches of the Service and their rôle in War, of its Mode of Fighting, etc., etc. Translated from the Corrected Edition, by permission of the author, by Colonel Edward Newdegate. Demy 8vo. 5s.

ASHANTEE WAR (The).
> A Popular Narrative. By the Special Correspondent of the "Daily News." Crown 8vo. 6s.

ASHE (T.) Author of "The Sorrows of Hypsipyle."
: **EDITH; OR, LOVE AND LIFE IN CHESHIRE.** Sewed. 6d.

ASHTON (John).
: **ROUGH NOTES OF A VISIT TO BELGIUM, SEDAN, AND PARIS,** in September, 1870-71. Crown 8vo. 3s. 6d.

AUNT MARY'S BRAN PIE.
: By the author of "St. Olave's," "When I was a Little Girl," etc. Illustrated. 3s. 6d.

: **SUNNYLAND STORIES.** Fcap. 8vo. Illustrated. 3s. 6d.

: Being two of Henry S. King and Co.'s Three and Sixpenny Series of Children's Books.

AURORA: A Volume of Verse. 5s.

AYRTON (J. C.)
: **A SCOTCH WOOING.** 2 vols. Crown 8vo.

BAGEHOT (Walter).
: **PHYSICS AND POLITICS;** or, Thoughts on the Application of the Principles of "Natural Selection" and "Inheritance" to Political Society. Third Edition. Crown 8vo. 4s.
: Volume II. of the International Scientific Series.

: **THE ENGLISH CONSTITUTION.** A New Edition, Revised and Corrected, with an Introductory Dissertation on Recent Changes and Events. Crown 8vo. 7s. 6d.

: **LOMBARD STREET.** A Description of the Money Market. Crown 8vo. Sixth Edition. 7s. 6d.

BAIN (Alexander), LL.D.
: **MIND AND BODY.** The Theories of their Relation. Fourth Edition. Crown 8vo. 4s.
: Volume IV. of the International Scientific Series.

BANKS (Mrs. G. Linnæus).
: **GOD'S PROVIDENCE HOUSE.** Crown 8vo. 3s. 6d.
: One of the volumes of the Cornhill Library of Fiction.

BARING (T. C.), M.P., late Fellow of Brasenose College, Oxford.
: **PINDAR IN ENGLISH RHYME.** Being an Attempt to render the Epinikian Odes with the principal remaining Fragments of Pindar into English Verse. Small quarto. Cloth, 7s.

BARLEE (Ellen).
>   **LOCKED OUT**; A Tale of the Strike. With a Frontispiece. 1s. 6d.

BAYNES (Rev. Canon R. H.), Editor of "Lyra Anglicana," etc.
>   **HOME SONGS FOR QUIET HOURS.** Second Edition. Fcap. 8vo. Cloth extra, 3s. 6d.
>   *** This may also be had handsomely bound in Morocco with gilt edges.*

BECKER (Bernard H.)
>   **THE SCIENTIFIC SOCIETIES OF LONDON.** 1 vol. Crown 8vo. 5s.

BENNETT (Dr. W. C.)
>   **SONGS FOR SAILORS.** Dedicated by Special Request to H.R.H. the Duke of Edinburgh. Crown 8vo. 3s. 6d. With Steel Portrait and Illustrations.
>   An Edition in Illustrated Paper Covers, 1s.
>
>   **BABY MAY. HOME POEMS AND BALLADS.** With Frontispiece. Cloth elegant. Crown 8vo. 6s.
>
>   **BABY MAY AND HOME POEMS.** Fcap. 8vo. Sewed in Coloured Wrapper. 1s.
>
>   **NARRATIVE POEMS AND BALLADS.** Fcap. 8vo. Sewed in Coloured Wrapper. 1s.

BENNIE (Rev. Jas. Noble), M.A.
>   **THE ETERNAL LIFE.** Sermons preached during the last twelve years. Crown 8vo. 6s.

BERNARD (Bayle).
>   **SAMUEL LOVER, THE LIFE AND UNPUBLISHED WORKS OF.** In 2 vols. Post 8vo. With a Steel Portrait. 21s.

BETHAM-EDWARDS (Miss M.)
>   **KITTY.** Crown 8vo. With a Frontispiece. 3s. 6d.
>   One of the volumes of the Cornhill Library of Fiction.
>
>   **MADEMOISELLE JOSEPHINE'S FRIDAYS, AND OTHER STORIES.** Crown 8vo. 7s. 6d.

BISCOE (A. C.)
>   **THE EARLS OF MIDDLETON,** Lords of Clermont and of Fettercairn, and the Middleton Family. 1 vol. Crown 8vo. 10s. 6d.

BLANC (Henry), M.D.
>   CHOLERA : HOW TO AVOID AND TREAT IT. Popular and Practical Notes. Crown 8vo. 4s. 6d.

BLUME (Major William).
>   THE OPERATIONS OF THE GERMAN ARMIES IN FRANCE, from Sedan to the end of the war of 1870–71. With Map. From the Journals of the Head-quarters Staff. Translated by the late E. M. Jones, Maj. 20th Foot, Prof. of Mil. Hist., Sandhurst. Demy 8vo. 9s.

BOGUSLAWSKI (Captain A. von).
>   TACTICAL DEDUCTIONS FROM THE WAR OF 1870-71. Translated by Colonel Sir Lumley Graham, Bart., late 18th (Royal Irish) Regiment. Third Edition, Revised and Corrected. Demy 8vo. 7s. A volume of Henry S. King and Co.'s Series of Military Works.

BONWICK (James).
>   THE TASMANIAN LILY. Cr. 8vo. With Frontispiece. 5s.
>   MIKE HOWE, THE BUSHRANGER OF VAN DIEMEN'S LAND. Crown 8vo. With Frontispiece. 5s.

BOSWELL (R. B.), M.A., Oxon.
>   METRICAL TRANSLATIONS FROM THE GREEK AND LATIN POETS, and other Poems. Crown 8vo. 5s.

BOTHMER (Countess Von).
>   CRUEL AS THE GRAVE. A Novel. 3 vols.

BOWRING (L.), C.S.I., Lord Canning's Private Secretary, and for many years Chief Commissioner of Mysore and Coorg.
>   EASTERN EXPERIENCES. Illustrated with Maps and Diagrams. Demy 8vo. 16s.

BRAVE MEN'S FOOTSTEPS. By the Editor of "Men who have Risen." A Book of Example and Anecdote for Young People. With Four Illustrations by C. Doyle. Third Edition. Crown 8vo. 3s. 6d.

BRIALMONT (Colonel A.)
>   HASTY INTRENCHMENTS. Translated by Lieut. Charles A. Empsom, R.A. With nine Plates. Demy 8vo. 6s.

BRIEFS AND PAPERS. Being Sketches of the Bar and the Press. By Two Idle Apprentices. Crown 8vo. 7s. 6d.

BROOKE (Rev. Stopford A.), M.A., Chaplain in Ordinary to Her Majesty the Queen.

THE LATE REV. F. W. ROBERTSON, M.A., LIFE AND LETTERS OF. Edited by Stopford Brooke, M.A.
I. In 2 vols., uniform with the Sermons. Steel Portrait. 7s. 6d.
II. Library Edition. 8vo. Two Steel Portraits. 12s.
III. A Popular Edition, in 1 vol. 8vo. 6s.

THEOLOGY IN THE ENGLISH POETS.—COWPER, COLERIDGE, WORDSWORTH, and BURNS. Second Edition. Post 8vo. 9s.

CHRIST IN MODERN LIFE. Sermons Preached in St. James's Chapel, York Street, London. Eighth Edition. Crown 8vo. 7s. 6d.

FREEDOM IN THE CHURCH OF ENGLAND. Six Sermons suggested by the Voysey Judgment. Second Edition. Crown 8vo. 3s. 6d.

SERMONS Preached in St. James's Chapel, York Street, London. Eighth Edition. Crown 8vo. 6s.

SERMONS Preached in St. James's Chapel, York Street, London. Second Series. Second Edition. Crown 8vo. 7s.

FREDERICK DENISON MAURICE: The Life and Work of. A Memorial Sermon. Crown 8vo. Sewed. 1s.

BROOKE (W. G.), M.A., Barrister-at-Law.

THE PUBLIC WORSHIP REGULATION ACT. With a Classified Statement of its Provisions, Notes, and Index. Third Edition, revised and corrected. Crown 8vo. 3s. 6d.

SIX PRIVY COUNCIL JUDGMENTS—1850-1872. Annotated by. Third Edition. Crown 8vo. 9s.

BROWN (Rev. J. Baldwin), B.A.

THE HIGHER LIFE. Its Reality, Experience, and Destiny. Fourth Edition. Crown 8vo. 7s. 6d.

THE DOCTRINE OF ANNIHILATION IN THE LIGHT OF THE GOSPEL OF LOVE. Five Discourses. Second Edition. Crown 8vo. 2s. 6d.

BROWN (John Croumbie), LL.D., etc.

REBOISEMENT IN FRANCE; or, Records of the Replanting of the Alps, the Cevennes, and the Pyrenees with Trees, Herbage, and Bush, with a view to arresting and preventing the destructive consequences and effects of Torrents. 1 vol. Demy 8vo. 12s. 6d.

THE HYDROLOGY OF SOUTHERN AFRICA. Demy 8vo. 10s. 6d.

BROWNE (Rev. Marmaduke E.)
    UNTIL THE DAY DAWN. Four Advent Lectures delivered in the Episcopal Chapel, Milverton, Warwickshire, on the Sunday evenings during Advent, 1870. Crown 8vo. 2s. 6d.

BRYANT (William Cullen).
    POEMS. Red-line Edition. Handsomely bound. With 24 Illustrations and Portrait of the Author. 7s. 6d.
    A Cheaper Edition, with Frontispiece. 3s. 6d.

BUCHANAN (Robert).
    POETICAL WORKS. Collected Edition, in 3 Vols., price 6s. each.
    Vol. I.—"Ballads and Romances;" "Ballads and Poems of Life," and a Portrait of the Author.
    Vol. II.—"Ballads and Poems of Life;" "Allegories and Sonnets."
    Vol. III.—"Cruiskeen Sonnets;" "Book of Orm;" "Political Mystics."
    MASTER-SPIRITS. Post 8vo. 10s. 6d.

BULKELEY (Rev. Henry J.)
    WALLED IN, and other Poems. Crown 8vo. 5s.

BUNNÈTT (F. E.)
    LEONORA CHRISTINA, MEMOIRS OF, Daughter of Christian IV. of Denmark; Written during her Imprisonment in the Blue Tower of the Royal Palace at Copenhagen, 1663-1685. Translated by F. E. Bunnètt. With an Autotype Portrait of the Princess. Medium 8vo. A New and Cheaper Edition. 5s.

    LINKED AT LAST. 1 vol. Crown 8vo.

    UNDER A CLOUD; OR, JOHANNES OLAF. By E. D. Wille. Translated by F. E. Bunnètt. 3 vols.

BURTON (Mrs. Richard).
    THE INNER LIFE OF SYRIA, PALESTINE, AND THE HOLY LAND. 2 vols. Demy 8vo. 24s.

BUTLER (Josephine E.)
    JOHN GREY (of Dilston): MEMOIRS. By his Daughter. New and Cheaper Edition. Crown 8vo. 3s. 6d.

CALDERON.
    CALDERON'S DRAMAS: The Wonder-Working Magician—Life is a Dream—The Purgatory of St. Patrick. Translated by Denis Florence MacCarthy. Post 8vo. 10s.

CAMDEN (Charles).
> HOITY TOITY, THE GOOD LITTLE FELLOW. With Eleven Illustrations. Crown 8vo. 3s. 6d.
>
> THE TRAVELLING MENAGERIE. With Ten Illustrations by J. Mahoney. Crown 8vo. 3s. 6d.
>
> The above form part of Henry S. King & Co.'s Three and Sixpenny Series of Children's Books.

CARLISLE (A. D.), B.A., Trin. Coll., Camb.
> ROUND THE WORLD IN 1870. A Volume of Travels, with Maps. New and Cheaper Edition. Demy 8vo. 6s.

CARNE (Miss E. T.)
> THE REALM OF TRUTH. Crown 8vo. 5s. 6d.

CARPENTER (E.)
> NARCISSUS AND OTHER POEMS. Fcap. 8vo. 5s.

CARPENTER (W. B.), LL.D., M.D., F.R.S., etc.
> THE PRINCIPLES OF MENTAL PHYSIOLOGY. With their Applications to the Training and Discipline of the Mind, and the Study of its Morbid Conditions. 8vo. Illustrated. 12s.

CARR (Lisle).
> JUDITH GWYNNE. 3 vols. Crown 8vo. Second Edition.

CHRISTOPHERSON (The late Rev. Henry), M.A., Assistant Minister at Trinity Church, Brighton.
> SERMONS. Crown 8vo. Cloth. 7s. 6d. With an Introduction by John Rae, LL.D., F.S.A.

CLAYTON (Cecil).
> EFFIE'S GAME; HOW SHE LOST AND HOW SHE WON. A Novel. 2 vols.

CLERK (Mrs. Godfrey), Author of "The Antipodes and Round the World."
> 'ILAM EN NAS. Historical Tales and Anecdotes of the Times of the Early Khalifahs. Translated from the Arabic Originals. Illustrated with Historical and Explanatory Notes. Crown 8vo. 7s.

CLERY (C.), Captain 32nd Light Infantry, Deputy Assistant Adjutant-General, late Professor of Tactics Royal Military College, Sandhurst.
> MINOR TACTICS. Demy 8vo. Second Edition. With 26 Maps and Plans. 16s.

CLODD (Edward), F.R.A.S.
THE CHILDHOOD OF THE WORLD: a Simple Account of Man in Early Times. New Edition. Crown 8vo. 3s.
A Special Edition for Schools. 1s.
THE CHILDHOOD OF RELIGIONS. Including a Simple Account of the Birth and Growth of Myths and Legends. Crown 8vo. 5s.

COLERIDGE (Sara).
PRETTY LESSONS IN VERSE FOR GOOD CHILDREN, with some Lessons in Latin, in Easy Rhyme. A New Edition. Illustrated. 3s. 6d.
PHANTASMION. A Fairy Romance. With an Introductory Preface by the Right Hon. Lord Coleridge of Ottery St. Mary. A New Edition. Illustrated. 7s. 6d.
MEMOIR AND LETTERS OF SARA COLERIDGE. Edited by her Daughter. Third Edition, Revised and Corrected. With Index. 2 vols. Crown 8vo. With Two Portraits. 24s.
Cheap Edition. With one Portrait. 7s. 6d.

COLLINS (Mortimer).
THE PRINCESS CLARICE. A Story of 1871. 2 vols.
SQUIRE SILCHESTER'S WHIM. By Mortimer Collins, Author of "Marquis and Merchant," etc. 3 vols.
MIRANDA. A Midsummer Madness. 3 vols.
THE INN OF STRANGE MEETINGS, AND OTHER POEMS. Crown 8vo. 5s.
THE SECRET OF LONG LIFE. Dedicated by special permission to Lord St. Leonard's. Fourth Edition. Large crown 8vo. 5s.

COLLINS (Rev. Richard), M.A.
MISSIONARY ENTERPRISE IN THE EAST. With special reference to the Syrian Christians of Malabar, and the results of modern Missions. With Four Illustrations. Crown 8vo. 6s.

CONWAY (Moncure D.)
REPUBLICAN SUPERSTITIONS. Illustrated by the Political History of the United States. Including a Correspondence with M. Louis Blanc. Crown 8vo. 5s.

CONYERS (Ansley).
CHESTERLEIGH. 3 vols. Crown 8vo.

COOKE (M. C.), M.A., LL.D.
FUNGI; their Nature, Influences, Uses, etc. Edited by the Rev. M. J. Berkeley, M.A., F.L.S. Second Edition. Crown 8vo. With Illustrations. 5s.
Being Vol. XIV. of the International Scientific Series.

COOKE (Professor Josiah P.), of the Harvard University.
>THE NEW CHEMISTRY. Second Edition. With Thirty-one Illustrations. 5s.
>Vol. IX. of the International Scientific Series.
>SCIENTIFIC CULTURE. Crown 8vo. Cloth. 1s.

COOPER (T. T.)
>THE MISHMEE HILLS: an Account of a Journey made in an Attempt to Penetrate Thibet from Assam, to open New Routes for Commerce. Second Edition. With Four Illustrations and Map. Demy 8vo. 10s. 6d.

CORNHILL LIBRARY OF FICTION, The. 3s. 6d. per Volume.
>HALF-A-DOZEN DAUGHTERS. By J. Masterman.
>THE HOUSE OF RABY. By Mrs. G. Hooper.
>A FIGHT FOR LIFE. By Moy Thomas.
>ROBIN GRAY. By Charles Gibbon.
>KITTY. By Miss M. Betham-Edwards.
>HIRELL. By John Saunders.
>ONE OF TWO; or, The Left-Handed Bride. By J. Hain Friswell.
>READY-MONEY MORTIBOY. A Matter-of-Fact Story.
>GOD'S PROVIDENCE HOUSE. By Mrs. G. L. Banks.
>FOR LACK OF GOLD. By Charles Gibbon.
>ABEL DRAKE'S WIFE. By John Saunders.

CORY (Lieutenant-Colonel Arthur).
>SHADOWS OF COMING EVENTS; or, The Eastern Menace. Crown 8vo. Cloth. 5s.

COSMOS. A Poem. Fcap. 8vo. 3s. 6d.
>SUBJECTS.—Nature in the Past and in the Present—Man in the Past and in the Present—The Future.

COTTON (Robert Turner).
>MR. CARINGTON. A Tale of Love and Conspiracy. 3 vols. Crown 8vo.

CUMMINS (Henry Irwin), M.A.
>PAROCHIAL CHARITIES OF THE CITY OF LONDON. Sewed. 1s.

CURWEN (Henry).
>SORROW AND SONG: Studies of Literary Struggle. Henry Mürger—Novalis—Alexander Petöfi—Honoré de Balzac—Edgar Allan Poe—André Chénier. 2 vols. Crown 8vo. 15s.

DAVIDSON (Samuel), D.D., LL.D.

THE NEW TESTAMENT, TRANSLATED FROM THE LATEST GREEK TEXT OF TISCHENDORF. Post 8vo. 10s. 6d.

DAVIES (G. Christopher).

MOUNTAIN, MEADOW, AND MERE: a Series of Outdoor Sketches of Sport, Scenery, Adventures, and Natural History. With Sixteen Illustrations by Bosworth W. Harcourt. Crown 8vo. 6s.

RAMBLES AND ADVENTURES OF OUR SCHOOL FIELD CLUB. Crown 8vo. With 4 Illustrations. 5s.

DAVIES (Rev. J. Llewelyn), M.A.

THEOLOGY AND MORALITY. Essays on Questions of Belief and Practice. Crown 8vo. 7s. 6d.

D'ANVERS (N. R.)

LITTLE MINNIE'S TROUBLES. An Every-day Chronicle. Illustrated by W. H. Hughes. Fcap. 3s. 6d.

A Simple Chronicle of a Child's Life.

DE KERKADEC (Vicomtesse Solange).

A CHEQUERED LIFE, being Memoirs of the Vicomtesse de Leoville Meilhan. Edited by. Crown 8vo. 7s. 6d.

Containing many recollections of the First Emperor Napoleon and his Court.

DE L'HOSTE (Colonel E. P.).

THE DESERT PASTOR, JEAN JAROUSSEAU. Translated from the French of Eugène Pelletan. In fcap. 8vo., with a Frontispiece. New Edition. 3s. 6d.

One of Henry S. King and Co.'s Three and Sixpenny Books for the Young.

DE LIEFDE (Jacob).

THE GREAT DUTCH ADMIRALS. Crown 8vo. With Eleven Illustrations by Townley Green and others. 5s.

One of Henry S. King and Co.'s Five Shilling Books for the Young.

DE REDCLIFFE (Viscount Stratford), P.C., K.G., G.C.B.

WHY AM I A CHRISTIAN? Fifth Edition. Crown 8vo. 3s.

DE TOCQUEVILLE (Alexis).

CORRESPONDENCE AND CONVERSATIONS OF, WITH NASSAU WILLIAM SENIOR. 2 vols. Post 8vo. 21s.

DE VERE (Aubrey).
> ALEXANDER THE GREAT. A Dramatic Poem. Small crown 8vo. 5s.
> THE INFANT BRIDAL, AND OTHER POEMS. A New and Enlarged Edition. Fcap. 8vo. 7s. 6d.
> THE LEGENDS OF ST. PATRICK, AND OTHER POEMS. Small crown 8vo. 5s.

DE WILLE (E.)
> UNDER A CLOUD; OR, JOHANNES OLAF. A Novel. Translated by F. E. Bunnètt. 3 vols. Crown 8vo.

DENNIS (John).
> ENGLISH SONNETS. Collected and Arranged. Fcap. 8vo. Elegantly bound. 3s. 6d.

DOBSON (Austin).
> VIGNETTES IN RHYME AND VERS DE SOCIÉTÉ. Second Edition. Fcap. 8vo. 5s.

DONNÉ (Alphonse), M.D.
> CHANGE OF AIR AND SCENE. A Physician's Hints about Doctors, Patients, Hygiene, and Society; with Notes of Excursions for Health in the Pyrenees, and amongst the Watering-places of France (Inland and Seaward), Switzerland, Corsica, and the Mediterranean. A New Edition. Large post 8vo. 9s.

DOWDEN (Edward), LL.D.
> SHAKSPERE: a Critical Study of his Mind and Art. Post 8vo. 12s.

DOWNTON (Rev. Henry), M.A.
> HYMNS AND VERSES. Original and Translated. Small crown 8vo. 3s. 6d.

DRAPER (John William), M.D., LL.D. Professor in the University of New York; Author of "A Treatise on Human Physiology."
> HISTORY OF THE CONFLICT BETWEEN RELIGION AND SCIENCE. Fifth Edition. 5s.
> Vol. XIII. of the International Scientific Series.

DREW (Rev. G. S.), M.A., Vicar of Trinity, Lambeth.
> SCRIPTURE LANDS IN CONNECTION WITH THEIR HISTORY. Second Edition. 8vo. 10s. 6d.
> NAZARETH: ITS LIFE AND LESSONS. Third Edition. Crown 8vo. 5s.
> THE DIVINE KINGDOM ON EARTH AS IT IS IN HEAVEN. 8vo. 10s. 6d.

DREW (Rev. G. S.), M.A.
    THE SON OF MAN: His Life and Ministry. Crown 8vo.
    7s. 6d.
DREWRY (G. Overend), M.D.
    THE COMMON-SENSE MANAGEMENT OF THE STOMACH.
    Fcap. 8vo. Second Edition. 2s. 6d.
DURAND (Lady).
    IMITATIONS FROM THE GERMAN OF SPITTA AND
    TERSTEGEN. Fcap. 8vo. 4s.
DU VERNOIS (Colonel von Verdy).
    STUDIES IN LEADING TROOPS. An authorized and accurate
    Translation by Lieutenant H. J. T. Hildyard, 71st Foot. Parts I.
    and II. Demy 8vo. 7s.
    This is one of Henry S. King and Co.'s Series of Military Works.
E. A. V.
    JOSEPH MAZZINI : A Memoir. With Two Essays by
    Mazzini—"Thoughts on Democracy," and "The Duties of
    Man." Dedicated to the Working Classes by P. H. Taylor, M.P.
    Crown 8vo. With Two Portraits. 3s. 6d.
EDEN (Frederic).
    THE NILE WITHOUT A DRAGOMAN. Second Edition.
    Crown 8vo. 7s. 6d.
EDWARDS (Rev. Basil).
    MINOR CHORDS; OR, SONGS FOR THE SUFFERING: a
    Volume of Verse. Fcap. 8vo. Cloth, 3s. 6d.; paper, 2s. 6d.
EILOART (Mrs.)
    LADY MORETOUN'S DAUGHTER. 3 vols. Crown 8vo.
ENGLISH CLERGYMAN.
    AN ESSAY ON THE RULE OF FAITH AND CREED OF
    ATHANASIUS. Shall the Rubric preceding the Creed be
    removed from the Prayer-book? 8vo. Sewed. 1s.
EROS AGONISTES. Poems. By E. B. D. Fcap. 8vo.
    3s. 6d.
EVANS (Mark).
    THE STORY OF OUR FATHER'S LOVE, told to Children;
    being a New and Enlarged Edition of Theology for Children.
    Fcap. 8vo. 3s. 6d.
    A BOOK OF COMMON PRAYER AND WORSHIP FOR
    HOUSEHOLD USE, compiled exclusively from the Holy Scrip-
    tures. Fcap. 8vo. Cloth, 2s. 6d.

EYRE (Maj.-Gen. Sir Vincent), C.B., K.C.S.I., etc.
 LAYS OF A KNIGHT-ERRANT IN MANY LANDS. Square crown 8vo. With Six Illustrations. 7s. 6d.
  Pharaoh Land. | Home Land. | Wonder Land. | Rhine Land.

FAITHFULL (Mrs. Francis G.)
 LOVE ME, OR LOVE ME NOT. 3 vols. Crown 8vo.

FARQUHARSON (Martha).
  I. ELSIE DINSMORE. Crown 8vo. 3s. 6d.
  II. ELSIE'S GIRLHOOD. Crown 8vo. 3s. 6d.
  III. ELSIE'S HOLIDAYS AT ROSELANDS. Crown 8vo. 3s. 6d.
 These are volumes of Henry S. King and Co.'s Series of Three and Sixpenny Books for the Young.

FAVRE (Mons. Jules).
 THE GOVERNMENT OF THE NATIONAL DEFENCE. From the 30th June to the 31st October, 1870. The Plain Statement of a Member. 1 vol. Demy 8vo. 10s. 6d.

FISHER (Alice).
 HIS QUEEN. 3 vols. Crown 8vo.

FORBES (Archibald).
 SOLDIERING AND SCRIBBLING. A Series of Sketches. Crown 8vo. 7s. 6d.

FOTHERGILL (Jessie).
 HEALEY. A Romance. 3 vols. Crown 8vo.

FOWLE (Rev. T. W.), M.A.
 THE RECONCILIATION OF RELIGION AND SCIENCE. Being Essays on Immortality, Inspiration, Miracles, and the Being of Christ. Demy 8vo. 10s. 6d.

FRASER (Donald), Accountant to the British-Indian Steam Navigation Company, Limited.
 EXCHANGE TABLES OF STERLING AND INDIAN RUPEE CURRENCY, upon a new and extended system, embracing Values from One Farthing to One Hundred Thousand Pounds, and at Rates progressing, in Sixteenths of a Penny, from 1s. 9d. to 2s. 3d. per Rupee. Royal 8vo. 10s. 6d.

FRERE (Sir H. Bartle E.), G.C.B., G.C.S.I., etc.
 THE THREATENED FAMINE IN BENGAL; How it may be Met, and the Recurrence of Famines in India Prevented. Being No. 1 of "Occasional Notes on Indian Affairs." Crown 8vo. With 3 Maps. 5s.

Friswell (J. Hain).

THE BETTER SELF. Essays for Home Life. Crown 8vo. 6s.
Contents:—Beginning at Home—The Girls at Home—The Wife's Mother—Pride in the Family—Discontent and Grumbling—Domestic Economy—On Keeping People Down—Likes and Dislikes—On Falling Out—Peace.

ONE OF TWO; or, The Left-Handed Bride. Crown 8vo. With a Frontispiece. 3s. 6d.
Being a Volume of the Cornhill Library of Fiction.

Gardner (John), M.D.

LONGEVITY; THE MEANS OF PROLONGING LIFE AFTER MIDDLE AGE. Third Edition, revised and enlarged. Small crown 8vo. 4s.

Garrett (Edward).

BY STILL WATERS. A Story for Quiet Hours. Crown 8vo. With Seven Illustrations. 6s.

Gibbon (Charles).

FOR LACK OF GOLD. Crown 8vo. With a Frontispiece. 3s. 6d.
ROBIN GRAY. Crown 8vo. With a Frontispiece. 3s. 6d.
The above Volumes form part of the Cornhill Library of Fiction.

Gilbert (Mrs.)

MRS. GILBERT, FORMERLY ANN TAYLOR, AUTOBIOGRAPHY AND OTHER MEMORIALS OF. Edited by Josiah Gilbert. In 2 vols. Post 8vo. With 2 Steel Portraits and several Wood Engravings. 24s.

Gill (Rev. W. W.)

MYTHS AND SONGS OF THE SOUTH PACIFIC. With a Preface by F. Max Müller, M.A., Professor of Comparative Philology at Oxford. 1 vol. Post 8vo.

Godkin (James).

THE RELIGIOUS HISTORY OF IRELAND: Primitive, Papal, and Protestant. Including the Evangelical Missions, Catholic Agitations, and Church Progress of the last half Century. 1 vol. 8vo. 12s.

Godwin (William).

WILLIAM GODWIN: HIS FRIENDS AND CONTEMPORARIES. By C. Kegan Paul. 2 vols. Demy 8vo. With Portraits.
THE GENIUS OF CHRISTIANITY UNVEILED. Being Essays never before published. Edited, with a Preface, by C. Kegan Paul. 1 vol. Crown 8vo. 7s. 6d.

B   b

GOETZE (Capt. A. von), Captain of the Prussian Corps of Engineers attached to the Engineer Committee, and Instructor at the Military Academy.

    OPERATIONS OF THE GERMAN ENGINEERS DURING THE WAR OF 1870-1871. Published by Authority, and in accordance with Official Documents. Translated from the German by Colonel G. Graham, V.C., C.B., R.E. Demy 8vo. Cloth. With 6 large Maps. 21s.

GOODMAN (Walter).

    CUBA, THE PEARL OF THE ANTILLES. Crown 8vo. 7s. 6d.

GOSSE (Edmund W.)

    ON VIOL AND FLUTE. With Title-page specially designed by William B. Scott. Crown 8vo. 5s.

GRANVILLE (A. B.), M.D., F.R.S., etc.

    AUTOBIOGRAPHY OF A. B. GRANVILLE, F.R.S., etc. Edited, with a brief account of the concluding years of his life, by his youngest Daughter, Paulina B. Granville. 2 vols. Demy 8vo. With a Portrait. 32s.

GRAY (Mrs. Russell).

    LISETTE'S VENTURE. A Novel. 2 vols. Crown 8vo. 21s.

GREEN (T. Bowden).

    FRAGMENTS OF THOUGHT. Dedicated by permission to the Poet Laureate. Crown 8vo. 7s. 6d.

GREENWOOD (James), "The Amateur Casual."

    IN STRANGE COMPANY; or, The Note Book of a Roving Correspondent. Second Edition. Crown 8vo. 6s.

GREY (John), of Dilston.

    JOHN GREY (of Dilston): MEMOIRS. By Josephine E. Butler. New and Cheaper Edition. Crown 8vo. 3s. 6d.

GRIFFITH (Rev. T.), A.M., Prebendary of St. Paul's.

    STUDIES OF THE DIVINE MASTER. Demy 8vo. 12s.

GRIFFITHS (Captain Arthur).

    THE QUEEN'S SHILLING. A Novel. 2 vols. 21s.

    MEMORIALS OF MILLBANK, AND CHAPTERS IN PRISON HISTORY. 2 vols. Post 8vo. 21s. With Illustrations.

GRUNER (M. L.)

    STUDIES OF BLAST FURNACE PHENOMENA. Translated by L. D. B. Gordon, F.R.S.E., F.G.S. Demy 8vo. 7s. 6d.

GURNEY (Rev. Archer Thompson).
> **WORDS OF FAITH AND CHEER.** A Mission of Instruction and Suggestion. 1 vol. Crown 8vo. 6s.
>
> **FIRST PRINCIPLES IN CHURCH AND STATE.** Demy 8vo. Sewed. 1s. 6d.

HAECKEL (Professor Ernst), of the University of Jena.
> **THE HISTORY OF CREATION.** A Popular Account of the Development of the Earth and its Inhabitants, according to the Theories of Kant, Laplace, Lamarck, and Darwin. The Translation revised by Professor E. Ray Lankester, M.A., F.R.S. With Coloured Plates and Genealogical Trees of the various groups of both plants and animals. 2 vols. Post 8vo. 32s.
>
> **THE HISTORY OF THE EVOLUTION OF MAN.** Translated by E. A. Van Rhyn and L. Elsberg. M.D. (University of New York), with Notes and Additions sanctioned by the Author. Post 8vo.

HARCOURT (Capt. A. F. P.)
> **THE SHAKESPEARE ARGOSY:** Containing much of the wealth of Shakespeare's Wisdom and Wit, alphabetically arranged and classified. Crown 8vo. 6s.

HAWEIS (Rev. H. R.), M.A.
> **SPEECH IN SEASON.** Third Edition. Crown 8vo. 9s.
>
> **THOUGHTS FOR THE TIMES.** Eighth Edition. Crown 8vo. 7s. 6d.
>
> **UNSECTARIAN FAMILY PRAYERS,** for Morning and Evening for a Week, with short selected passages from the Bible. Square crown 8vo. 3s. 6d.

HAWTHORNE (Julian).
> **BRESSANT.** A Romance. 2 vols. Crown 8vo. 21s.
>
> **IDOLATRY.** A Romance. 2 vols. Crown 8vo. 21s.

HAWTHORNE (Nathaniel).
> **NATHANIEL HAWTHORNE.** A Memoir, with Stories now first published in this country. By H. A. Page. Post 8vo. 7s. 6d.
>
> **SEPTIMIUS.** A Romance. Second Edition. Crown 8vo. 9s.

HAYMAN (Henry), D.D., late Head Master of Rugby School.
> **RUGBY SCHOOL SERMONS.** With an Introductory Essay on the Indwelling of the Holy Spirit. Crown 8vo. 7s. 6d.

HEATHERGATE. A Story of Scottish Life and Character. By a New Author. 2 vols. Crown 8vo. 21s.

HELLWALD (Baron F. Von).
> **THE RUSSIANS IN CENTRAL ASIA.** A Critical Examination, down to the present time, of the Geography and History of Central Asia. Translated by Lieut.-Col. Theodore Wirgman, LL.B. In 1 vol. Large post 8vo. With Map. 12s.

HELVIG (Captain Hugo).
> **THE OPERATIONS OF THE BAVARIAN ARMY CORPS.** Translated by Captain G. S. Schwabe. With Five large Maps. In 2 vols. Demy 8vo. 24s.
> This is one of Henry S. King and Co.'s Series of Military Books.

HINTON (James), late Aural Surgeon to Guy's Hospital.
> **THE PLACE OF THE PHYSICIAN.** Being the Introductory Lecture at Guy's Hospital, 1873-74; to which is added ESSAYS ON THE LAW OF HUMAN LIFE, AND ON THE RELATION BETWEEN ORGANIC AND INORGANIC WORLDS. Second Edition. Crown 8vo. 3s. 6d.
> **PHYSIOLOGY FOR PRACTICAL USE.** By various writers. Second Edition. With 50 Illustrations. 2 vols. Crown 8vo. 12s. 6d.
> **AN ATLAS OF DISEASES OF THE MEMBRANA TYMPANI.** With Descriptive Text. Post 8vo. £6 6s.
> **THE QUESTIONS OF AURAL SURGERY.** Post 8vo. With Illustrations. 2 vols. 12s. 6d.

HOCKLEY (W. B.)
> **TALES OF THE ZENANA**; or, A Nuwab's Leisure Hours. By the Author of "Pandurang Hari." With a Preface by Lord Stanley of Alderley. 2 vols. Crown 8vo. 21s.
> **PANDURANG HARI**; or, Memoirs of a Hindoo. A Tale of Mahratta Life sixty years ago. With a Preface by Sir H. Bartle E. Frere, G.C.S.I., etc. 2 vols. Crown 8vo. 21s.

HOFFBAUER (Captain).
> **THE GERMAN ARTILLERY IN THE BATTLES NEAR METZ.** Based on the official reports of the German Artillery. Translated by Capt. E. O. Hollist. Demy 8vo. With Map and Plans. 21s.
> This is one of the volumes in Henry S. King and Co.'s Military Series.

HOLROYD (Major W. R. M.), Bengal Staff Corps, Director of Public Instruction, Punjab.
> **TAS-HIL UL KALAM**; or, Hindustani made Easy. Crown 8vo. 5s.

HOPE (Lieut. James).
> **IN QUEST OF COOLIES.** With Illustrations. Crown 8vo. 6s.

HOOPER (Mrs. G.)
THE HOUSE OF BABY. With a Frontispiece. Crown 8vo. 3s. 6d.
One of the volumes of the Cornhill Library of Fiction.

HOOPER (Mary).
LITTLE DINNERS: HOW TO SERVE THEM WITH ELEGANCE AND ECONOMY. Ninth Edition. 1 vol. Crown 8vo. 5s.
COOKERY FOR INVALIDS. Crown 8vo. 3s. 6d.

HOPKINS (Manley).
THE PORT OF REFUGE; or, Counsel and Aid to Shipmasters in Difficulty, Doubt, or Distress. Crown 8vo. 6s.

HOWARD (Mary M.), Author of "Brampton Rectory."
BEATRICE AYLMER, AND OTHER TALES. Crown 8vo. 6s.

HOWARD (Rev. G. B.)
AN OLD LEGEND OF ST. PAUL'S. Fcap. 8vo. 4s. 6d.

HOWE (Cupples), Master Mariner.
THE DESERTED SHIP. A real story of the Atlantic. Illustrated by Townley Green. Crown 8vo. 3s. 6d.
One of Henry S. King and Co.'s Three and Sixpenny Books for the Young.

HOWELL (James).
A TALE OF THE SEA, SONNETS, AND OTHER POEMS. Fcap. 8vo. 5s.

HUGHES (Allison).
PENELOPE, AND OTHER POEMS. Fcap. 8vo. 4s. 6d.

HULL (Edmund C. P.)
THE EUROPEAN IN INDIA. A Handbook of Practical Information for those proceeding to, or residing in, the East Indies, relating to Outfits, Routes, Time for Departure, Indian Climate, etc. With a MEDICAL GUIDE FOR ANGLO-INDIANS. By R. R. S. Mair, M.D., F.R.C.S.E., late Deputy Coroner of Madras. Second Edition, Revised and Corrected. In 1 vol. Post 8vo. 6s.

HUMPHREY (Rev. W.), of the Congregation of the Oblates of St. Charles.
MR. FITZJAMES STEPHEN AND CARDINAL BELLARMINE. Demy 8vo. Sewed. 1s.

HUTTON (James).
MISSIONARY LIFE IN THE SOUTHERN SEAS. With Illustrations. Crown 8vo. 7s. 6d.

INTERNATIONAL SCIENTIFIC SERIES (The).

    I. **THE FORMS OF WATER IN CLOUDS AND RIVERS, ICE AND GLACIERS.** By J. Tyndall, LL.D., F.R.S. With 14 Illustrations. Fifth Edition. 5s.

   II. **PHYSICS AND POLITICS**; or, Thoughts on the Application of the Principles of "Natural Selection" and "Inheritance" to Political Society. By Walter Bagehot. Third Edition. 4s.

  III. **FOODS.** By Edward Smith, M.D., LL.B., F.R.S. Profusely Illustrated. Third Edition. 5s.

  IV. **MIND AND BODY**: The Theories of their Relation. By Alexander Bain, LL.D. Fourth Edition. With Four Illustrations. 4s.

   V. **THE STUDY OF SOCIOLOGY.** By Herbert Spencer. Fourth Edition. 5s.

  VI. **ON THE CONSERVATION OF ENERGY.** By Balfour Stewart, M.D., LL.D., F.R.S. With 14 Engravings. Third Edition. 5s.

 VII. **ANIMAL LOCOMOTION**; or, Walking, Swimming, and Flying. By J. B. Pettigrew, M.D., F.R.S. Second Edition. With 119 Illustrations. 5s.

VIII. **RESPONSIBILITY IN MENTAL DISEASE.** By Henry Maudsley, M.D. Second Edition. 5s.

  IX. **THE NEW CHEMISTRY.** By Professor J. P. Cooke, of the Harvard University. Second Edition. With 31 Illustrations. 5s.

   X. **THE SCIENCE OF LAW.** By Professor Sheldon Amos. Second Edition. 5s.

  XI. **ANIMAL MECHANISM.** A Treatise on Terrestrial and Aerial Locomotion. By Professor E. J. Marey. With 117 Illustrations. Second Edition. 5s.

 XII. **THE DOCTRINE OF DESCENT AND DARWINISM.** By Professor Oscar Schmidt (Strasburg University). Second Edition. With 26 Illustrations. 5s.

XIII. **THE HISTORY OF THE CONFLICT BETWEEN RELIGION AND SCIENCE.** By Professor J. W. Draper. Fifth Edition. 5s.

INTERNATIONAL SCIENTIFIC SERIES (The).

XIV. FUNGI; their Nature, Influences, Uses, etc. By M. C. Cooke, M.A., LL.D. Edited by the Rev. M. J. Berkeley, M.A., F.L.S. Second Edition. With numerous Illustrations. 5s.

XV. THE CHEMICAL EFFECTS OF LIGHT AND PHOTOGRAPHY. By Dr. Hermann Vogel (Polytechnic Academy of Berlin). Third Edition, translation thoroughly revised. With 100 Illustrations. 5s.

XVI. THE LIFE AND GROWTH OF LANGUAGE. By William Dwight Whitney, Professor of Sanskrit and Comparative Philology in Yale College, New Haven. Second Edition. 5s.

XVII. MONEY AND THE MECHANISM OF EXCHANGE. By Prof. W. Stanley Jevons. Second Edition. 5s.

XVIII. THE NATURE OF LIGHT: With a General Account of Physical Optics. By Dr. Eugene Lommel, Professor of Physics in the University of Erlangen. Second Edition. With 188 Illustrations and a table of Spectra in Chromolithography. 5s.

XIX. ANIMAL PARASITES AND MESSMATES. By Monsieur Van Beneden, Professor of the University of Louvain, Correspondent of the Institute of France. With 83 Illustrations. 5s.

XX. THE FIVE SENSES OF MAN. By Professor Bernstein, of the University of Halle. Crown 8vo.

XXI. ON FERMENTATION. By Professor Schutzenberger, Director of the Chemical Laboratory at the Sorbonne. Crown 8vo.

INTERNATIONAL SCIENTIFIC SERIES (The).

Forthcoming Volumes.

Prof. W. KINGDON CLIFFORD, M.A. The First Principles of the Exact Sciences explained to the Non-mathematical.

Prof. T. H. HUXLEY, LL.D., F.R.S. Bodily Motion and Consciousness.

Dr. W. B. CARPENTER, LL.D., F.R.S. The Physical Geography of the Sea.

Prof. WILLIAM ODLING, F.R.S. The Old Chemistry viewed from the New Standpoint.

W. LAUDER LINDSAY, M.D., F.R.S.E. Mind in the Lower Animals.

Sir JOHN LUBBOCK, Bart., F.R.S. On Ants and Bees.

Prof. W. T. THISELTON DYER, B.A., B.Sc. Form and Habit in Flowering Plants.

Mr. J. N. LOCKYER, F.R.S. Spectrum Analysis.

Prof. MICHAEL FOSTER, M.D. Protoplasm and the Cell Theory.

H. CHARLTON BASTIAN, M.D., F.R.S. The Brain as an Organ of Mind.

Prof. A. C. RAMSAY, LL.D., F.R.S. Earth Sculpture: Hills, Valleys, Mountains, Plains, Rivers, Lakes; how they were Produced, and how they have been Destroyed.

Prof. RUDOLPH VIRCHOW (Berlin Univ.) Morbid Physiological Action.

Prof. CLAUDE BERNARD. History of the Theories of Life.

Prof. H. SAINTE-CLAIRE DEVILLE. An Introduction to General Chemistry.

Prof. WURTZ. Atoms and the Atomic Theory.

Prof. DE QUATREFAGES. The Human Race.

Prof. LACAZE-DUTHIERS. Zoology since Cuvier.

Prof. BERTHELOT. Chemical Synthesis.

INTERNATIONAL SCIENTIFIC SERIES (The).
(Forthcoming Volumes.)

Prof. J. ROSENTHAL. General Physiology of Muscles and Nerves.

Prof. JAMES D. DANA, M.A., LL.D. On Cephalization; or, Head-Characters in the Gradation and Progress of Life.

Prof. S. W. JOHNSON, M.A. On the Nutrition of Plants.

Prof. AUSTIN FLINT, Jr. M.D. The Nervous System, and its Relation to the Bodily Functions.

Prof. FERDINAND COHN (Breslau Univ.) Thallophytes (Algæ, Lichens, Fungi).

Prof. HERMANN (University of Zurich). Respiration.

Prof. LEUCKART (University of Leipsic). Outlines of Animal Organization.

Prof. LIEBREICH (University of Berlin). Outlines of Toxicology.

Prof. KUNDT (University of Strasburg). On Sound.

Prof. REES (University of Erlangen). On Parasitic Plants.

Prof. STEINTHAL (University of Berlin). Outlines of the Science of Language.

P. BERT (Professor of Physiology, Paris). Forms of Life and other Cosmical Conditions.

E. ALGLAVE (Professor of Constitutional and Administrative Law at Douai, and of Political Economy at Lille). The Primitive Elements of Political Constitutions.

P. LORAIN (Professor of Medicine, Paris). Modern Epidemics.

Mons. FREIDEL. The Functions of Organic Chemistry.

Mons. DEBRAY. Precious Metals.

Prof. CORFIELD, M.A., M.D. (Oxon.) Air in its relation to Health.

Prof. A. GIARD. General Embryology.

IGNOTUS.
> CULMSHIRE FOLK. A Novel. New and Cheaper Edition. In 1 vol. Crown 8vo. 6s.

INGELOW (Jean).
> THE LITTLE WONDER-HORN. A Second Series of "Stories Told to a Child." With Fifteen Illustrations. Square 24mo. 3s. 6d.
>
> OFF THE SKELLIGS. (Her First Romance.) 4 vols. Crown 8vo. 42s.

JACKSON (T. G.)
> MODERN GOTHIC ARCHITECTURE. Crown 8vo. 5s.

JACOB (Maj.-Gen. Sir G. Le Grand), K.C.S.I., C.B.
> WESTERN INDIA BEFORE AND DURING THE MUTINIES. Pictures drawn from life. Second Edition. Crown 8vo. 7s. 6d.

JENKINS (E.) and RAYMOND (J.), Esqs.
> A LEGAL HANDBOOK FOR ARCHITECTS, BUILDERS, AND BUILDING OWNERS. Second Edition Revised. Crown 8vo. 6s.

JENKINS (Rev. R. C.), M.A., Rector of Lyminge, and Honorary Canon of Canterbury.
> THE PRIVILEGE OF PETER, Legally and Historically Examined, and the Claims of the Roman Church compared with the Scriptures, the Councils, and the Testimony of the Popes themselves. Fcap. 8vo. 3s. 6d.

JENKINS (Edward), M.P.
> GLANCES AT INNER ENGLAND. A Lecture delivered in the United States and Canada. Crown 8vo. 5s.
>
> GINX'S BABY: His Birth and other Misfortunes. Thirty-fourth Edition. Crown 8vo. 2s.
>
> LUCHMEE AND DILLO. A Story of West Indian Life. 2 vols. Demy 8vo. Illustrated. [*Preparing.*
>
> LITTLE HODGE. A Christmas Country Carol. Fourteenth Thousand. With Five Illustrations. Crown 8vo. 5s.
> A Cheap Edition in paper covers, price 1s.
>
> LORD BANTAM. Seventh Edition. Crown 8vo. 2s. 6d.

JEVONS (Prof. W. Stanley).
> MONEY AND THE MECHANISM OF EXCHANGE. Second Edition. Crown 8vo. 5s.
> Vol. XVII. of the International Scientific Series.

KAUFMANN (Rev. M.), B.A.
>   **SOCIALISM**: Its Nature, its Dangers, and its Remedies considered. Crown 8vo. 7s. 6d.

KEATING (Mrs.)
>   **HONOR BLAKE**: The Story of a Plain Woman. 2 vols Crown 8vo. 21s.

KER (David).
>   **ON THE ROAD TO KHIVA.** Illustrated with Photographs of the Country and its Inhabitants, and a copy of the Official Map in use during the Campaign, from the Survey of Captain Leusilin. 1 vol. Post 8vo. 12s.
>
>   **THE BOY SLAVE IN BOKHARA.** A Tale of Central Asia. Crown 8vo. With Illustrations. 5s.
>
>   **THE WILD HORSEMAN OF THE PAMPAS.** Crown 8vo. Illustrated. 5s.
>
>   Two of Henry S. King and Co.'s Five Shilling Books for the Young.

KING (Alice).
>   **A CLUSTER OF LIVES.** Crown 8vo. 7s. 6d.

KING (Mrs. Hamilton).
>   **THE DISCIPLES.** A New Poem. Second Edition, with some Notes. Crown 8vo. 7s. 6d.
>
>   **ASPROMONTE, AND OTHER POEMS.** Second Edition. Cloth. 4s. 6d.

KINGSFORD (Rev. F. W.), M.A., Vicar of St. Thomas's, Stamford Hill; late Chaplain H. E. I. C. (Bengal Presidency).
>   **HARTHAM CONFERENCES**; or, Discussions upon some of the Religious Topics of the Day. "Audi alteram partem." Crown 8vo. 3s. 6d.

KNIGHT (Annette F. C.)
>   **POEMS.** Fcap. 8vo. Cloth. 5s.

LACORDAIRE (Rev. Père).
>   **LIFE**: Conferences delivered at Toulouse. Crown 8vo. A New and Cheaper Edition. 3s. 6d.

LADY OF LIPARI (The).
>   A Poem in Three Cantos. Fcap. 8vo. 5s.

LAURIE (J. S.), of the Inner Temple, Barrister-at-Law; formerly H.M. Inspector of Schools, England; Assistant Royal Commissioner, Ireland; Special Commissioner, African Settlement; Director of Public Instruction, Ceylon.

EDUCATIONAL COURSE OF SECULAR SCHOOL BOOKS FOR INDIA.

The following Works are now ready :—

THE FIRST HINDUSTANI READER. Stiff linen wrapper, 6d.

THE SECOND HINDUSTANI READER. Stiff linen wrapper, 6d.

GEOGRAPHY OF INDIA; with Maps and Historical Appendix, tracing the growth of the British Empire in Hindustan. 128 pp. fcap. 8vo. Cloth. 1s. 6d.

In the Press :—

ELEMENTARY GEOGRAPHY OF INDIA.

FACTS AND FEATURES OF INDIAN HISTORY, in a series of alternating Reading Lessons and Memory Exercises.

LAYMANN (Captain), Instructor of Tactics at the Military College, Neisse.

THE FRONTAL ATTACK OF INFANTRY. Translated by Colonel Edward Newdigate. Crown 8vo. 2s. 6d.

L. D. S.

LETTERS FROM CHINA AND JAPAN. 1 vol. Crown 8vo., with Illustrated Title-page. 7s. 6d.

LEANDER (Richard).

FANTASTIC STORIES. Translated from the German by Paulina B. Granville. With Eight full-page Illustrations by M. E. Fraser-Tytler. Crown 8vo. 5s.

One of Henry S. King and Co.'s Five Shilling Books for the Young.

LEATHES (Rev. Stanley), M.A.

THE GOSPEL ITS OWN WITNESS. Being the Hulsean Lectures for 1873. 1 vol. Crown 8vo. 5s.

LEE (Rev. Frederick George), D.C.L.

THE OTHER WORLD; or, Glimpses of the Supernatural. Being Facts, Records, and Traditions, relating to Dreams, Omens, Miraculous Occurrences, Apparitions, Wraiths, Warnings, Second-sight, Necromancy, Witchcraft, etc. 2 vols. A New Edition. Crown 8vo. 15s.

LEE (Holme).
> **HER TITLE OF HONOUR.** A Book for Girls. New Edition. Crown 8vo. With a Frontispiece. 5s.

LENOIR (J.).
> **FAYOUM;** or, Artists in Egypt. A Tour with M. Gérome and others. Crown 8vo. A New and Cheaper Edition. With 13 Illustrations. 3s. 6d.

LISTADO (J. T.).
> **CIVIL SERVICE.** A Novel. 2 vols. Crown 8vo.

LORIMER (Peter), D.D.
> **JOHN KNOX AND THE CHURCH OF ENGLAND:** His work in her Pulpit and his influence upon her Liturgy, Articles, and Parties. Demy 8vo. 12s.

LOVER (Samuel), R.H.A.
> **THE LIFE OF SAMUEL LOVER, R.H.A.;** Artistic, Literary, and Musical. With Selections from his Unpublished Papers and Correspondence. By Bayle Bernard. 2 vols. Post 8vo. With a Portrait. 21s.

LOWER (Mark Antony), M.A., F.S.A.
> **WAYSIDE NOTES IN SCANDINAVIA.** Being Notes of Travel in the North of Europe. Crown 8vo. 9s.

LYONS (R. T.), Surgeon-Major, Bengal Army.
> **A TREATISE ON RELAPSING FEVER.** Post 8vo. 7s. 6d.

MACAULAY (James), M.A., M.D., Edin.
> **IRELAND.** A Tour of Observation, with Remarks on Irish Public Questions. Crown 8vo. A New and Cheaper Edition. 3s. 6d.

MAC CARTHY (Denis Florence).
> **CALDERON'S DRAMAS.** Translated from the Spanish. Post 8vo. Cloth, gilt edges. 10s.

MAC DONALD (George).
> **GUTTA-PERCHA WILLIE, THE WORKING GENIUS.** With Nine Illustrations by Arthur Hughes. Second Edition. Crown 8vo. 3s. 6d.
>
> One of Henry S. King and Co.'s Three and Sixpenny Books for the Young.
>
> **MALCOLM.** A Novel. Second Edition. 3 vols. Crown 8vo.
>
> **ST. GEORGE AND ST. MICHAEL.** 3 vols. Crown 8vo.
>
> **MY SISTER ROSALIND.** By the author of "Christina North." A Novel. 2 vols.

MAC KENNA (Stephen J.)

    PLUCKY FELLOWS. A Book for Boys. With Six Illustrations. Second Edition. Crown 8vo. 3s. 6d.

    One of Henry S. King and Co.'s Three and Sixpenny Books for the Young.

    AT SCHOOL WITH AN OLD DRAGOON. Crown 8vo. With Six Illustrations. 5s.

    One of Henry S. King and Co.'s Five Shilling Books for the Young.

MACLACHLAN (Archibald Neil Campbell), M.A.

    WILLIAM AUGUSTUS, DUKE OF CUMBERLAND; being a Sketch of his Military Life and Character, chiefly as exhibited in the General Orders of his Royal Highness, 1745—1747. Post 8vo. With Illustrations. 15s.

MAIR (R. S.), M.D., F.R.C.S.E., late Deputy Coroner of Madras.

    THE MEDICAL GUIDE FOR ANGLO-INDIANS. Being a Compendium of Advice to Europeans in India, relating to the Preservation and Regulation of Health. With a Supplement on the Management of Children in India. Crown 8vo. Limp cloth. 3s. 6d.

MANNING (His Eminence).

    ESSAYS ON RELIGION AND LITERATURE. By various Writers. Demy 8vo. 10s. 6d.

    CONTENTS:—The Philosophy of Christianity—Mystic Elements of Religion—Controversy with the Agnostics—A Reasoning Thought—Darwinism brought to Book—Mr. Mill on Liberty of the Press—Christianity in relation to Society—The Religious Condition of Germany—The Philosophy of Bacon—Catholic Laymen and Scholastic Philosophy.

MAREY (E. J.)

    ANIMAL MECHANICS. A Treatise on Terrestrial and Aerial Locomotion. Second Edition. With 117 Illustrations. 5s.

    Volume XI. of the International Scientific Series.

MARKEWITCH (B.)

    THE NEGLECTED QUESTION. Translated from the Russian, by the Princess Ourousoff, and dedicated by Express Permission to Her Imperial and Royal Highness Marie Alexandrovna, the Duchess of Edinburgh. 2 vols. Crown 8vo. 14s.

MARRIOTT (Maj.-Gen. W. F.), C.S.I.
> A GRAMMAR OF POLITICAL ECONOMY. Crown 8vo. 6s.

MARSHALL (Hamilton).
> THE STORY OF SIR EDWARD'S WIFE. A Novel. 1 vol. Crown 8vo. 10s. 6d.

MARZIALS (Theophile).
> THE GALLERY OF PIGEONS, and other Poems. Crown 8vo. 4s. 6d.

MASTERMAN (J.)
> HALF-A-DOZEN DAUGHTERS. Crown 8vo. With a Frontispiece. 3s. 6d.
> One of the Cornhill Library of Fiction.

MAUDSLEY (Dr. Henry).
> RESPONSIBILITY IN MENTAL DISEASE. Second Edition. 5s.
> Vol. VIII. of the International Scientific Series.

MAUGHAN (William Charles).
> THE ALPS OF ARABIA; or, Travels through Egypt, Sinai, Arabia, and the Holy Land. Demy 8vo. With Map. A New and Cheaper Edition. 5s.

MAURICE (C. Edmund).
> LIVES OF ENGLISH POPULAR LEADERS. No. 1.—STEPHEN LANGTON. Crown 8vo. 7s. 6d.
> No. 2.—TYLER, BALL, and OLDCASTLE. Crown 8vo. 7s. 6d.

MEDLEY (Lieut.-Col. J. G.), Royal Engineers.
> AN AUTUMN TOUR IN THE UNITED STATES AND CANADA. Crown 8vo. 5s.

MENZIES (Sutherland).
> MEMOIRS OF DISTINGUISHED WOMEN. 2 vols. Post 8vo.

MICKLETHWAITE (J. T.), F.S.A.
> MODERN PARISH CHURCHES: Their Plan, Design, and Furniture. Crown 8vo. 7s. 6d.

MIRUS (Major-General von).
> CAVALRY FIELD DUTY. Translated by Major Frank S. Russell, 14th (King's) Hussars. Crown 8vo. Cloth limp. 7s. 6d.
> This work is one of Henry S. King and Co.'s Military Series.

MOORE (Rev. Daniel), M.A.
> CHRIST AND HIS CHURCH. A Course of Lent Lectures, delivered in the Parish Church of Holy Trinity, Paddington. By the author of "The Age and the Gospel: Hulsean Lectures," etc. Crown 8vo. 3s. 6d.

MOORE (Rev. Thomas), Vicar of Christ Church, Chesham.
> SERMONETTES: on Synonymous Texts, taken from the Bible and Book of Common Prayer, for the Study, Family Reading, and Private Devotion. Small Crown 8vo. 4s. 6d.

MORELL (J. R.)
> EUCLID SIMPLIFIED IN METHOD AND LANGUAGE. Being a Manual of Geometry. Compiled from the most important French Works, approved by the University of Paris and the Minister of Public Instruction. Fcap. 8vo. 2s. 6d.

MORICE (Rev. F. D.), M.A., Fellow of Queen's College, Oxford.
> THE OLYMPIAN AND PYTHIAN ODES OF PINDAR. A New Translation in English Verse. Crown 8vo. 7s. 6d.

MORLEY (Susan).
> AILEEN FERRERS. A Novel. 2 vols. Crown 8vo.
> THROSTLETHWAITE. A Novel. 3 vols. Crown 8vo.

MORSE (Edward S.), Ph. D., late Professor of Comparative Anatomy and Zoology in Bowdoin College.
> FIRST BOOK OF ZOOLOGY. With numerous Illustrations.

MOSTYN (Sydney).
> PERPLEXITY. A Novel. 3 vols. Crown 8vo.

MUSGRAVE (Anthony).
> STUDIES IN POLITICAL ECONOMY. 6s.

NAAKÈ (John T.), of the British Museum.
> SLAVONIC FAIRY TALES. From Russian, Servian, Polish, and Bohemian Sources. With Four Illustrations. Crown 8vo. 5s.

NEWMAN (John Henry), D.D.
> CHARACTERISTICS FROM THE WRITINGS OF DR. J. H. NEWMAN. Being Selections, Personal, Historical, Philosophical, and Religious, from his various Works. Arranged with the Author's personal approval. Second Edition. Crown 8vo. With Portrait. 6s.
>
> *⁎* A Portrait of the Rev. Dr. J. H. Newman, mounted for framing, can be had, price 2s. 6d.

NEWMAN (Mrs.)
>   TOO LATE. A Novel. 2 vols. Crown 8vo.

NOBLE (James Ashcroft).
>   THE PELICAN PAPERS. Reminiscences and Remains of a Dweller in the Wilderness. Crown 8vo. 6s.

NORMAN PEOPLE (The).
>   THE NORMAN PEOPLE, and their Existing Descendants in the British Dominions and the United States of America. One handsome volume. 8vo. 21s.

NORRIS (Rev. A.)
>   THE INNER AND OUTER LIFE POEMS. Fcap. 8vo. 6s.

NOTREGE (John), A.M.
>   THE SPIRITUAL FUNCTION OF A PRESBYTER IN THE CHURCH OF ENGLAND. Crown 8vo. Red edges. 3s. 6d.

ORIENTAL SPORTING MAGAZINE (The).
>   THE ORIENTAL SPORTING MAGAZINE. A Reprint of the first 5 Volumes, in 2 Volumes. Demy 8vo. 28s.

PAGE (H. A.)
>   NATHANIEL HAWTHORNE, A MEMOIR OF, with Stories now first published in this country. Large post 8vo. 7s. 6d.

PAGE (Capt. S. Flood).
>   DISCIPLINE AND DRILL. Four Lectures delivered to the London Scottish Rifle Volunteers. Cheaper Edition. Crown 8vo. 1s.

PALGRAVE (W. Gifford).
>   HERMANN AGHA. An Eastern Narrative. 2 vols. Crown 8vo. Cloth, extra gilt. 18s.

PARKER (Joseph), D.D.
>   THE PARACLETE: An Essay on the Personality and Ministry of the Holy Ghost, with some reference to current discussions. Demy 8vo. 12s.

PARR (Harriett).
>   ECHOES OF A FAMOUS YEAR. Crown 8vo. 8s. 6d.

PAUL (C. Kegan).
>   GOETHE'S FAUST. A New Translation in Rime. Crown 8vo. 6s.
>   WILLIAM GODWIN: HIS FRIENDS AND CONTEMPORARIES. 2 vols. With Portraits. Demy 8vo.

PAYNE (John).
SONGS OF LIFE AND DEATH. Crown 8vo. 5s.

PAYNE (Professor).
LECTURES ON EDUCATION. 6d. each.
I. Pestalozzi: the Influence of His Principles and Practice.
II. Fröbel and the Kindergarten System. Second Edition.
III. The Science and Art of Education.
IV. The True Foundation of Science Teaching.

PELLETAN (Eugène).
THE DESERT PASTOR, JEAN JAROUSSEAU. Translated from the French. By Colonel E. P. De L'Hoste. With a Frontispiece. Fcap. 8vo. New Edition. 3s. 6d.

PENRICE (Major J.), B.A.
A DICTIONARY AND GLOSSARY OF THE KO-RAN. With copious Grammatical References and Explanations of the Text. 4to. 21s.

PERCEVAL (Rev. P.)
TAMIL PROVERBS, WITH THEIR ENGLISH TRANSLATION. Containing upwards of Six Thousand Proverbs. Third Edition. 8vo. Sewed. 9s.

PERRIER (Amelia).
A WINTER IN MOROCCO. With Four Illustrations. Crown 8vo. A New and Cheaper Edition. 3s. 6d.
A GOOD MATCH. A Novel. 2 vols. Crown 8vo.

PESCHEL (Dr.)
MANKIND: A Scientific Study of the Races and Distribution of Man, considered in their Bodily Variations, Languages, Occupations, and Religions.

PETTIGREW (J. B.), M.D., F.R.S.
ANIMAL LOCOMOTION; or, Walking, Swimming, and Flying. Second Edition. With 119 Illustrations. 5s.
Volume VII. of the International Scientific Series.

PIGGOT (John), F.S.A, F.R.G.S.
PERSIA—ANCIENT AND MODERN. Post 8vo. 10s. 6d.

POUSHKIN (Alexander Serguevitch).
RUSSIAN ROMANCE. Translated from the Tales of Belkin, etc. By Mrs. J. Buchan Telfer (née Mouravieff). Cr. 8vo. 7s. 6d.

POWER (Harriet).
> OUR INVALIDS: HOW SHALL WE EMPLOY AND AMUSE THEM? Fcap 8vo. 2s. 6d.

POWLETT (Lieut. Norton), Royal Artillery.
> EASTERN LEGENDS AND STORIES IN ENGLISH VERSE. Crown 8vo. 5s.

PRESBYTER.
> UNFOLDINGS OF CHRISTIAN HOPE. An Essay showing that the Doctrine contained in the Damnatory Clauses of the Creed commonly called Athanasian is unscriptural. Small crown 8vo. Cloth. 4s. 6d.

PRICE (Prof. Bonamy).
> CURRENCY AND BANKING. One Vol. Crown 8vo. 6s.

PROCTOR (Richard A.)
> OUR PLACE AMONG INFINITIES. A Series of Essays contrasting our little abode in space and time with the Infinities around us. To which are added "Essays on Astrology," and "The Jewish Sabbath." Crown 8vo. 6s.
>
> THE EXPANSE OF HEAVEN. A Series of Essays on the Wonders of the Firmament. With a Frontispiece. Second Edition. Crown 8vo. 6s.

RANKING (B. Montgomerie).
> STREAMS FROM HIDDEN SOURCES. Crown 8vo. 6s.

READY-MONEY MORTIBOY.
> READY-MONEY MORTIBOY. A Matter-of-Fact Story. Crown 8vo. With frontispiece. 3s. 6d.
> This is one of the volumes of the Cornhill Library of Fiction.

REANEY (Mrs. G. S.)
> WAKING AND WORKING; OR, FROM GIRLHOOD TO WOMANHOOD. With a Frontispiece. Crown 8vo. 5s.
> One of Henry S. King and Co.'s Five Shilling Books for the Young.
>
> SUNBEAM WILLIE, AND OTHER STORIES, for Home Reading and Cottage Meetings. Small square, uniform with "Lost Gip," etc. 3 Illustrations. 1s. 6d.

REGINALD BRAMBLE.
> REGINALD BRAMBLE. A Cynic of the Nineteenth Century. An Autobiography. 1 vol. Crown 8vo. 10s. 6d.

REID (T. Wemyss).
> **CABINET PORTRAITS.** Biographical Sketches of Statesmen of the Day. 1 vol. Crown 8vo. 7s. 6d.

RHOADES (James).
> **TIMOLEON.** A Dramatic Poem. Fcap. 8vo. 5s.

RIBOT (Professor Th.)
> **CONTEMPORARY ENGLISH PSYCHOLOGY.** La. post 8vo. 9s. An analysis of the views and opinions of the following metaphysicians, as expressed in their writings:—James Mill, Alexander Bain, John Stuart Mill, George H. Lewes, Herbert Spencer, Samuel Bailey.
>
> **HEREDITY:** A Psychological Study on its Phenomena, its Laws, its Causes, and its Consequences. 1 vol. Large crown 8vo. 9s.

ROBERTSON (The Late Rev. F. W.), M.A.
> **THE LATE REV. F. W. ROBERTSON, M.A., LIFE AND LETTERS OF.** Edited by the Rev. Stopford Brooke, M.A., Chaplain in Ordinary to the Queen.
> I. 2 vols., uniform with the Sermons. With Steel Portrait. 7s. 6d.
> II. Library Edition, in Demy 8vo. with Two Steel Portraits. 12s.
> III. A Popular Edition, in 1 vol. 6s.
>
> *New and Cheaper Editions:—*
>
> **SERMONS.**
>> Vol. I. Small crown 8vo. 3s. 6d.
>> Vol. II. Small crown 8vo. 3s. 6d.
>> Vol. III. Small crown 8vo. 3s. 6d.
>> Vol. IV. Small crown 8vo. 3s. 6d.
>
> **EXPOSITORY LECTURES ON ST. PAUL'S EPISTLE TO THE CORINTHIANS.** Small crown 8vo. 5s.
>
> **AN ANALYSIS OF MR. TENNYSON'S "IN MEMORIAM."** (Dedicated by Permission to the Poet-Laureate.) Fcap. 8vo. 2s.
>
> **THE EDUCATION OF THE HUMAN RACE.** Translated from the German of Gotthold Ephraim Lessing. Fcap. 8vo. 2s. 6d.
>
> *The above Works can also be had bound in half morocco.*
>
> *** A Portrait of the late Rev. F. W. Robertson, mounted for framing, can be had, price 2s. 6d.
>
> **NOTES ON GENESIS.** Uniform with the Sermons.
>
> **LECTURES AND ADDRESSES,** with other literary remains. A New Edition. 5s.

Ross (Mrs. Ellen), ("Nelsie Brook.")
>   **DADDY'S PET.** A Sketch from Humble Life. Square crown 8vo. Uniform with "Lost Gip." With Six Illustrations. 1s.

Roxburghe Lothian.
>   **DANTE AND BEATRICE FROM 1282 TO 1290.** A Romance. 2 vols. Post 8vo. Cloth. 24s.

Russell (William Clark).
>   **MEMOIRS OF MRS. LÆTITIA BOOTHBY.** Crown 8vo. 7s. 6d.

Russell (E. R.)
>   **IRVING AS HAMLET.** Demy 8vo. Second Edition. Sewed. 1s.

Sadler (S. W.), R.N., Author of "Marshall Vavasour."
>   **THE AFRICAN CRUISER.** A Midshipman's Adventures on the West Coast. A Book for Boys. With Three Illustrations. Second Edition. Crown 8vo. 3s. 6d.
>
>   One of Henry S. King and Co.'s Three and Sixpenny Books for the Young.

Samarow (Gregor).
>   **FOR SCEPTRE AND CROWN.** A Romance of the Present Time. Translated by Fanny Wormald. 2 vols. Crown 8vo. 15s.

Saunders (Katherine).
>   **THE HIGH MILLS.** A Novel. 3 vols. Crown 8vo.
>
>   **GIDEON'S ROCK,** and other Stories. 1 vol. Crown 8vo. 6s.
>
>   **JOAN MERRYWEATHER,** and other Stories. 1 vol. Crown 8vo. 6s.
>
>   **MARGARET AND ELIZABETH.** A Story of the Sea. 1 vol. Crown 8vo. 6s.
>
>   **TOO LONG UNTOLD,** and other Stories. 2 vols. Crown 8vo.
>
>   Contents:—Too Long Untold—The Harpers of Men-y-don—Ida's Story—Little Missy—The Shaken Nest.

Saunders (John).
>   **HIRELL.** Crown 8vo. With Frontispiece. 3s. 6d.
>
>   **ABEL DRAKE'S WIFE.** Crown 8vo. With Frontispiece. 3s. 6d.
>
>   These works form separate volumes of the Cornhill Library of Fiction.
>
>   **ISRAEL MORT, OVERMAN.** The Story of the Mine. 3 vols. Crown 8vo.

SCHELL (Major von).
>   THE OPERATIONS OF THE FIRST ARMY UNDER GEN. VON GOEBEN. Translated by Col. C. H. von Wright. Four Maps. Demy 8vo. 9s.
>
>   THE OPERATIONS OF THE FIRST ARMY UNDER GEN. VON STEINMETZ. Translated by Captain E. O. Hollist. Demy 8vo. 10s. 6d.
>
>   These works form separate volumes of Henry S. King and Co.'s Military Series.

SCHERFF (Major W. von).
>   STUDIES IN THE NEW INFANTRY TACTICS. Parts I. and II. Translated from the German by Colonel Lumley Graham. Demy 8vo. 7s. 6d.
>
>   This work is one of Henry S. King and Co.'s Military Series.

SCHMIDT (Prof. Oscar), Strasburg University.
>   THE DOCTRINE OF DESCENT AND DARWINISM. Second Edition. 26 Illustrations. 5s.
>
>   Being Vol. XII. of the International Scientific Series.
>
>   HANDBOOK OF COMPARATIVE ANATOMY. Crown 8vo.

SCOTT (Patrick).
>   THE DREAM AND THE DEED, and other Poems. Fcap. 8vo. 5s.

SEEKING HIS FORTUNE, and other Stories.
>   SEEKING HIS FORTUNE, and other Stories. Crown 8vo. With Four Illustrations. 3s. 6d.
>
>   One of Henry S. King and Co.'s Three and Sixpenny Books for the Young.

SENIOR (Nassau William).
>   ALEXIS DE TOCQUEVILLE. Correspondence and Conversations with Nassau W. Senior, from 1833 to 1859. Edited by M. C. M. Simpson. 2 vols. Large post 8vo. 21s.
>
>   JOURNALS KEPT IN FRANCE AND ITALY. From 1848 to 1852. With a Sketch of the Revolution of 1848. Edited by his Daughter, M. C. M. Simpson. 2 vols. Post 8vo. 24s.

SEVEN AUTUMN LEAVES.
>   SEVEN AUTUMN LEAVES FROM FAIRYLAND. Illustrated with 9 Etchings. Square crown 8vo. 3s. 6d.

SHADWELL (Major-General), C.B.
> **MOUNTAIN WARFARE.** Illustrated by the Campaign of 1799 in Switzerland. Being a Translation of the Swiss Narrative compiled from the Works of the Archduke Charles, Jomini, and others. Also of Notes by General H. Dufour on the Campaign of the Valtelline in 1635. With Appendix, Maps, and Introductory Remarks. Demy 8vo. 16s.

SHELDON (Philip).
> **WOMAN'S A RIDDLE;** or, Baby Warmstrey. A Novel. 3 vols. Crown 8vo.

SHERMAN (Gen. W. T.)
> **MEMOIRS OF GEN. W. T. SHERMAN,** Commander of the Federal Forces in the American Civil War. By Himself. 2 vols Demy 8vo. With Map. 24s. *Copyright English Edition.*

SHELLEY (Lady).
> **SHELLEY MEMORIALS FROM AUTHENTIC SOURCES.** With (now first printed) an Essay on Christianity by Percy Bysshe Shelley. Third Edition. Crown 8vo. With Portrait. 5s.

SHIPLEY (Rev. Orby), M.A.
> **STUDIES IN MODERN PROBLEMS.** By various Writers. Crown 8vo. 2 vols. 5s. each.

CONTENTS.—VOL. I.

Sacramental Confession.
Abolition of the Thirty-nine Articles. Part I.
The Sanctity of Marriage.
Creation and Modern Science.
Retreats for Persons Living in the World.
Catholic and Protestant.
The Bishops on Confession in the Church of England.

CONTENTS.—VOL. II.

Some Principles of Christian Ceremonial.
A Layman's View of Confession of Sin to a Priest. Parts I. and II.
Reservation of the Blessed Sacrament.
Missions and Preaching Orders.
Abolition of the Thirty-nine Articles. Part II.
The First Liturgy of Edward VI. and our own office contrasted and compared.

SMEDLEY (M. B.)
> **BOARDING-OUT AND PAUPER SCHOOLS FOR GIRLS.** Crown 8vo. 3s. 6d.

SMITH (Edward), M.D., LL.B., F.R.S.
> **HEALTH AND DISEASE,** as influenced by the Daily, Seasonal, and other Cyclical Changes in the Human System. A New Edition. 7s. 6d.
> **FOODS.** Third Edition. Profusely Illustrated. 5s.
> Volume III. of the International Scientific Series.
> **PRACTICAL DIETARY FOR FAMILIES, SCHOOLS, AND THE LABOURING CLASSES.** A New Edition. 3s. 6d.
> **CONSUMPTION IN ITS EARLY AND REMEDIABLE STAGES.** A New Edition. 7s. 6d.

SMITH (Hubert).
> **TENT LIFE WITH ENGLISH GIPSIES IN NORWAY.** With Five full-page Engravings and Thirty-one smaller Illustrations by Whymper and others, and Map of the Country showing Routes. Second Edition. Revised and Corrected. 8vo. 21s.

SONGS FOR MUSIC.
> **SONGS FOR MUSIC.** By Four Friends. Square crown 8vo. 5s.
> Containing Songs by Reginald A. Gatty, Stephen H. Gatty, Greville J. Chester, and Juliana H. Ewing.

SOME TIME IN IRELAND.
> **SOME TIME IN IRELAND.** A Recollection. Crown 8vo. 7s. 6d.

SONGS OF TWO WORLDS.
> **SONGS OF TWO WORLDS.** By a New Writer. First Series. Second Edition. Fcap. 8vo. 5s.
> **SONGS OF TWO WORLDS.** By a New Writer. Second Series. Second Edition. Fcap. 8vo. 5s.
> **SONGS OF TWO WORLDS.** By a New Writer. Third Series. Second Edition. Fcap. 8vo. 5s.

SPENCER (HERBERT).
> **THE STUDY OF SOCIOLOGY.** Fourth Edition. Crown 8vo. 5s.
> Volume V. of the International Scientific Series.

STEVENSON (Rev. W. Fleming).
> **HYMNS FOR THE CHURCH AND HOME.** Selected and Edited by the Rev. W. Fleming Stevenson.
> The most complete Hymn Book published.
> The Hymn Book consists of Three Parts:—I. For Public Worship.—II. For Family and Private Worship.—III. For Children.
> *₊* *Published in various forms and prices, the latter ranging from 8d. to 6s. Lists and full particulars will be furnished on application to the Publishers.*

STEWART (Professor Balfour).
> ON THE CONSERVATION OF ENERGY. Third Edition. With Fourteen Engravings. 5s.
> Volume VI. of the International Scientific Series.

STONEHEWER (Agnes).
> MONACELLA : A Poem. Fcap. 8vo. Cloth, 3s. 6d.

STRETTON (Hesba). Author of "Jessica's First Prayer."
> CASSY. Twenty-fourth Thousand. With Six Illustrations. Square crown 8vo. 1s. 6d.
> THE KING'S SERVANTS. Thirtieth Thousand. With Eight Illustrations. Square crown 8vo. 1s. 6d.
> LOST GIP. Forty-third Thousand. With Six Illustrations. Square crown 8vo. 1s. 6d.
> *** Also a handsomely-bound Edition, with Twelve Illustrations, price 2s. 6d.
> THE WONDERFUL LIFE. Eighth Thousand. Fcap. 8vo. 2s. 6d.
> FRIENDS TILL DEATH. With Frontispiece. Limp cloth, 6d.
> TWO CHRISTMAS STORIES. With Frontispiece. Limp cloth, 6d.
> HESTER MORLEY'S PROMISE. 3 vols. Crown 8vo.
> THE DOCTOR'S DILEMMA. 3 vols. Crown 8vo.

STUBBS (Lieut.-Col. Francis W.), Royal (late Bengal) Artillery.
> THE REGIMENT OF BENGAL ARTILLERY : The History of its Organization, Equipment, and War Services. With Maps and Plans. 2 vols. 8vo. [*Preparing*.

SULLY (James).
> SENSATION AND INTUITION. Demy 8vo. 10s. 6d.

TAYLOR (Rev. J. W. Augustus), M.A.
> POEMS. Fcap. 8vo. 5s.

TAYLOR (Sir Henry).
> EDWIN THE FAIR AND ISAAC COMNENUS. 3s. 6d.
> A SICILIAN SUMMER AND OTHER POEMS. 3s. 6d.

TAYLOR (Colonel Meadows), C.S.I., M.R.I.A.
> SEETA. A Novel. 3 vols.
> THE CONFESSIONS OF A THUG.
> TARA : a Mahratta Tale.
> RALPH DARNELL.
> TIPPOO SULTAN.
> A NOBLE QUEEN. 3 vols. Crown 8vo.
> New and Cheaper Edition in one vol. crown 8vo. with Frontispiece. Each 6s.

TENNYSON (Alfred).
    QUEEN MARY. A Drama. New Edition. Crown 8vo. 6s.

TENNYSON'S (Alfred) Works. Cabinet Edition. Ten Volumes. Each with Portrait. 2s. 6d.
    CABINET EDITION. 10 vols. Complete in handsome Ornamental Case. 28s.

TENNYSON'S (Alfred) Works. Author's Edition. Complete in Five Volumes. Cloth gilt, 6s. each; half-morocco, Roxburgh style, 7s. 6d. each.
    EARLY POEMS, and ENGLISH IDYLLS.—VOL. I.
    LOCKSLEY HALL, LUCRETIUS, and other Poems.—VOL. II.
    THE IDYLLS OF THE KING (*Complete*).—VOL. III.*
    THE PRINCESS, and MAUD.—VOL. IV.
    ENOCH ARDEN, and IN MEMORIAM.—VOL. V.

    TENNYSON'S IDYLLS OF THE KING, and other Poems. Illustrated by Julia Margaret Cameron. 1 vol. Folio. Half-bound morocco, cloth sides. Six Guineas.

TENNYSON'S (Alfred) Works. Original Editions.
    POEMS. Small 8vo. 6s.
    MAUD, and other Poems. Small 8vo. 3s. 6d.
    THE PRINCESS. Small 8vo. 3s. 6d.
    IDYLLS OF THE KING. Small 8vo. 5s.
    IDYLLS OF THE KING. Collected. Small 8vo. 6s.
    THE HOLY GRAIL, and other Poems. Small 8vo. 4s. 6d.
    GARETH AND LYNETTE. Small 8vo. 3s.
    ENOCH ARDEN, etc. Small 8vo. 3s. 6d.
    SELECTIONS FROM THE ABOVE WORKS. Square 8vo. Cloth, 3s. 6d. Cloth gilt, extra, 4s.
    SONGS FROM THE ABOVE WORKS. Square 8vo. Cloth extra, 3s. 6d.
    IN MEMORIAM. Small 8vo. 4s.
    LIBRARY EDITION. In 6 vols. 8vo. 10s. 6d. each.
    POCKET VOLUME EDITION. 11 vols. In neat case, 31s. 6d.
        Ditto, ditto. Extra cloth gilt, in case, 35s.
    POEMS. Illustrated Edition. 4to. 25s.

---

* On and after the 1st of January, 1876, the price of this volume will be 7s. 6d. cloth, and 9s. Roxburgh.

THOMAS (Moy).
　　A FIGHT FOR LIFE. Crown 8vo. With Frontispiece. 3s. 6d.
　　This is one of the volumes of the Cornhill Library of Fiction.

THOMSON (J. T.), F.R.G.S.
　　HAKAYIT ABDULLA. The Autobiography of a Malay Munshi, between the years 1808 and 1843. Demy 8vo. 12s.

THOMPSON (A. C.)
　　PRELUDES. A Volume of Poems. Illustrated by Elizabeth Thompson (Painter of "The Roll Call"). 8vo. 7s. 6d.

THOMPSON (Rev. A. S.), British Chaplain at St. Petersburg.
　　HOME WORDS FOR WANDERERS. A Volume of Sermons. Crown 8vo. 6s.

THOUGHTS IN VERSE. Small crown 8vo. 1s. 6d.

THRING (Rev. Godfrey), B.A.
　　HYMNS AND SACRED LYRICS. 1 vol. Fcap. 8vo. 5s.

TODD (Herbert), M.A.
　　ARVAN; or, The Story of the Sword. A Poem. Crown 8vo. 7s. 6d.

TRAHERNE (Mrs. Arthur).
　　THE ROMANTIC ANNALS OF A NAVAL FAMILY. Crown 8vo. A New and Cheaper Edition. 5s.

TRAVERS (Mar.)
　　THE SPINSTERS OF BLATCHINGTON. A Novel. 2 vols. Crown 8vo.

TREVANDRUM OBSERVATIONS.
　　OBSERVATIONS OF MAGNETIC DECLINATION MADE AT TREVANDRUM AND AGUSTIA MALLEY in the Observatories of his Highness the Maharajah of Travancore, G.C.S.I., in the Years 1852 to 1860. Being Trevandrum Magnetical Observations, Volume I. Discussed and Edited by John Allan Brown, F.R.S., late Director of the Observatories. With an Appendix. Imp. 4to. Cloth. £3 3s.
　　⁎ *The Appendix, containing Reports on the Observatories and on the Public Museum, Public Park, and Gardens at Trevandrum, pp. xii.-116, may be had separately.* 21s.

TURNER (Rev. Charles).
> SONNETS, LYRICS, AND TRANSLATIONS. Crown 8vo. 4s. 6d.

TYNDALL (J.), LL.D., F.R.S.
> THE FORMS OF WATER IN CLOUDS AND RIVERS, ICE AND GLACIERS. With Twenty-six Illustrations. Fifth Edition. Crown 8vo. 5s.
> Volume I. of the International Scientific Series.

UMBRA OXONIENSIS.
> RESULTS OF THE EXPOSTULATION OF THE RIGHT HONOURABLE W. E. GLADSTONE, in their Relation to the Unity of Roman Catholicism. Large fcap. 8vo. 5s.

UPTON (Roger D.), Captain late 9th Royal Lancers.
> NEWMARKET AND ARABIA. An Examination of the Descent of Racers and Coursers. With Pedigrees and Frontispiece. Post 8vo. 9s.

VAMBERY (Prof. Arminius), of the University of Pesth.
> BOKHARA: Its History and Conquest. Demy 8vo. 18s.

VANESSA. By the Author of "Thomasina," etc. A Novel. Second Edition. 2 vols. Crown 8vo.

VAUGHAN (Rev. C. J.), D.D.
> WORDS OF HOPE FROM THE PULPIT OF THE TEMPLE CHURCH. Third Edition. Crown 8vo. 5s.
>
> THE SOLIDITY OF TRUE RELIGION, and other Sermons Preached in London during the Election and Mission Week, February, 1874. Crown 8vo. 3s. 6d.
>
> FORGET THINE OWN PEOPLE. An Appeal for Missions. Crown 8vo. 3s. 6d.
>
> THE YOUNG LIFE EQUIPPING ITSELF FOR GOD'S SERVICE. Being Four Sermons Preached before the University of Cambridge, in November, 1872. Fourth Edition. Crown 8vo. 3s. 6d.

VINCENT (Capt. C. E. H.), late Royal Welsh Fusiliers.
> ELEMENTARY MILITARY GEOGRAPHY, RECONNOITRING, AND SKETCHING. Compiled for Non-Commissioned Officers and Soldiers of all Arms. Square crown 8vo. 2s. 6d.
>
> RUSSIA'S ADVANCE EASTWARD. Based on the Official Reports of Lieutenant Hugo Stumm, German Military Attaché to the Khivan Expedition. With Map. Crown 8vo. 6s.

VIZCAYA; or, Life in the Land of the Carlists.
> VIZCAYA; or, Life in the Land of the Carlists at the Outbreak of the Insurrection, with some Account of the Iron Mines and other Characteristics of the Country. With a Map and Eight Illustrations. Crown 8vo. 9s.

VOGEL (Prof.), Polytechnic Academy of Berlin.
> THE CHEMICAL EFFECTS OF LIGHT AND PHOTOGRAPHY, in their application to Art, Science, and Industry. Third Edition. The translation thoroughly revised. With 100 Illustrations, including some beautiful Specimens of Photography. 5s.
> Volume XV. of the International Scientific Series.

VYNER (Lady Mary).
> EVERY DAY A PORTION. Adapted from the Bible and the Prayer Book, for the Private Devotions of those living in Widowhood. Collected and Edited by Lady Mary Vyner. Square crown 8vo. Elegantly bound. 5s.

WAITING FOR TIDINGS.
> WAITING FOR TIDINGS. By the Author of "White and Black." 3 vols. Crown 8vo.

WARTENSLEBEN (Count Hermann von), Colonel in the Prussian General Staff.
> THE OPERATIONS OF THE SOUTH ARMY IN JANUARY AND FEBRUARY, 1871. Compiled from the Official War Documents of the Head-quarters of the Southern Army. Translated by Colonel C. H. von Wright. With Maps. Demy 8vo. 6s.
>
> THE OPERATIONS OF THE FIRST ARMY UNDER GEN. VON MANTEUFFEL. Translated by Colonel C. H. von Wright. Uniform with the above. Demy 8vo. 9s.
> These works form separate volumes of Henry S. King and Co.'s Military Series.

WEDMORE (Frederick).
> TWO GIRLS. 2 vols. Crown 8vo.

WELLS (Captain John C.), R.N.
> SPITZBERGEN—THE GATEWAY TO THE POLYNIA; or, A Voyage to Spitzbergen. With numerous Illustrations by Whymper and others, and Map. 8vo. 21s.

WETMORE (W. S.).
> COMMERCIAL TELEGRAPHIC CODE. Post 4to. Boards. 42s.

WHAT 'TIS TO LOVE. By the Author of "Flora Adair," "The Value of Fostertown." 3 vols. Crown 8vo.

WHITNEY (William Dwight). Professor of Sanskrit and Comparative Philology in Yale College, New Haven.
> THE LIFE AND GROWTH OF LANGUAGE. Second Edition. Crown 8vo. 5s. *Copyright Edition.*
> Volume XVI. of the International Scientific Series.

WHITTLE (J. Lowry), A.M., Trin. Coll., Dublin.
> CATHOLICISM AND THE VATICAN. With a Narrative of the Old Catholic Congress at Munich. Second Edition. Crown 8vo. 4s. 6d.

WILBERFORCE (Henry W.)
> THE CHURCH AND THE EMPIRES. Historical Periods. Preceded by a Memoir of the Author by John Henry Newman, D.D., of the Oratory. With Portrait. Post 8vo. 10s. 6d.

WILKINSON (T. Lean).
> SHORT LECTURES ON THE LAND LAWS. Delivered before the Working Men's College. Crown 8vo. 2s.

WILLIAMS (Rev. Rowland), D.D.
> LIFE AND LETTERS OF ROWLAND WILLIAMS, D.D., with Selections from his Note-books. Edited by Mrs. Rowland Williams. With a Photographic Portrait. 2 vols. Large post 8vo. 24s.

WILLOUGHBY (The Hon. Mrs.)
> ON THE NORTH WIND—THISTLEDOWN. A Volume of Poems. Elegantly bound. Small crown 8vo. 7s. 6d.

WILSON (H. Schütz).
> STUDIES AND ROMANCES. Crown 8vo. 7s. 6d.

WINTERBOTHAM (Rev. R.), M.A., B.Sc.
> SERMONS AND EXPOSITIONS. Crown 8vo. 7s. 6d.

WOOD (C. F.)
> A YACHTING CRUISE IN THE SOUTH SEAS. Demy 8vo. With Six Photographic Illustrations. 7s. 6d.

WRIGHT (Rev. W.), of Stoke Bishop, Bristol.
> MAN AND ANIMALS: A Sermon. Crown 8vo. Stitched in wrapper. 1s.
>
> WAITING FOR THE LIGHT, AND OTHER SERMONS. Crown 8vo. 6s.

WYLD (R. S.), F.R.S.E.
>THE PHYSICS AND PHILOSOPHY OF THE SENSES; or, The Mental and the Physical in their Mutual Relation. Illustrated by several Plates. Demy 8vo. 16s.

YONGE (C. D.), Regius Professor, Queen's College, Belfast.
>HISTORY OF THE ENGLISH REVOLUTION OF 1688. Crown 8vo. 6s.

YORKE (Stephen), Author of "Tales of the North Riding."
>CLEVEDEN. A Novel. 2 vols. Crown 8vo.

YOUMANS (Eliza A.)
>AN ESSAY ON THE CULTURE OF THE OBSERVING POWERS OF CHILDREN, especially in connection with the Study of Botany. Edited, with Notes and a Supplement, by Joseph Payne, F.C.P., Author of "Lectures on the Science and Art of Education," etc. Crown 8vo. 2s. 6d.
>
>FIRST BOOK OF BOTANY. Designed to cultivate the Observing Powers of Children. With 300 Engravings. New and Enlarged Edition. Crown 8vo. 5s.

YOUMANS (Edward L.), M.D.
>A CLASS BOOK OF CHEMISTRY, on the Basis of the new System. With 200 Illustrations.

ZIMMERN (Helen).
>STORIES IN PRECIOUS STONES. With Six Illustrations. Third Edition. Crown 8vo. 5s.

FORTHCOMING WORKS.

SIR THOMAS MUNRO, BART., K.C.B., sometime Governor of Madras. A Selection from his Minutes and other Official Writings. Edited by Sir Alexander Arbuthnot, K.C.S.I.

ALDYTH. A Novel. By the Author of "Healey." 3 vols. Crown 8vo.

IDA CRAVEN. A Novel. By Mrs. M. H. Cadell. 3 vols. Crown 8vo.

SCIENTIFIC INTRODUCTION TO GREEK AND LATIN. By Ferdinand Baur, Ph D., Professor at Maulbronne. Translated and adapted by C. Kegan Paul, M.A., and E. B. Stone, M.A., late Fellow of King's College, Cambridge, and Assistant-Master at Eton College.

TOO LONG UNTOLD, and other Stories. By Katherine Saunders. 2 vols. Crown 8vo.
    CONTENTS:—Too Long Untold—The Harpers of Men-y-don—Ida's Story—Little Missy—The Shaken Nest.

www.ingramcontent.com/pod-product-compliance
Lightning Source LLC
Chambersburg PA
CBHW031857220426
43663CB00006B/662